EXPERIENCE AND THE ANALYTIC

Have you ever watched children trying to divide a quantity of quicksilver into a certain number of parts? The more they squeeze it and torment it and try to force it to obey them, the more they provoke the freedom of that noble metal; it escapes their ingenuity and keeps scattering into little particles beyond all reckoning.

MONTAIGNE, "Of Experience"

EXPERIENCE AND THE ANALYTIC

A Reconsideration of Empiricism

By ALAN PASCH

THE UNIVERSITY OF CHICAGO PRESS

The Library of Congress Catalog Card

PASCH, ALAN.
    Experience and the analytic; a reconsideration
of empiricism. [Chicago] University of Chicago
Press [1958]
    275 p. 24 cm.
    Includes bibliography.
    1. Experience.
    B816.P3   *190 144   58–11953‡
    Library of Congress

THE UNIVERSITY OF CHICAGO PRESS, CHICAGO 37
Cambridge University Press, London, N.W. 1, England
The University of Toronto Press, Toronto 5, Canada

© 1958 by The University of Chicago. Published 1958
Composed and printed by THE UNIVERSITY OF CHICAGO PRESS
Chicago, Illinois, U.S.A.

To
E. B. P.

Preface

BACK TO EXPERIENCE" is the slogan of philosophic empiricism in modern times, and though no slogan can communicate more than a whisper of any philosophy worthy of the name, this one does suggest empiricism's most distinctive feature. It points, too, to what is paradoxical about empiricism, for the more rigorously and conscientiously empiricists have tried to work out their position the further that position has become removed from anything easily recognizable as experience. To examine and resolve this paradox is the aim of the following work. The examination, occupying the first half of the book, encompasses several problems that have recently been engaging the attention of empiricist and near-empiricist philosophers. The remainder of the book is devoted to a sketch of the direction empiricism must take if it is to resolve its difficulties without flouting altogether the intentions of its most eminent practitioners.

More particularly, in the first of three parts the problem of the distinction between analytic and synthetic truths is examined, and it is found that the distinction may be maintained in a sharp and rigid form only within a correspondingly sharp and rigid linguistic framework. It is found also that the empiricist principle that all nonanalytic ideas should be derived from experience may be maintained in the way in which empiricists have wanted to maintain it only within the kind of linguistic framework that supports a sharp and rigid analytic-synthetic distinction. The empiricism that results, as exemplified by the philosophy which proceeds through the rational reconstruction of knowledge within an ideal language, rests on a series of conventions, the interesting ones being conventions about the line to be drawn between analytic and synthetic truths, and about the nature of the experience to which empiricists have wanted

to connect all nonanalytic knowledge. This is a conventionalism which scarcely lends substance to the spirit of empiricism.
In the second part an investigation is made of the claim of
many epistemologists to be able to locate a kind of perceptual
experience which possesses "epistemological priority" and could
therefore serve as a unique and indubitable basis for a reconstruction of knowledge that is both rational and empirical—rational because purged of all nonrational elements and sequences
of elements, and empirical because confined within a framework
whose roots are undeniably experiential. The investigation leads
to the counterclaim that no kind of experience may be said with
justification to be epistemologically prior to every other kind of
experience, or even to any other kind of experience. (Summary
passages of the discussion up to this point may be found beginning on pages 82, 112, and 128.) Turning to an examination of
cognitive experience in general, the following beliefs are expressed: All cognitive experience happens contextually; each
context within which experience occurs is uniquely characterized by the distinction between its formal and its nonformal
elements; this is true both of low-level contexts and of such
high-level contexts as artificial languages, whose formal and nonformal elements consist in analytic and synthetic statements,
respectively.

In the final part the empiricist criterion of significance is
loosened, so that it becomes a contextual criterion, dependent
on the particular context within which significance is sought.
Any such context is limited, so that we can keep it under control, and it is accepted only provisionally, so that we need keep
it at all only so long as it suits our purpose. The philosophic
method which adopts such limited and provisional contexts as
its media is called "pragmatic reconstruction." An important
methodological principle of pragmatic reconstruction is the
"principle of significant precision," and the crucial concept of
empiricism, incorporated in a general but not intransigent requirement, turns out to be intersubjectivity.

The kind of empiricism that emerges from the considerations
just summarized is neither psychological, as was the empiricism

of Hume, nor linguistic, as have been more recent brands of empiricism, but methodological. Its experiential reference is not to the primitive elements of experience, whether psychological or linguistic, but rather to the way experience happens. Empiricists, by attending more to the way experience happens and less to its alleged constituent elements, might achieve that intimacy between philosophy and primitive experience that has been supposed to be the motivating goal of empiricism and that has tantalized empiricists by remaining always just beyond their reach. My own view is that since experience happens contextually, and since this is as true at advanced levels as at primitive levels of experience, empiricists, to give philosophy the experiential reference they have always wanted it to have, must pay continual and careful regard to the contexts within which their philosophy is done, the kind of regard that "pragmatic reconstruction," as a way of doing philosophy, insures.

It may be that the direction I have indicated leads so far afield from what has customarily been called empiricism that, by using one word to cover two such different points of view, a terminological disservice has been done. If so, then another word may be appropriated to designate the position rooted in the philosophic method I have called "pragmatic reconstruction." But it may also be that to stretch the meaning of "empiricism" as I have done is in point of historical fact to recognize the drastic transitions undergone by philosophic empiricism in the last two hundred and fifty years, and that to use the word thus, though in some respects an abrupt departure from normal usage, is in other respects a closer approximation to its original significance in modern philosophy.

To stretch the meaning of a word is to blur a distinction. It has been said that the philosopher's art is the art of making distinctions, and it will be objected to many of the arguments which follow that they depend on blurring important distinctions philosophers have made. In addition to making distinctions, though, the philosopher's art lies in keeping them under control once made, and to keep a distinction under control is to preserve it within domains in which it is significant and to obliterate it elsewhere. In large measure this book represents an attempt to keep certain crucial philosophic distinctions under control.

Probably what is most original about the book is the way in which I have combined and extended other men's ideas, some of which have been unfashionable long enough to sound original. To such an extent is the work derivative that I have been unable except in a comparatively few instances to credit the sources of the ideas I have borrowed, much less of the attitudes I have adopted. Readers of the philosophers on whom I have leaned will be able to gauge the degree to which my obligations have outrun my acknowledgments.

In the case of some of these philosophers, more needs to be said. I am well aware of a similarity between my general outlook in philosophy and that of James and Dewey, and in fact I meant, by naming the position spelled out in the final pages of the book "pragmatic reconstruction," to call attention to the similarity (as well as to the semiotic sense in which this reconstruction is pragmatic). When addressing the problems considered in the book, however, I seem to be operating within a quite different framework—swayed by different winds of doctrine and looking in different directions for guidance. As a result I find myself incapable of estimating the extent of the similarity between my views and those of the pragmatists named, or even of determining whether the similarity involves anything more specific than the sharing of a Weltanschauung—which, of course, is ultimately the most important kind of similarity.

I am afraid, too, that I have been equally unsuccessful in avoiding a corresponding error of commission, the error of attributing to philosophers ideas and attitudes unrecognizable to them as their own. It frequently comes about, when I attempt to formulate the principles underlying certain philosophic positions or methods, that, due either to my inadequate understanding of them or to some defect in the positions or methods themselves, I end up with what can be only a caricature of a position men could seriously entertain or of a method they could deliberately employ. But the price of eliminating some of the apparent theoretic grotesqueries is an equally apparent distortion of the positions or methods as they emerge from actual philosophic practice, and since much of the criticism that follows is directed against the gap which separates philosophic theory from philosophic practice, this is a price I have been unwilling to pay.

Among the debts I must single out for explicit acknowledgment are those I owe to Professor Hilary Putnam, who has saved me from a number of stylistic, logical, and philosophic errors, and to Professor John W. Yolton, who has devoted much time and thought to this book from its beginning, suggesting ideas to be explored and approaches to be followed and enabling me to understand my own ideas more clearly. I am deeply grateful to Mr. Yolton, not only for his philosophic interest and advice, but also for sounding a note of encouragement at a time when it was badly needed. My debt to Professor Horace M. Kallen is as vast as his influence on me has been pervasive, and no less difficult to itemize. Though my philosophic views have diverged from his in important respects, it is from him that I have got my general philosophic outlook, and it is from him that I have learned the uses of philosophy.

I wish to express my gratitude to the department of philosophy in Princeton University for the Bamford Fellowship which enabled me, in 1955–56, to carry out extensive revisions on a dissertation—revisions that must otherwise have waited a depressing number of years. Several people have very kindly concerned themselves over the fate of my manuscript, and I am much indebted to them. That the book is no worse than it is should be attributed largely to the people who, in one way or another, have helped me with it; that it is no better should be attributed entirely to me.

Finally, I wish to acknowledge permission by Methuen and Company, Ltd., to include in my book the quotation from H. H. Price's *Perception*, and by Charles Scribner's Sons to include the quotation from *Tender Is the Night* by F. Scott Fitzgerald. Pages 11–12 of the present work appeared, with differences, in the April 26, 1956, issue of the *Journal of Phi-*

losophy, and pages 145–51 appeared, with slight differences, and with material from pages 135–36 and 162–63 included, in the June, 1957, issue of *Philosophical Studies*; the editors of both journals have kindly consented to my reprinting the material in these articles.

ALAN PASCH

Contents

PART II

EMPIRICISM AND EXPERIENCE

Chapter III

PART I

EMPIRICISM

AND

ANALYTICITY

CHAPTER I

The Analytic-Synthetic Distinction
and Its Significance for Empiricism

1. EMPIRICISM AND ANALYTICITY:
THE BACKGROUND

"EMPIRICISM" is one of those words, like "material-
ism," "naturalism," "idealism," and a host of others, which suffer so much from excessive meaning that they are in danger of
having no meaning at all. Presumably a descriptive term, it has
become overladen with emotional overtones to the point of belonging, in one way or another, to the value vocabularies of lit-
erary critics, scientists (especially social scientists), theologians,
and political commentators, not to mention philosophers. The
charge of being either empirical or unempirical has been held
sufficient to damn into the fringe areas of intellectual integrity
writers on almost any subject and of almost any persuasion. Even
eliminating all but the word's descriptive uses, its various nuances of meaning are so numerous that only when confined explicitly to a narrow and specific context is it more than vaguely
suggestive. A recent dictionary of philosophy follows up nine
definitions of empiricism with references to fourteen different
articles, ranging from "scepticism," "sensationalism," and "pluralism" to "idealism," "transcendentalism," and "scientific empiricism," all fourteen apparently intended to shed light on
"empiricism." The ranks of philosophers who have been called
empiricists, at one time or another, include couples of such dubious ideological compatibility as Bacon and Hobbes, Hume
and Kant, James and Bergson, Carnap and Husserl.

In view of this unpromising state of terminological affairs it
might appear that any discussion of empiricism is doomed to
play itself out simply trying to designate unambiguously what

the discussion was to have been about. Nevertheless, there seems to be enough common ground among present-day philosophers who call themselves empiricists, and the sense in which "empiricism" is to be used here is a loose enough one, so that only a brief characterization of empiricism is necessary. Moreover, since I will argue that the position I am about to characterize as empiricist is an untenable position as it stands, and since I will urge that it be replaced by a similar position which I would like also to call empiricism, it is desirable to provide beforehand for a certain flexibility of usage.[1]

Briefly then, the empiricism I want to talk about is the empiricism associated with the names of Locke, Hume, Mach, James, and Russell; the empiricism that led to the verification and operationist theories of meaning; the empiricism that has more recently been the topic of such urgent discussions as Quine's "Two Dogmas of Empiricism,"[2] Bergmann's "Two Cornerstones of Empiricism,"[3] Carnap's "Empiricism, Semantics, and Ontology,"[4] and the symposium by Reichenbach, Goodman, and Lewis on "The Experiential Element in Knowl-

[1] The account which follows lays no claim to accuracy of historical detail. The history of empiricism is itself an interesting and rewarding topic for inquiry, but what follows is merely a historical background for an analysis of empiricism.

[2] W. V. Quine, "Two Dogmas of Empiricism," *Philosophical Review*, LX (1951), 20–43; reprinted in his *From a Logical Point of View* (Cambridge, Mass.: Harvard University Press, 1953), pp. 20–46. References throughout the present book will be to the latter.

[3] Gustav Bergmann, "Two Cornerstones of Empiricism," *Synthèse*, VIII (1953), 435–52; reprinted in his *The Metaphysics of Logical Positivism* (New York: Longmans, Green & Co., 1954), pp. 78–105. References throughout the present book will be to the latter.

[4] Rudolf Carnap, "Empiricism, Semantics, and Ontology," *Revue internationale de philosophie*, XI (1950), 20–40; reprinted in his *Meaning and Necessity* (enlarged ed.; Chicago: University of Chicago Press, 1956), pp. 205–21; reprinted in *Semantics and the Philosophy of Language*, ed. Leonard Linsky (Urbana: University of Illinois Press, 1952), pp. 208–28; reprinted in *Readings in Philosophy of Science*, ed. Philip P. Wiener (New York: Charles Scribner's Sons, 1953), pp. 509–22; reprinted in *Contemporary Philosophy*, ed. James L. Jarrett and Sterling M. McMurrin (New York: Henry Holt & Co., 1954), pp. 377–90. References throughout the present book will be to *Semantics and the Philosophy of Language*.

edge."[5] It is true that among the philosophers just named there
are enough disagreements and inconsistencies to provide material for several additional volumes; that quite likely no two empiricists have ever conceived operationism or the verification
principle in the same fashion; and that the articles mentioned
are characterized more by their explicit disagreement with each
other, if not with empiricism itself, than by their agreement.
Nevertheless, a community of opinion can be found here, if not
about the validity of empiricism, then at least about certain fundamental aspects of the empiricism whose validity is in question.

The most basic principle of this "minimal" empiricism is that
all ideas are derived from experience, and the vagueness and ambiguity of the expressions "ideas," "derived from," and "experience" pretty well account for the history of modern empiricism.
The effort to clarify "idea" has led to a host of problems, involving not only the original expression but such others as "concept," "term," "judgment," "proposition," "sentence," and
"statement," as well as "basic" or "expressive" or "protocol"
instances of these. Operationism and the verification theory of
meaning have both risen from attempts to sharpen the expression "derived from," the former concerning itself with concepts
and the latter with propositions. The same attempt has led, on
a more comprehensive scale, to what is known as rational reconstruction, a reconstruction of the whole body of scientific knowledge within the framework of a language system such that, as
Quine puts it, "each meaningful statement is equivalent to some
logical construct upon terms which refer to immediate experience."[6] "Derived from" has thus had the sense of "reducible
to," whether this sense is linguistic or extralinguistic, and in fact
Quine has designated the whole movement as *reductionism*,
reserving "empiricism" for a broader usage. Corresponding to
the ambiguity of the term "experience," or, as it is customarily

[5] Symposium, "The Experiential Element in Knowledge," *Philosophical
Review*, LXI (1952), 147–75. (Hans Reichenbach, "Are Phenomenal Reports Absolutely Certain?" 147–59; Nelson Goodman, "Sense and Certainty,"
160–67; C. I. Lewis, "The Given Element in Empirical Knowledge,"
168–75.)

[6] *Op. cit.*, p. 20.

qualified, "immediate experience," the primitive terms of a language system may be of various kinds; they may, for example, designate physical things or sensory data, and the sensory data may comprise appearances of physical things or the primitive elements out of which physical things are constituted. Inquiries into the nature of "immediate experience" do not, of course, all proceed within the linguistic framework of rational reconstruction, but may be psychological or, in the sense of the "historical, plain method" of Locke, epistemological.

It is seen that empiricism of the kind I am trying to talk about is above all a theory of meaning, or rather of meaningfulness or significance. When it is said that all ideas are derived from experience, it is meaningful or significant ideas that are meant: if a given idea is not derived from experience, then it is (or should be regarded as) meaningless. It is at this point that the empiricist is confronted with logic and mathematics, which are not derived from experience in any obvious sense. Are mathematical ideas to be regarded as derived from experience in some less-than-obvious sense? Two considerations hinge on the answer to this question. If the answer is no, then mathematics seems to be nonsignificant, a notion only a lunatic or a philosopher could entertain seriously; if yes, then what is the nature of the significance characterized in terms of the concept—suddenly become very deep—of being derived from experience, and how are mathematical ideas to be distinguished from the chimerical ideas that empiricists have wanted to brand as nonsignificant but that are conceivably also derived in some less-than-obvious sense from experience?

Second, there is a property which belongs essentially to true mathematical propositions but which empiricists have not wanted to predicate of true propositions derived from experience—the property of being true necessarily. Part of the motivation of the early empiricists was the conviction that a major philosophic error lay in attributing to true propositions about matters of fact the same certainty or necessity that was attributed to propositions such as mathematical propositions, which refer only to relations among ideas. True propositions about factual matters are contingently, not necessarily, true, and at best they can be known with high probability, never with certainty.

It is in terms of this distinction between *matters of fact* and *relations among ideas* that Hume, for example, was able to clarify the empiricist position. The significance that an idea has by virtue of being derived from experience is what may be called empirical significance. The principle of empiricism could thus be reformulated as the principle that all factual ideas, or ideas referring to experience, are empirical, or derived from experience. If we desire to speak of true propositions rather than significant "ideas," we may say that all true propositions which say anything about experience are derived from experience. Such truths are contingent, and can be known with probability only. Truths, on the other hand, which are necessary and which can be known with certainty are about relations among ideas. Such truths are neither factual nor empirical, which is to say they neither refer to experience nor need be derived from experience. If it be objected that by the empiricists' criterion of significance these truths are nonsignificant, the reply is that the empiricists' criterion does not apply to truths about relations among ideas but only to truths about matters of fact.[7]

For Hume, therefore, the universe of significant discourse is exhausted by the two classes of factual propositions and mathematical propositions. "If we take in our hand any volume . . . let us ask, Does it contain any abstract reasoning concerning quantity or number? No. Does it contain any experimental rea-

---

[7] Empiricism of meaning, with which I am concerned, must not be confounded with empiricism of knowledge or of truth, the kind of empiricism which admits no knowledge unless inductively arrived at. An empiricist of the latter kind must either deny that mathematical propositions can be true and can constitute knowledge, or else he must deny that there is any such sharp distinction as Hume thought between matters of fact and relations among ideas. Mill, an empiricist of knowledge, took the position that mathematical propositions are inductive generalizations. In large measure the problems to be dealt with in the present work are precisely those generated by the attempt to formulate an empiricist position which maintains the noninductive or a priori character of logic and mathematics—the attempt to formulate an empiricism of meaning.

soning concerning matter of fact and existence? No. Commit it then to the flames: for it can contain nothing but sophistry and illusion."[8]

It is not to be thought, however, that empiricist philosophers monopolized the distinction between these two kinds of truth. After all, the distinction between a realm of ideas and a realm of things is central in Plato, and Leibniz relied heavily on a rigid boundary between truths of reason and truths of fact, which are necessary and contingent, respectively. What is different about the distinction as conceived by empiricists is the epistemological significance attributed to it. For Plato, broadly speaking, the realm of ideas was the prototype of the realm of things, and knowledge about the latter was to be had only by considering the former. This is exactly what empiricists denied, and Hume insisted that no knowledge about matters of fact could be gained by inquiring into relations among ideas; only in this way could he maintain the necessity of logical and mathematical truths as against the contingency of truths about matters of fact. Before examining more closely the relationship between the empiricist principle and the distinction between truths of reason and those of fact, it will be helpful to glance at Kant's way of marking the distinction.

Whereas the philosophers before Kant made only the general distinction mentioned above—the distinction between truths of reason (necessary truths, relations among ideas) and truths of fact (contingent truths, matters of fact)—Kant found it necessary to make a second distinction, the distinction between analytic and synthetic truths. There was no question with Leibniz, for example, of distinguishing either in intension or extension between statements true by virtue of the principle of contradiction and statements necessarily true; hence Leibniz needed only one pair of terms, "necessary" and "contingent." But Kant, in order even to articulate the possibility that some statements are necessary besides those Leibniz thought necessary, needed the

[8] *An Enquiry concerning Human Understanding*, ed. L. A. Selby-Bigge (2d ed.; Oxford: Clarendon Press, 1951), p. 165. Italics omitted.

additional pair of terms, "analytic" and "synthetic." Still a third
pair of terms was used by Kant when he distinguished between
judgments which are true a priori and those which are true
a posteriori.[9] This was a distinction based on the sources of cognition, a priori judgments stemming from pure reason and pure
understanding (and hence being validated independently of experience), and a posteriori judgments stemming from experience
(and requiring experience for their validation).

Thus there are in Kant three relevant distinctions, the distinctions between (1) necessary and contingent, (2) a priori and
a posteriori, and (3) analytic and synthetic judgments. Necessity, according to Kant, cannot be obtained from experience,
and therefore necessary judgments are a priori judgments.[10] Necessity, in fact, is for Kant a mark of the a priori, along with
what he calls strict universality,[11] and it is tempting to say that
there was no real difference for Kant between distinctions (1)
and (2). To begin with, Kant tells us that necessity and strict
universality, the two marks of the a priori, are coextensive, and
since his only reason for distinguishing them is apparently that
sometimes necessity is more easily demonstrated and sometimes
universality, they may be more than coextensive. At any rate,
"strictly universal" will be taken here in the sense of Leibniz'
"true in all possible worlds,"[12] which in turn will be taken as
identical with "necessary." But, second, if no ground exists for
distinguishing between necessity and strict universality, then on
what grounds are necessity and apriority to be distinguished? It
might have been said that the latter includes both necessity and
strict universality, but these are no longer distinguishable. It
would seem that no such ground is to be found, and, indeed,

9 Kant uses the terms "judgment" and "proposition" interchangeably.

10 ". . . all proper mathematical judgments are a priori, and not empirical,
because they carry with them necessity, which cannot be obtained from experience" (Prolegomena, trans. Paul Carus [Chicago, Ill.: Open Court Publishing Co., 1902], p. 16).

11 Critique of Pure Reason, trans. Norman Kemp Smith (London: Macmillan & Co., 1953), p. 44.

12 ". . . with strict universality, that is, in such manner that no exception
is allowed as possible" (ibid).

Kant's only reason for using both distinction (1) and distinction (2) is apparently in order to preserve verbal continuity with earlier writers who had used both sets of expressions.

However, not merely the identity, but the coextension, of distinctions (1) and (2) on the one hand, and (3) on the other, has been the focal point of much modern philosophy beginning with Kant.[13] Kant's reason for using the extra pair of terms "analytic" and "synthetic" was, as seen, in order to deny that it divides the world of statements into the same two camps that the pair "a priori" and "a posteriori" divides it into—in order, that is, to be able to say that some truths which are necessary in one of Leibniz' senses of necessity are not necessary in another sense. The sense in which these truths are necessary is the sense marked by the term "a priori," and the sense in which they are not is marked by the term "analytic." Kant was thus able to spare his readers the laborious circumlocution I have just gone through, simply by asserting that there are synthetic judgments a priori.

The analytic-synthetic distinction, according to Kant, is "a distinction in judgments, as to their content, according to which they are either merely explicative, adding nothing to the content of the cognition, or expansive, increasing the given cognition: the former may be called analytical, the latter synthetical, judgments."[14] The distinction, when made on this basis, is seen to agree with the distinction Hume wanted to make between matters of fact and relations among ideas, according to which reasoning about relations among ideas could give us no knowledge about matters of fact. Care must be taken, however, about identifying "empirical" with "synthetic." For Hume, of course, there is nothing wrong with such an identification, but for Kant "empirical" is properly identified with "a posteriori," not with "synthetic." Expressed in Kantian terms, the empiricist principle is

[13] In calling two distinctions coextensive I mean their corresponding terms are coextensive. If, for example, the distinctions between A and B and between C and D are coextensive, it is because A and C are coextensive and B and D are coextensive.

[14] *Prolegomena*, p. 14.

the principle that all factual, or synthetic, truths are empirical,
or a posteriori, and Kant's denial of the empiricist principle took
the form of the assertion that there are synthetic truths which
are a priori. It is, as a matter of historical fact, characteristic of
most philosophic empiricists, at least until recently, to hold the
three distinctions designated by the pairs of terms "analytic"-
"synthetic," "a priori"-"a posteriori," and "necessary"-"contingent" to be coextensive, and "empirical" to be coextensive with
the second term in each pair.[15] I say "most" empiricists, partly
because there is at least a question whether these distinctions
are coextensive for Mill, and partly because, if pragmatists are
considered to be philosophic empiricists (as I would like to consider them), then either pragmatists must be excepted or else it
must be made clear that the distinctions held by them to be
coextensive are called distinctions by courtesy only. And I say
"at least until recently" because cases have recently been made
for the existence of the synthetic a priori by philosophers who,
whether or not they call themselves empiricists, qualify, in my
opinion, to be called empiricists on other grounds.[16]

2. EMPIRICISM AND ANALYTICITY: ONE
   "DOGMA" OR TWO?

In the controversy touched off by Quine's "Two
Dogmas of Empiricism" and evidenced by the extraordinary
spate of articles that has appeared on the subject in the little
more than four or five years following, only one writer so far as

[15] See Alan Gewirth, "The Distinction between Analytic and Synthetic
Truths," *Journal of Philosophy*, L (1953), 397–425. Gewirth also cites the
distinctions verbal-real and essential-accidental as belonging with the rest,
that is, as being held by empiricists to be coextensive with the three already
mentioned. (Strictly speaking, "empirical" is coextensive not with "synthetic"
but with "synthetic and meaningful.")

[16] See, e.g., the following: Irving M. Copi, "Modern Logic and the Synthetic A Priori," *Journal of Philosophy*, XLVI (1949), 243–45; Alonzo
Church, review of Copi's article in *Journal of Symbolic Logic*, XV (1950),
221; C. H. Langford, "A Proof That Synthetic A Priori Propositions Exist,"
Journal of Philosophy, XLVI (1949), 20–24; Arthur Pap, "Are All Necessary Propositions Analytic?" *Philosophical Review*, LVIII (1949), 299–320,
and "Logic and the Synthetic A Priori," *Philosophy and Phenomenological
Research*, X (1949–50), 500–14; S. E. Toulmin, "A Defence of 'Synthetic
Necessary Truth.'" *Mind*, LVIII (1949), 164–77.

I know, Hofstadter in his study of Quine's epistemology, has questioned Quine's claim that the two dogmas are "at root identical."[17] Without, for the present, drawing any conclusions about whether the views characterized by Quine as dogmas are adequately so characterized, or about whether, dogmas or not, they are ill-founded, I want to examine the proposition, asserted by Quine and denied by Hofstadter, that they are identical.

Quine characterizes the dogmas as, first, that there is "some fundamental cleavage" between analytic and synthetic truths, and, second, that "each meaningful statement is equivalent to some logical construct upon terms which refer to immediate experience."[18] For brevity's sake these may be called (after Quine) the dogmas of analyticity and reductionism, respectively. Historically, as has been seen, the concept of reductionism is by itself an attempt to explicate what has been traditionally called empiricism, while the belief in a distinction between analytic and synthetic truths has been held in one form or another by philosophers who could in no appropriate sense be called empiricists. Hence, to call analyticity and reductionism two dogmas of empiricism is to use "empiricism" in a different and broader sense than I have used it so far. But it is not necessary to examine this sense in detail in order to investigate the claim that reductionism, or empiricism in the narrow sense, and analyticity are "at root identical," though I will have to examine the broader sense of "empiricism" before I have finished stating my case.

Whether or not analyticity and reductionism are in any sense identical, it has been shown that they are at least intimately bound up with each other. A convenient conceptual device for exhibiting this intimacy is the verification theory of meaning,

[17] Albert Hofstadter, "The Myth of the Whole: A Consideration of Quine's View of Knowledge," *Journal of Philosophy*, LI (1954), 397–417. Recent doubts about the analytic-synthetic distinction had been expressed before the appearance of Quine's article; see, e.g., J. R. Reid, "Analytic Statements in Semiosis," *Mind*, LII (1943), 314–30, and John Wild and J. L. Cobitz, "On the Distinction between the Analytic and the Synthetic," *Philosophy and Phenomenological Research*, VIII (1947–48), 651–67.

[18] *Op. cit.*, p. 20.

the theory, according to Quine, that "the meaning of a statement is the method of empirically confirming or infirming it."[19]
If it is significance, or meaningfulness, rather than meaning for
which the criterion is wanted, the verification theory can be said
to be the theory that a statement is significant if there is a
method of empirically confirming or infirming it. The reason
why the verification theory is a convenient device for exhibiting
the intimacy between analyticity and reductionism is that the
verification theory is itself intimate with both.

It is intimate with analyticity because it defines empirical
significance and therefore defines the fundamental cleavage
which is thought to exist between analytic and synthetic truths.
It is intimate with reductionism because reductionism defines
the nature of verification, the nature, in Quine's words, "of the
relation between a statement and the experiences which contribute to or detract from its confirmation."[20] Moreover, the
verification theory helps clarify analyticity because, in terms of
the theory, an analytic statement would seem to be "a limiting
kind of statement which is vacuously confirmed, *ipso facto*,
come what may."[21]

In these terms, however, it is certainly not obvious that the
two beliefs are really the same belief. Though it be maintained
that the nature of empirical significance is adequately expressed
by the verification theory, there is no necessity for also maintaining that there is a limiting kind of statement which is confirmed vacuously, *ipso facto*, and come what may. But even if
this latter assertion did follow from proclaiming the verification
theory as dogma, it is not the same as the assertion that there
is a fundamental cleavage between analytic and synthetic truths.
And in fact, not only is it not the same as the fundamental
cleavage assertion, it is the denial of that assertion. To say of a
statement that it is a limiting case of a certain class of statements is—though perhaps not to include it in that class—to
suggest, at any rate, that there is some sort of continuity between the statements in the class and the statement of the
limiting kind and, therefore, to deny that a fundamental cleav-

[19] *Ibid.*, p. 37.   [20] *Ibid.*, p. 38.   [21] *Ibid.*, p. 41.

age separates them. Thus, on the view under consideration, the statement "no bachelor is married" is a perfectly good empirical, and hence synthetic, statement whose empirical significance happens to reside in the fact that it is confirmed no matter what.

Nor does it help to travel the other direction, to start with analyticity and work toward reductionism, both conceived in terms of the verification theory, because now, instead of arriving at an inconsistency, I begin with one, the inconsistency of asserting that some true statements, namely, analytic statements, are devoid of empirical significance and that their empirical significance resides in their vacuous confirmation.

The trouble lies in characterizing analytic statements as a limiting kind of statement confirmed no matter what. It is as though one were to assert that a fundamental cleavage exists between two kinds of vessels, surface vessels and submarines, to view submarines as vessels having the ability to become unsubmerged without aid, and then to characterize surface vessels as a limiting kind of submarine which is unsubmerged no matter what.[22] True, surface vessels are unsubmerged no matter what, and to that extent, if one forces the issue, a limiting kind of submarine, but this is not enlightening with respect to the nature of the alleged fundamental cleavage between surface vessels and submarines. It is rather the sort of argument a carrier skipper might use to persuade a submarine-minded appropriations committee.

Instead of re-examining the verification theory of meaning for clues to the identification of analyticity and reductionism, I will weaken Quine's claim and investigate Hofstadter's counterclaim.

---

[22] The analogy may be made more exact by demanding that all recognized vessels be "surfaceful," and defining "surfacefulness" as the ability to become unsubmerged without aid. The characterization of surface vessels as a limiting kind of submarine then becomes necessary to explain why surface vessels are recognized. What has happened, of course, is that a criterion framed in terms of one kind of object has been unjustifiably extended to apply without qualification to a second kind, and balance is then restored by means of a distorted characterization of the second kind—a perfect example of Vaihinger's "method of antithetic error."

Quine's arguments in favor of the root identity of the two dogmas are confined to the "limiting kind" or "extreme case" sort of argument based on the verification theory and already found unsatisfactory. In its final form, this is the argument that the truth of statements depends both on language and on extralinguistic fact; that this double dependency "carries in its train, not logically but all too naturally," a twofold constituency of the truth of a statement, one linguistic and the other (which must for empiricists "boil down to a range of confirmatory experiences") factual; and that an analytic statement is the "extreme case" where the linguistic constituent is "all that matters."[23] One still wonders what sort of relationship this identity relationship can be.

Moreover, Quine does not speak of the two dogmas as "at root identical" throughout his article: at times he says only that they are "intimately connected" or that one "clearly supports" the other.[24] And in all probability I am looking for far more significance than Quine intended the word "identical" to have. Furthermore, Quine might well reply that the expression in question is not "identical" but rather "at root identical," that no such simple and literal sense of identity is intended as the one I seem to be demanding but some deeper sense which is "at the root" of the whole matter. Hofstadter, in fact, suggests that what is at the root of the matter is the supposition, common to the two dogmas, that "the statement is the unit of significance," and the suggestion is certainly supported by Quine in his discussion of what empiricism is like without the dogmas. However—and quite apart from Quine—the simple and literal relationship between the dogmas is an intriguing problem by itself, and I will continue to examine it.

Clearly, it is not being argued, and no case could be made for the position, that the dogmas are identical in some intensional sense of identity. I shall assume, therefore, that what is being claimed is that the analyticity and reductionism dogmas are extensionally equivalent, that if either is denied the other cannot be consistently affirmed.

[23] Op. cit., p. 41.   [24] Ibid.

But Hofstadter shows that even this claim is false. Suppose, he requests, that there is a sharp distinction in our language between analytic and synthetic, and that the statement "the current in this galvanometer coil is 2 amperes" is clearly and distinctly synthetic. Still, according to Hofstadter, in order to isolate the observable consequences or factual constituent of the statement—for example, a deviation of the galvanometer mirror—other statements, of theory and of antecedent conditions, are required, as Duhem has shown. The statement does not, in other words, by itself "boil down to a range of confirmatory experiences," and hence there is a statement which is both synthetic and nonempirical. Hofstadter shows that the claim of extensional equivalence is false by demonstrating that reductionism could be denied and analyticity, nevertheless, affirmed.[25]

There is another possibility, though doubtless far from what Quine had in mind when he said the two dogmas are at root identical. This is the even weaker claim that reductionism cannot be affirmed at the same time analyticity is denied though analyticity can be affirmed at the same time reductionism is denied, which is to say that reductionism implies analyticity or, in still other words, that analyticity is a necessary condition for reductionism.

Can this claim be defended? Suppose the statement "the current in this galvanometer coil is 2 amperes" does have "its own isolable counterpart in experience" (Hofstadter's expression)—say, a deviation of the galvanometer mirror. In this case it is empirically significant according to what Quine calls the "attenuated form" of the dogma of reductionism,[26] and it is undeniably synthetic by any criterion admitting a connection between a statement's meaning and its experiential counterpart. Nevertheless, that there is a statement which is clearly and distinctly synthetic is no reason why there must be a sharp distinction between synthetic and analytic statements—no reason

---

[25] Hofstadter is not arguing explicitly against the claim of extensional equivalence, but in showing that one dogma may be maintained and the other rejected without inconsistency, he implicitly denies that claim.

[26] Op. cit., p. 41.

why, say, "2 amperes is 2 amperes" must be clearly and distinctly analytic.[27] It seems legitimate on the basis of this argument, therefore, to affirm the dogma of reductionism while denying that of analyticity, and the claim that the former implies the latter is apparently proved false.

Before quitting this latter claim, however, let me call attention to a feature of the argument against it which strikes me as odd. The argument rests on a hypothetical state of affairs characterized, first, by the absence of any "fundamental cleavage" between truths which are analytic and truths which are synthetic, and, second, by the validity of the principle that every significant synthetic statement and no other statement is empirical, that is, has its own "range of confirmatory experiences." What strikes me as odd about this is that when there is no sharp distinction between analytic and synthetic statements the significance of a principle about synthetic statements but not analytic ones becomes questionable. A digression will clarify the point.

To deny that "no bachelor is married" may be distinguished on the basis of experiential meaningfulness from "no bachelor is sentimental" is to make a strong assertion. But the claim being denied—that the statements are distinguishable on that basis—is correspondingly weak. A much stronger claim, and one that most philosophers seem in fact to be making when they draw the analytic-synthetic distinction, is that these two statements may be distinguished along with all statements *of the same kind.* The claim, in other words, is that there is a distinction not simply between two statements but between two classes of statements. This is a claim, moreover, which may be rejected without denying the distinction between "no bachelor is married" and "no bachelor is sentimental," so that the rejection constitutes a relatively weak counterclaim. Some philosophers do deny the distinction in question between these two state-

27 It has recently been maintained (by Richard Rudner, "A Note on Likeness of Meaning," *Analysis,* X [1949–50], 115–18) that repetitive statements such as "2 amperes is 2 amperes" are not analytic because not only are no two words ever synonymous but no two tokens of the same word ever have the same meaning in every respect. But see p. 36 n. below.

ments, usually on the ground that the nature of the distinction cannot be specified in detail. Since to specify the nature of the distinction in detail would probably amount to a specification of two class characteristics, however, what purports to be the denial of a distinction between two statements may really be only the denial of a distinction between two classes. But most rejections of the analytic-synthetic distinction consist in the weak counterclaim that the attempt to maintain a sharp distinction, on the basis in question, between statements that resemble "no bachelor is married" and statements that resemble "no bachelor is sentimental" is unsatisfactory; most rejections do not consist in the strong counterclaim that the paradigm statements are on a par so far as their having or failing to have experiential import is concerned.

Any of several reasons may be given for the rejection of the attempt to maintain a sharp distinction between the class of statements called analytic and the class called synthetic, and in every case the status of a principle about all and only synthetic statements is peculiar. It may, for example, be claimed that there are statements that are both analytic and synthetic, in which case a principle attributing a characteristic to every synthetic statement and withholding it from every analytic one is self-contradictory. It may be claimed that there are statements that might be either analytic or synthetic—statements we do not know how to classify or are, for some other reason, unable to classify; in this case, though a principle about all synthetic statements or about only synthetic statements would be significant to us (since we could either include or exclude unclassified statements), a principle about all and only synthetic statements would have its significance seriously impaired. Again, it may be claimed simply that no satisfactory specification of the distinction, other than partial inventories of the extensions of its terms, has been given, in which case the principle about all and only synthetic statements would be held to be equally unsatisfactory.

The principle could be reformulated, it is true, in such a way that synthetic statements are not alluded to and rejection

of the analytic-synthetic distinction would not inhibit acceptance of the principle. It could, for example, be reformulated
simply as the principle that "every significant statement has its
own range of confirmatory experiences." But this would be not
so much a reformulation as a return to the original formulation,
except that instead of "all (empirical) ideas are derived from
experience" the principle now states that "all (empirical) statements have their own ranges of confirmatory experiences." And
the empiricist is faced all over again with the problem about
logical and mathematical statements.[28]

Either "no bachelor is married" has its own range of confirmatory experiences, just as "no bachelor is sentimental" has,
or else it hasn't. If the latter is the case, then a second principle
is needed to distinguish the "no bachelor is married" kind of
nonempirical statement from another kind of nonempirical
statement which also does not have its own range of confirmatory experiences but to which empiricists have been most
anxious to deny significance. This second principle, however,
would bear a suspicious resemblance to the analyticity principle
that, on the present hypothesis, is rejected.[29] If, on the other
hand, "no bachelor is married" is linked with "no bachelor is
sentimental" in having its own range of confirmatory experiences, then the reductionist principle appears to be compromised by the difficulty encountered in attempting to explain
how "no bachelor is married" is able to have its own range of
confirmatory experiences and, moreover, to have it in a way in
which certain other statements, to which empiricists have
wanted to deny significance, cannot. By formulating the prin-

[28] See above, pp. 6–7.

[29] Thus Carnap, in an early paper ("Formal and Factual Science," translated by Herbert Feigl and May Brodbeck and reprinted in their *Readings in
the Philosophy of Science* [New York: Appleton-Century-Crofts, 1953], pp.
123–28), spoke of analytic statements as "auxiliary statements," "mere calculational devices" which "facilitate linguistic transformations in the factual
sciences" (italics omitted). The second principle required would, on this
view, have to distinguish between two kinds of nonempirical statements, those
which facilitate calculation and those which do not—or, to point up the
moral, it would have to distinguish between nonempirical statements which
have "calculational significance" and those which have not.

ciple of reductionism so that it is applicable to synthetic statements alone, empiricists avoid these problems—but they also
put themselves in a position of dependence, as I am suggesting,
on the analytic-synthetic distinction.

Thus, although the simultaneous affirmation of reductionism
and denial of analyticity cannot be said to be contradictory
(unless the denial takes the form of the assertion that some
statements are both analytic and synthetic), without analyticity
the principle of reductionism is very much weakened. A principle which exhorts us to accept as empirically significant certain members of the class of synthetic statements and no members of the class of nonsynthetic statements is, in the absence
of a clear division between those classes or even of adequate
assurance that there is a division at all, a strange kind of principle. Whatever form the rejection of the analyticity principle
takes, the least that must be said against the reductionist principle is that it has lost its empirical usefulness. The principle
will be said, on that account, to be pragmatically invalid.
Analyticity, in other words, is a necessary condition for the
pragmatic validity of reductionism.

Moreover, it may be noted that a corresponding weakened
conclusion cannot be drawn from the argument which denies
that reductionism is a necessary condition for analyticity: it
cannot be said that reductionism is a necessary condition for
the pragmatic validity of analyticity. To assume that reductionism is false is to assume that not all significant synthetic statements have their own ranges of confirmatory experiences. But
nevertheless it may be true in every sense required that there
is a sharp distinction between analytic and synthetic statements.
The tentative conclusion, therefore, is that analyticity is a
necessary condition for the pragmatic validity of reductionism,
but reductionism is not a necessary condition for the pragmatic
validity of analyticity.

Perhaps if the problem were exhibited in the more traditional
terms of the early empiricists, or better yet in Kantian terms,
which to my mind are the clearest yet devised as far as this

aspect of empiricism is concerned, the conclusion I have reached may be made less tentative. Kant, it will be remembered, made a helpful distinction between the content of a statement and its sources, or between the property a statement has by virtue of being or not being about experience and the property it has by virtue of being or not being derived from (or, as we may say, validated in terms of) experience. Statements which are about experience are synthetic statements; statements which are not are, if true, analytic. Statements which are derived from or validated in terms of experience are a posteriori statements; statements which are not are a priori.

Empiricism may now be formulated as the principle that the distinction between analytic and synthetic and the distinction between a priori and a posteriori are coextensive: all and only statements about experience are (if recognized by empiricism) derived from experience and hence validated in terms of experience. The denial of empiricism may take, and has taken, the form of the assertion that there are significant synthetic statements a priori—that there are meaningful statements about experience which nevertheless are neither derived from experience nor to be experientially validated. Analyticity is simply the principle that there is a sharp distinction, a "fundamental cleavage," between statements which are about experience and statements which are not. The relationship between these two principles, at least when interpreted extensionally, may now be seen quite easily.

Suppose, first, that the principle of empiricism is rejected. This is to suppose that there is at least one statement—say, "every event has a cause"—which is about experience (synthetic) but not derived from or validated in terms of experience (not a posteriori) and which is significant. There is nothing in this supposition to militate against the existence of a distinction between truths which are about experience and truths which are not. In short, the principle of empiricism is not a necessary condition for the pragmatic validity of the principle of analyticity.

Now suppose that the principle of analyticity is rejected. Whatever form this rejection may take, it must be said as a very minimum that the extensions of "analytic" and of "synthetic" are vague in the sense that borderline cases exist for which no decision procedure is available. The empiricist principle cannot, on this assumption, be asserted in the form involving the coextension of the analytic-synthetic and a priori–a posteriori distinctions, because this coextension would entail the coextension of the corresponding terms of the distinctions, and there could be no justification for saying that a term whose extension is vague has the same extension as a term whose extension is not vague. One might, to be sure, also reject the a priori–a posteriori distinction in an effort to preserve the coextension, but this would be to assume that the terms involved are systematically vague in identical ways—one might just as well assume the validity of empiricism to begin with and not bother about all these details. At any rate, on the assumption that analyticity is false, to assert the principle of empiricism in the form which denies the existence of meaningful synthetic truths that are a priori is, once more, to make a claim having no pragmatic validity. The principle of empiricism, when pragmatically valid, implies the principle of analyticity.

I conclude that the result tentatively arrived at earlier in this section is correct. The dogma of analyticity is a necessary condition for the pragmatic validity of the dogma of reductionism (or of empiricism in its traditional sense), but the dogma of reductionism is not a necessary condition for the pragmatic validity of the dogma of analyticity. One who believes there is a sharp distinction between analytic and synthetic may or may not be a reductionist, as he chooses, but one who is a reductionist (and this includes those who call themselves, on that account, empiricists) has no choice: he must either accept the existence of a sharp and rigid analytic-synthetic distinction as a consequence of his reductionism or else accept the alternative consequence that, as it stands, his reductionism is, if it is consistent, a position serving no useful function for empiricists.

I am now in a position to map out the direction I want to take. If it can be agreed, on the basis of such recent attacks on the distinction as Quine's, that no clear and distinct boundary separates analytic from synthetic truths—at least in any way customarily associated with empiricism—then the appropriate conclusion may be drawn about empiricism itself or, at any rate, about empiricism in the narrow "reductionist" sense in which it has thus far been considered.

Moreover, if from a careful review of methods used for impugning the tenability of the analyticity principle, anything can be learned about the real significance of the analytic-synthetic distinction, this may be taken to be a clue to the manner in which empiricism must be reconceived if it is not to be discarded altogether.

However, I do not want to rest my conclusions about empiricism on the argument that empiricism implies analyticity and analyticity is untenable, or that, analyticity being a necessary condition for empiricism, the real nature of analyticity is an indication of the real nature of empiricism. I will, instead, try subsequently (in chapters iii and iv) to offer independent reasons why empiricism, to be tenable, must be conceived along radically different lines than most empiricists have conceived it, and in particular along certain lines suggested by what will have been said about the analytic-synthetic distinction.

3. CONTAINMENT AND C. I. LEWIS' INTENSIONAL
THEORY OF MEANING AND ANALYTICITY

It will be helpful if I begin the discussion of the analytic-synthetic distinction and of recent attacks on it—especially Quine's—by taking a closer look at Kant's way of conceiving it. The distinction according to Kant, as has been seen, is an exhaustive division of judgments on the basis of their content and not, like the a priori–a posteriori distinction, on the basis of their sources. Analytic judgments (or, as they will hereafter be called, analytic statements or truths) "express nothing in the predicate but what has been already actually thought in the concept of the subject, though not so distinctly or with the same (full) consciousness." An analytic statement is a subject-predicate statement whose predicate belongs to the subject "as something which is (covertly) contained" in it, or is connected with the subject in a way that is "thought through identity." Analytic truths "depend wholly on the law of Contradiction" because their predicates, since they are "constituent concepts" of their subjects, cannot be denied of them without contradiction. (This, incidentally, is the ground of their necessity and hence of their apriority.) Synthetic truths, on the other hand, are "ampliative" rather than "explicative" in that they predicate of the concept of the subject a new concept "which has not been in any wise thought in it, and which no analysis could possibly extract from it," and whose connection with the subject is "thought without identity." True statements whose truth does not derive solely from the law of contradiction are synthetic statements (whether or not their truth derives in part from the law of contradiction—as Kant thinks is the case with those synthetic statements he calls a priori).[30]

What emerges from Kant's discussion of analyticity is chiefly the idea of containment. An analytic statement says nothing about the world because (the concept of) its predicate is contained in (the concept of) its subject. Because its predicate is contained in its subject, the two are thought through identity, which is to say that once I have the subject in mind I can have

---

[30] *Prolegomena*, pp. 14 f.; *Critique of Pure Reason*, pp. 48 f. Kant's indebtedness to earlier writers, especially Leibniz, can be seen in this discussion of analytic and synthetic truths. Locke speaks of identical propositions which, though true and self-evident and in a sense basic to all our knowledge, are nevertheless "trifling," since "they add no light to our understandings, bring no increase to our knowledge." Another sort of trifling proposition, according to Locke, is "when a part of the complex idea is predicated of the name of the whole; a part of the definition, of the word defined" (*An Essay concerning Human Understanding*, abridged and edited by A. S. Pringle-Pattison [Oxford: Clarendon Press, 1950], pp. 306 f. [italics omitted]). Leibniz calls primitive truths of reason "by the general name of *identical*, because they seem only to repeat the same thing without giving us any information" (*New Essays concerning Human Understanding*, trans. Alfred G. Langley [3d ed.; La Salle, Ill.: Open Court Publishing Co., 1949], p. 404), and the reason for a necessary truth, which is founded on the law of contradiction, "can be found by analysis, resolving it into more simple ideas and truths, until we come to those which are primary" (*Monadology*, trans. Robert Latta [London: Oxford University Press, 1951], p. 236). See F. Ueberweg, *System of Logic*, trans. T. M. Lindsay (London: Longmans, Green & Co., 1871), pp. 289–94 (cited by Gewirth, *op. cit.*, p. 398).

the predicate in mind without having anything different in
mind than I had before. And again, an analytic statement cannot be denied without inconsistency, because to deny it would
be to say, in effect, that its predicate, which is contained in its
subject, is not contained in its subject. It is on this account that
Kant appropriated Leibniz' description of the statements in
question as true by virtue of the law of contradiction.

Having elicited the notion of containment as central to the
analytic-synthetic distinction, at least so far as that distinction is
made by Kant, I must now face the objection made by almost
everyone who has written lately on the question, that the notion
of containment is not a very precise one. It is easy to see, as
Waismann points out, that the word "contain" is used primarily in a spatial sense, and that even if not taken in this sense it
can be used in a great many different ways; in fact one is inclined to agree with Quine that Kant leaves the notion at a
metaphorical level.[31] But before condemning "containment" as
a concept by means of which the analytic-synthetic distinction
may be seen, I will present a more recent treatment of the problem of analyticity, one utilizing the very similar concept of *inclusion*. This is Lewis' treatment in *An Analysis of Knowledge
and Valuation*.[32] And I will present the objections to Lewis'
treatment which can be gleaned from Quine's "Two Dogmas of
Empiricism."

Lewis distinguishes between two kinds of analytic statements,
which he calls *explicitly* analytic and *implicitly* analytic. An explicitly analytic statement is an analytic statement which asserts
the necessity of something; an implicitly analytic statement is
an analytic statement which asserts something that is logically
necessary but does not assert *that* it is logically necessary.[33]

[31] F. Waismann, "Analytic-Synthetic," Part I, *Analysis*, X (1949–50), 26.
Quine, *op. cit.*, pp. 20–21.

[32] Lewis, *An Analysis of Knowledge and Valuation* (2d printing; La Salle,
Ill.: Open Court Publishing Co., 1950), Book I.

[33] *Ibid.*, p. 89. Other writers have made a totally different distinction between implicitly and explicitly analytic statements. For example, Pap (*Elements of Analytic Philosophy* [New York: Macmillan Co., 1949], pp. 474–

Thus, "all cats are animals" asserts that every existent cat is an animal, but gives no clue to whether the statement belongs with analytic or synthetic truths. The latter is known only when we know whether or not the corresponding explicitly analytic statement is true—the statement, in this case, that "all cats are necessarily animals," or "a cat is by definition an animal," or "that anything should be a cat but not an animal, is logically impossible." The first, in other words, tells us that the denotation or extension of "cat" is *included* in the extension of "animal," while the second tells us that the connotation or intension of "cat" *includes* the intension of "animal." And this corresponds with a requirement of analytic truths that seems to be universally accepted: the requirement that they be true in all possible worlds. If a statement is true in all possible worlds, then it is true in the actual world, and it is the latter only that is expressed by an implicitly analytic statement. But before we can know a statement to be analytic, we must be able to make its analyticity explicit, or else we could not distinguish it from a statement that is true in the actual world but not in all possible worlds.

Quine's difficulty with what has been said so far is that he feels the burden to have been shifted from the problem of analyticity to the problem of intensional language. To condone a language rich enough to contain such adverbs as "necessarily," according to Quine, presupposes a prior understanding of analyticity. He accordingly looks to extensional languages and finds —as could be predicted on the basis of the discussion above— that the most that can be said of a true statement in an extensional language is that it is true, not that it is analytic. In Lewis' terms, only implicitly analytic statements can appear in an extensional language, and consequently we have no way of determining whether the corresponding explicitly analytic statement

---

75) distinguishes between statements, such as "nobody knows what is not the case," which we *feel* to be analytically true and statements which have been *demonstrated* by philosophic analysis to be analytically true, for example, the same statement together with the partial analysis of "I know *p*" into "I believe *p*, and *p*." The former Pap calls implicitly analytic and the latter explicitly analytic, though it will be noticed that, unlike Lewis' distinction, Pap's depends on the context within which the statement is asserted.

is true, or, in other words, whether the statement is true in all possible worlds.

However, Lewis purports to provide an explanatory framework within which an independent understanding can be gained of the intensional adverbs which Quine claims rest on a prior notion of analyticity. Moreover, Lewis' framework also sharpens the meaning of inclusion, and so affords a direct insight into the nature of analyticity.

There are, according to Lewis, two ways in which intensional meaning may be understood, and these may be marked by the expressions "linguistic meaning" and "sense meaning."[34] The intension of an expression in the sense of its *linguistic meaning* Lewis describes as "that property which is common to all expressions which could be substituted for the one in question without altering the truth or falsity of any statement, or altering the signification of any other context in which this expression in question should be constituent." (By "signification" Lewis means the property of a thing which determines whether a term does or does not correctly apply to the thing.) The linguistic meaning of a linguistic entity is thus other linguistic entities. The intension of an expression in the sense of its *sense meaning*, on the other hand, is "a *criterion in mind*, by reference to which one is able to apply or refuse to apply the expression in question in the case of presented, or imagined, things or situations."

Analyticity may now be seen to involve what Lewis calls sense meaning, or what an expression means intensionally as a "criterion in mind." In Lewis' view, whether the analytic truth "all cats are animals" is meant to affirm a relation of classes and is thus correctly stated as implicitly analytic, or is meant to affirm a relation of intensional meanings and should thus be stated as explicitly analytic, it is the latter relation that must be known before the truth can be known to be analytic. The epistemological question of analyticity, according to Lewis, concerns the nature of the necessity in "all cats are necessarily animals," and

34 *An Analysis of Knowledge and Valuation*, pp. 131 ff.

how we know it. And the question can be answered only by reference to the sense meanings of "cat" and "animal." "The compatibility or incompatibility of sense-recognizable characters, and the inclusion of one in another or its exclusion by another, is thus the root of the matter."[35]

The upshot of Lewis' analysis, then, oversimplified as this account of it has been, is that the analyticity implicit in "all cats are animals" and explicit in "all cats are necessarily animals" rests ultimately on our refusal to apply the term "cat" to any sense-recognizable character to which we would not also apply the term "animal."

Furthermore, the analysis given provides Lewis with defensive weapons against current attacks on the principle that there is a basic distinction between analytic and synthetic truths. Since relations among sense-recognizable characters are fixed and irrevocable, as are relations among the meanings that are grounded in these characters, the determination of analyticity is not subject to any convention or decision, nor relative to how we express the relations. The incorrect view that analyticity is more or less arbitrarily determined stems, Lewis thinks, from confusing the determination of ways of classifying and expressing linguistically, which does involve decision, with the determination of the meanings classified and expressed, which does not.

It might be objected that analyticity, as Lewis views it, no longer involves that independence of matters of fact which was the original motive for introducing the concept. This objection could not be sustained, however, for two reasons. First, the sense in which an analytic statement has experiential meaning, and can thus be verified as analytic, must be distinguished from the sense in which it has none, or rather from the sense in which it has the same meaning as every other analytic statement. The latter Lewis calls "holophrastic" meaning and the former "analytic." ("Analytic meaning" must not be confounded with "analytic truth," despite Lewis' unfortunate terminology; an analytically true statement has two kinds of meaning, of which analytic

[35] *Ibid.*, p. 154.

meaning is one.) The analytic meaning of a complex expression Lewis defines as a "resultant of the meaning of its elementary constituents together with the syntactic relations of these in the whole expression."[36] Thus, while in the sense of holophrastic meaning, "all cats are animals" and "all squares are rectangles" have the same intension, namely zero (or, in another vocabulary, "*p* or not-*p*"), their analytic meanings are as different as the situations to which we would apply the terms "cat" and "square." But the meaning which attaches peculiarly to complex expressions as units rather than composites is holophrastic meaning, and it is holophrastic meaning which could be damaging to Lewis' position if found to depend—as it does not—on matters of fact even when the complex expressions to which it attaches are analytic statements. The original conception of analytic statements as statements whose truth is independent of matters of fact is therefore preserved, contrary to the present objection, through the distinction between holophrastic and analytic meaning.

Second, the objection could not be sustained because the question of existence or nonexistence is, according to Lewis, irrelevant to sense meaning. Determination of sense meaning does not require application, but only applicability. Whether or not the occasion for applying an expression ever presents itself, so long as we know in advance of the occasion that we would apply or refuse to apply the expression, we know its sense meaning. It is for this reason that Lewis calls sense meanings "criteria in mind."

The foregoing has been a rough characterization of a conception of meaning and of analyticity which relies on the concept of inclusion, similar to the concept of containment appealed to by Kant's treatment of analyticity, and which might even escape the indictment that so many recent writers have leveled against the classic conception of analyticity. According to Lewis, analyticity is to be viewed properly only in intensional terms, as involving expressions like "necessarily" and "by definition." Quine's objection to this is that these expressions can be under-

36 *Ibid.*, p. 82.

stood only with a prior understanding of analyticity. And Lewis, in turn, offers a theory of meaning intended to explain these intensional expressions independently of analyticity. Whether his theory is satisfactory must now be seen.

What Lewis has done is to push the necessity associated with the analytic farther back in the epistemological scale, at least as far back (it is tempting to add) as is consonant with the empiricism that is at stake. The procedure can be condoned if, first, it can be shown that there *is* the requisite necessity in relations among sense meanings defined as criteria in mind, and if, second, the connection of sense meaning with linguistic meaning is established in such a way that we can get easily from the former to the latter; that is, if the necessity can be carried over from criteria in mind to communicable and intersubjective meanings. Without fulfilment of the latter condition the empiricism thus defended would not seem to be the philosophic position we wanted to defend; moreover, it is hard to see how the former condition could then be fulfilled.

Lewis' views on "an incorrigible datum-element underlying empirical beliefs which are justified,"[37] and on an expressive language within which this datum-element is articulated, are of importance here. Rather than give a detailed exposition of these views, however, it will suffice for the present to extract what is crucial in order to determine the point under discussion. What is crucial is that sense meanings and their relationships cannot, according to Lewis, be exactly expressed in words, or "exhibited by exhibiting words and the relations of words."[38] It follows from our inability to express sense meanings exactly that an examination of linguistic entities—in particular, statements—can give us no exact conception of meanings and their relationships and, hence, of the necessity in terms of which we could understand analyticity.

But it might be objected here that exactness is not required. Either we would or we would not apply the term "animal" to

[37] "The Given Element in Empirical Knowledge," p. 168.
[38] An Analysis of Knowledge and Valuation, p. 140.

every sense-recognizable character to which we would apply the term "cat." This is not a quantitative affair, it might be said, but only a topological one. And Lewis encourages the objection, as well as the metaphor, by stating explicitly that "patterns of linguistic relation can only serve as a kind of map, for location of the empirical item meant in terms of sense-experience."[39]

But the counterobjection is available that, while it is true that exactness of the translation of sense meaning into linguistic meaning may not be required to assure the truth of "all cats are necessarily animals" and therefore the analyticity of "all cats are animals," nevertheless a guarantee of topological accuracy is required, and even this cannot be had. As Lewis admits, "use of the same expressions in the presence of the same objective facts does not necessarily imply the same sense-criteria of application."[40] He goes on to maintain that induction is possible on the basis of behavior, including linguistic behavior, and that if what is wanted in this context is certainty, it is an unreasonable request. No such certainty is required of scientific induction; moreover, we are forced to rely on induction even in the case of linguistic meanings, so that "any supposed advantage in this respect is illusory."[41] However, Lewis' comparison of the problem of getting at sense meanings with the problem of scientific induction is less than proper; what we seek in the latter activity is truth, whereas what Lewis must be able to provide through the former activity is analyticity, and analyticity, involving as it does necessity, is quite a different matter. The certainty that is sought is required not by any unjust demands on the part of Lewis' opponents but rather by Lewis' own setting of the problem.

As it happens, scientific induction is precisely the method, and the only method, by which sense meanings can be examined. The project of investigating sense meanings is a valid and

[39] *Ibid.*, pp. 140–41.

[40] *Ibid.*, p. 143.

[41] "As what we *intend* at the moment at least, a meaning seems to be as open to direct examination as anything we are likely to discover" (*ibid.*, p. 145). (The word "direct" does not occur in the first printing.)

important one and corresponds to the branch of semiotic called pragmatics.[42] Being a scientific endeavor, however, pragmatics must suffer from the limitations of science: in this case, of being unable to provide knowledge that is more than probable. And probable knowledge, however high the degree of probability, could provide the necessity in terms of which we can understand analyticity only if it were known independently that the necessity is there, underneath language and behavior, ready to be revealed with probability. Any independent knowledge of necessary relations among sense meanings, however, is not empirical knowledge; therefore, probability itself is all empiricists have to go on and it is as far as they can get.

At any rate, the second condition mentioned above, that we have a way of getting back and forth between sense meaning and linguistic meaning, is not satisfied; therefore the first condition, that sense meanings and the relations among them be shown to involve the necessity on which analyticity is said to rest, cannot be satisfied either. So it is found that Lewis' theory of meaning is not satisfactory, and his treatment of analyticity in terms of a necessity that is at the sensory end of the epistemological enterprise must be rejected. It would thus appear that Quine is justified in his claim that the understanding of intensional adverbs—those in terms of which Lewis analyzes the concept of analyticity—itself presupposes a prior understanding of analyticity. Moreover, since I was led to inquire into Lewis' treatment of the problem of analyticity because he utilizes "inclusion," which is similar to the unclear "containment" Kant employs, I must look for some other conception of analyticity to investigate.

The conceptions open to investigation are limited now in still a different respect, namely, that involving meanings as something "known" in the sense of "had in mind." For unless an interpretation can be given to "having in mind" that differs from Lewis' in carrying with it its own bridge for the gap between

[42] See Charles W. Morris, *Foundations of the Theory of Signs*, Vol. I, No. 2, of *International Encyclopedia of Unified Science* (Chicago: University of Chicago Press, 1938), and *Signs, Language and Behavior* (New York: Prentice-Hall, 1946).

mental phenomena that are linguistic and those that are not, any conception of analyticity that depends on having meanings in mind will suffer from the same fatal flaw. This is not, of course, to say the last word on the relation of language to thinking, though it hints at the position to be taken; the problem of this relationship will assume greater importance as I go along. But for the time being, the basis for distinguishing between analytic and synthetic statements must itself be linguistic if it is to be acceptable to empiricists.

4. DEFINITION AND SYNONYMY

In thinking of analytic truths as truths whose subjects conceptually contain their predicates, or as truths whose predicates cannot without inconsistency be denied of their subjects, or as statements which are true by virtue of the law of contradiction, we come easily to the concept of definition as central to analyticity. In fact, as already seen, Lewis takes "by definition" to be one of those intensional expressions whose presence in a true statement makes the statement explicitly analytic. Schlick is quoted by Waismann as maintaining that to say a predicate is contained in the concept of its subject "can only mean that it is part of its definition," or in other words that "a judgment is analytic if the ground for its truth lies solely in the definitions of the terms which occur in it."[43]

To borrow Quine's example, "no bachelor is married" is analytic because the ground for its truth lies solely in the definition of "bachelor" as "unmarried man." As it stands, however, the analyticity of "no bachelor is married" does not shine forth as one would like it to. For that, "unmarried man" must be substituted for "bachelor," to produce "no unmarried man is married." This latter statement is transparently analytic, and the reason is that it is logically true. To say of a true statement that it is logically true is to say that only its logical terms occur essentially, or as Quine puts it, that it remains true under all reinterpretations of its nonlogical terms. Schlick's conception of analyticity may be refined now into the assertion that a state-

[43] Waismann, *op. cit.*, p. 28.

ment is analytic if it can be transformed into a logical truth by means of definitions.[44]

A concept even more central than definition, however, might be the concept of synonymy. When we transform statements into logical truths (or falsehoods) by means of definitions, what we are doing is "putting synonyms for synonyms." And though it is through synonymy that definitions account for the transformations, it is not apparent that definitions alone can account for every pair of synonyms allowing such a transformation. Waismann suggests that, besides definitions, there are logical operations, which derive from logical equivalences, as well as what he calls linguistic or idiomatic operations, which are less formal and less systematic than definitions; all these can be used to transform an analytic statement into a logical truth. Logical equivalence might be considered as a logical kind of definition, but instead of talking about "idiomatic definitions" it might be less of a strain to stop talking about definitions altogether and talk instead about synonymy. Now an analytic statement is one that can be transformed into a logical truth by putting synonyms for synonyms, and the indicated procedure is to discover exactly what makes a pair of expressions synonymous.

A pair of expressions is said to be synonymous when both have the same meaning; what is needed is an understanding of "having the same meaning," which presumably can be had by understanding "having a meaning" at all. Lewis defines synonymy in terms of having the same intension,[45] and if the kind of intension he is talking about were what he calls linguistic meaning, his would be a definition requiring investigation. However, what he has in mind is sense meaning, on which, according to him, all linguistic meaning depends, and the same objections would have to be brought to bear on sense meanings in this

[44] See Quine, op. cit., pp. 22 ff.; Morton G. White, "The Analytic and the Synthetic: An Untenable Dualism," John Dewey: Philosopher of Science and Freedom, ed. Sidney Hook (New York: Dial Press, 1950), pp. 316–30; reprinted in Semantics and the Philosophy of Language, ed. Linsky, pp. 272–86; and Waismann, op. cit., pp. 28 ff.

[45] An Analysis of Knowledge and Valuation, p. 86.

connection as have already been made in connection with analyticity.

Goodman, in a recent discussion of synonymy, examines briefly a succession of classic theories of meaning in terms of which synonymy could be understood and discards them all for much the same reasons that Lewis' theory must be discarded (by empiricists, at least). Thus, it has been maintained at one time or another that two expressions have the same meaning if they stand for the same essence, platonic idea, mental idea, image, or concept.[46] If any one of these were a permissible characterization of sameness of meaning, analyticity could be understood easily in terms of synonymy—as far as that goes, if any one of these were a permissible concept at all, analyticity could be understood directly, without the mediation of synonymy.

If intensional meanings are ruled out as clues to the understanding of synonymy, it is extensions that must be examined, in particular the possibility that two expressions are synonymous if they have the same extension.[47] But as Goodman points out, any two expressions with zero extension—for example, "centaur" and "unicorn"—are then synonymous. Goodman goes on to make the claim that nevertheless there are extensional differences between terms with different meanings which would forbid such declarations of synonymy as that between "centaur" and "unicorn." This is to suppose, of course, that we already know that these expressions are not synonymous, but the supposition is perfectly proper; no one, not even a philosopher looking for an understanding of synonymy, can profess ignorance of a difference in meaning between "centaur" and "unicorn." Goodman's claim is supported by the consideration that coextensive terms which differ in meaning will be found to belong to certain compound expressions by virtue of which the

[46] Goodman, "On Likeness of Meaning," *Analysis*, X (1949–50), 1–7; reprinted in *Semantics and the Philosophy of Language*, ed. Linsky, pp. 67–74. References throughout the present book will be to the latter; present reference is to pp. 67 f.

[47] Strictly speaking, it is Lewis' comprehensional mode of meaning which should be used, rather than the more customary mode of denotation, in order to avoid difficulties about extensional fluctuation.

terms may be said to have "secondary extension" and which are not coextensive; in the examples at hand, "centaur-picture" and "unicorn-picture" are such compound expressions.

What Goodman has come up with is a criterion for comparing meanings extensionally, with no reference to intension. No two terms not ordinarily thought to be synonymous are, on this criterion, synonymous. But a further effect of this criterion is that no two terms whatever are synonymous, because for any pair of terms whatever, different secondary extensions may be found; as Goodman points out, given any two terms "p" and "q," a part of the extension of "p-description" (say, "a p that is not a q") can be found which is not part of the extension of "q-description." The result of this analysis therefore is that no two terms are synonymous, and the criterion for analyticity in terms of synonymy—that an analytic statement is one that can be transformed into a logical truth by putting synonyms for synonyms—breaks down.[48]

However, regardless of whether Goodman's analysis is acceptable or not, and even if a perfectly sound extensional interpretation of synonymy were to be had, a case for analyticity could not be made out on the basis of extensional equivalence. As we saw earlier, extensional equivalence can provide only for the truth of a statement, not for its analyticity. This is to say we could not know whether it would be true in possible but non-actual worlds. This same limitation militates against Leibniz' *salva veritate* test of synonymy, because, as Quine points out, when applied to an extensional language, this too could insure only extensional equivalence.

[48] Rudner, as mentioned above (p. 17 n.), carries Goodman's analysis a step further by showing that tokens, or word inscriptions, as well as words, have secondary extensions, so that different secondary extensions can be found for any two word inscriptions. And if a synonymy criterion were to be given for logical truth, not even logically true statements, including purely repetitive statements, would retain their analytic integrity. However, Robbins points out, with Goodman's sanction, that every two inscriptions which are "replicas" of each other, that is, which are "instances of the same sign-design," will have the same secondary extension whenever they have the same primary extension, so that only word inscriptions that are not replicas of each other will differ in meaning (see B. L. Robbins, "On Synonymy of Word-Events," *Analysis*, XII [1951–52], 100, and Goodman, "On Some Differences about Meaning," *Analysis*, XIII [1952–53], 92).

Any hope of getting to know analyticity on the basis of an acquaintance with synonymy seems groundless. To try to characterize synonymy as sameness of intension leads to the unempirical results found in connection with Lewis' theory of meaning, and consideration of synonymy as sameness of extension has got us no nearer to analyticity. Perhaps, therefore, it would pay to backtrack a few steps to the concept of definition, since it was this concept that led to synonymy in the first place. Can an understanding of definition be gained independently of synonymy, analyticity, and intensional adverbs like "necessarily," by means of which the analytic character of "all cats are by definition animals" spells itself out?

Among the first things one thinks of in connection with definition is the dictionary. But dictionaries are compiled from previously existing synonymies, or at least from what are taken on faith by lexicographers to be synonymies. What dictionaries give us, as a matter of fact, are reports on usage, and any theory of synonymy based on dictionary definitions would amount simply to a majority-rule synonymy. The concept of *degree of synonymy*, incidentally, is not unknown in recent literature. Goodman, for example, states that although no two words are synonymous, many pairs of words are very much alike in meaning, or have a high degree of synonymy; in fact the function of a dictionary, according to Goodman, is to join expressions having a high degree of synonymy.[49] The concern at present is with analyticity, however, and what is needed for analyticity is, as Quine makes clear, cognitive synonymy (which differs from psychological and poetic synonymy and is the kind of synonymy which, if we could understand it, would enable us to understand analyticity).

Another kind of definition, which Quine mentions and which

49 "On Likeness of Meaning," p. 73, and "On Some Differences about Meaning," p. 93. See also Benson Mates, "Synonymity," *University of California Publications in Philosophy*, XXV (1950), 201–26 (esp. 225); reprinted in *Semantics and the Philosophy of Language*, ed. Linsky (1952), pp. 111–36 (esp. 135).

Carnap develops in some detail,[50] is explication. Since the concept of explication will assume a certain importance in the present work, a brief sketch of it now will prove beneficial. In Carnap's words, explication is the "task of making more exact a vague or not quite exact concept used in everyday life or in an earlier stage of scientific or logical development, or rather replacing it by a newly constructed, more exact concept." The earlier concept or the term used for it is called the explicandum; the proposed concept or the term used for it is an explicatum of the old one. Examples of explication are Frege's and Russell's explication of "two" as the class of all couples, Tarski's explication of "truth" as the semantic conception of truth, and Carnap's explication of "analytic" as "L-true." An explicatum need not, according to Carnap, correspond very closely in meaning to the explicandum, so long as it is able to replace the explicandum within a certain context. Mention of "context" is a reminder that precision is not the only aim of explication; in addition to being precise an explicatum must function within a context of some sort, whether a scientific theory or a philosophic system. As Hempel writes, "the assignment of precise meanings to the terms under explication becomes a matter of judicious synthesis, of rational reconstruction, rather than of merely descriptive analysis."[51]

However, the concept of explication is of little help in trying to understand definition, or synonymy, or analyticity. Even though the correspondence between explicatum and explicandum need not be anywhere near exact, nevertheless some correspondence there must be; Quine points out that some favored contexts which are "clear and precise enough to be useful" are preserved, and since to preserve a context is to rely on previously established synonymies, this is enough to destroy any aid explication could render at present.

[50] Carnap, *Meaning and Necessity* (Chicago: University of Chicago Press, 1947), pp. 7–8, and *Logical Foundations of Probability* (Chicago: University of Chicago Press, 1950), pp. 1–8; Quine, op. cit., p. 25.

[51] Carl G. Hempel, *Fundamentals of Concept Formation in Empirical Science*, Vol. II, No. 7, of *International Encyclopedia of Unified Science* (Chicago: University of Chicago Press, 1952), p. 11.

The one kind of definition which Quine thinks does establish synonymy and does not rely on any previous synonymy is what he calls "the explicitly conventional introduction of novel notations for purposes of sheer abbreviation."[52] Abbreviation establishes synonymy because the definiendum has no other function than to be synonymous with the definiens. But examples of such definition in natural languages are relatively infrequent and can hardly be said to reveal the nature of the synonymy of "bachelor" and "unmarried man."

5. LOGICAL AND NONLOGICAL

The attempt to arrive at an understanding of the fundamental difference that exists, according to the dogma of analyticity, between analytic statements, which depend for their truth solely on the meanings involved, and synthetic statements, which, when true, depend also on fact, has been frustrated at every turn. Kant's appeal to a relation of "containment" between meanings in analytic statements was found to be a vague appeal; even when sharpened by Lewis' conception of analyticity as grounded in sense meanings—or more specifically, in a relation of "inclusion" between applications of the terms in an analytic statement, to sense-recognizable characters—it was found to lack the inspectable qualities an empiricist criterion ought to have. Analyticity characterized by transformability into logical truth was no clearer, because the transformation had to occur by means of definition or synonymy, and no clear understanding of definition or synonymy was found. As matters stand, therefore, the only kind of analytic statement that can be clearly conceived is a logically true statement, a statement all of whose unreplaceable terms are logical terms.

But let me see whether even the idea of a logically true statement can hold up under investigation. What is needed now is the kind of characterization of logical truth that was unobtainable for analyticity. A logical truth is an analytic truth because its truth depends only on the meanings of the words in it, but an analytic truth is not a logical truth unless all the words on

[52] *Op. cit.,* p. 26.

whose meanings its truth depends are logical words. All that is needed for an adequate understanding of logical truth, therefore, is an adequate understanding of logical words.[53]

If I am presented with a list of logical words—words like "or," "and," "all," and "not"—I understand perfectly well why these words are on the list and why words like "green," "jump," and "Indianapolis" are not. However, when the attempt is made to formulate the difference between the two kinds of words, the difference becomes blurred. To say that a logical word is a word which can occur essentially in a logically true statement[54] is no help because it is for the sake of understanding logically true statements that I am examining logical words.

Suppose that a logical word be distinguished from nonlogical words on the basis of factual or descriptive significance. A logical truth is a true statement in which only logical words occur essentially, and a logical word is a word which lacks descriptive significance. The possible objections to this characterization of logical words are of two kinds: it could be claimed that there are nonlogical words that lack descriptive significance or that there are logical words that do not lack descriptive significance.

Such words as "green" and "Indianapolis" will certainly not support the first claim, because their descriptive significance is undeniable. Nor can nonsense words like "frabjous" or metaphysical words like "thing-in-itself" be invoked; the latter has a descriptive significance by virtue at least of its historical status as a significant element of a philosophic system, and either a similar statement can be made about the former or it can be refused wordhood. But what about words such as "but," "though," and "nevertheless"? These are not found in the vocabularies of purely logical systems and yet they seem to lack

[53] For another discussion of the problem of characterizing logical words, see pp. 58–59 below.

[54] It could not be said, even circularly, that logical words must occur essentially in logically true statements whenever they do occur in logically true statements. See, e.g., Pap, "Logic and the Synthetic A Priori," pp. 507 ff., and "Logic and the Concept of Entailment," *Journal of Philosophy*, XLVII (1950), 382.

descriptive significance. The answer is that there is no reason
except convenience why these words do not appear in purely
logical vocabularies; therefore they may be considered logical
words. The difference between "and" and "but," Quine points
out, is rhetorical, not logical;[55] there is no difference so far as
truth values are concerned. Both are symbolized by "•", and "•"
has only one truth table. The same can be said for "though"
and "nevertheless"; they differ from each other and from "and"
and "but," if at all, only rhetorically. In fact, "but" finds its
way into logical vocabularies as well as "and"; the latter is
merely a suggested English translation of "•", and the English
translation suggested by Church for the denial of the expression
translated by "if A then B" is "A but not B."[56]

In brushing off the counterclaim that there are nonlogical
words that lack descriptive significance, however, I may inad-
vertently have supported the other counterclaim, that there are
logical words that do not lack descriptive significance. Quine
pins the difference between "and" and "but" on rhetoric, not
logic. What is the nature of this rhetorical difference? In addition to a difference in "naturalness of idiom," there may, according to Quine, be a difference in the speaker's mind—and, I
may add, a difference in the hearer's mind also. If I am re-
quested to purchase cigarettes and am told, as an afterthought,
"but get some matches, too," I may very well feel, however
dimly, that something is wrong about the remark. But I would
not ordinarily feel anything to be wrong, or at least not in anything like the same way, about "but get some cigars, too" or
about "and get some matches, too." This difference between
"and" and "but," whether or not only "in the speaker's mind,"
and however elusive it may be, I take to be a factual or descriptive difference, on the basis of which these logical words must
be said to have descriptive significance. It is true that "and" and
"but," in the sense that they have the same truth table, are
identical, but this is to be attributed to the factual paucity of

55 Quine, *Methods of Logic* (New York: Henry Holt & Co., 1950), p. 41.
56 Church, *Introduction to Mathematical Logic*, Vol. I (Princeton: Princeton University Press, 1956), p. 37.

truth tables as definitional instruments rather than to the alleged factual nonsignificance of "and" and "but." "And" normally conjoins only statements already related by the additional bond of relevance, and "but" does not simply conjoin statements, but conjoins them unexpectedly; yet when defined truth-functionally each word has simple conjunction as its sole function, and it may conjoin any statements whatever. The statement "p but q" is intended more as a denial of "if p, then not q" than simply as an affirmative restatement of "p and q"—an intention which is frustrated and ignored when that denial and that affirmation are defined by identical truth tables. From the logical point of view, to be sure, to demand equal representation for "and" and "but," and in a way that will retain the unique significance of each, is like demanding that editorial opinion be reflected in the news columns of a newspaper. Editorial opinion often *is* reflected in the news columns, but this is taken to be a symptom of sloppy journalism or worse; by the same token, the demand that logical meaning reflect every nuance of descriptive meaning stems from a misunderstanding of the nature of logic. Nevertheless, the belief that logical words have no descriptive meaning is as mistaken as the belief that the journalist has no opinion about the facts he is describing, or that he is able directly to "report" the facts while preventing the slightest element of interpretation from creeping in. The conscientious journalist chooses words that will best enable him to keep interpretation to a minimum, and the logician chooses words that are most useful in calculating truth conditions. The significance words possess for calculating truth conditions, furthermore, entirely apart from descriptive significance, is exactly what truth tables give us. All this is to say no more for present purposes than that logical words lack descriptive significance in so far as their descriptive significance is ignored—but this is true of all words, and can scarcely be adduced in support of the contention that a sharp and deep-rooted difference separates logical from nonlogical words.

Moreover, I have until now been considering only those logical words which lend themselves to truth-table definition, the

binary connectives of the statement calculus. When logical
words from the higher-order calculuses are taken into account—
words such as "all," "some," and "is a member of"—the attempt
to maintain a rigid logical-nonlogical distinction on the basis of
descriptive significance becomes even more questionable. If descriptive significance may be attached to "but" and "or," then
there should be no difficulty, or anyway less difficulty, in attaching it to "some" and "is a member of."[57]

To say that logical words have descriptive significance, however, is not to specify the kind they have or the way they have
it. That specification poses a harder problem. Its solution, moreover, may indicate that there is such a basic difference between
the way in which logical words have descriptive significance and
the way in which nonlogical words have it that the basic distinction between logical and nonlogical words is justified after
all.

Russell and Price have attempted at least one answer to the
question I am now asking. "Psychologically," Russell has written, " 'or' corresponds to a state of hesitation,"[58] and Price
shows how logical notions such as "not," "or," and "if . . . then
. . ." could be incipiently present in preverbal thinking.[59] The
difference between mental and physical states may of course be
emphasized, and the objection raised that while this answer
points to a *kind* of descriptive significance that logical words
have, the mental kind, there is a kind which they lack, the physical kind, and this is what differentiates them from nonlogical

[57] The latter word—"is a member of"—might conceivably be regarded as
logically dispensable (but see n. 60 below); the assertion still holds, however,
for "all" and "some." Even if these two should be considered to be defined
by, or expanded into, conjunction and disjunction, respectively (see, e.g.,
Quine, *Methods of Logic*, p. 88), they are nevertheless logical words, being
eliminable in favor of logical words, and they are logical words whose descriptive significance is undeniable, if subtle. But to replace "all" and "some" by
conjunction and disjunction requires either that the conjunction and disjunction be infinite (a requirement posing a few problems of its own), or else,
as Quine says (*ibid.*, p. 89), that we be "willing to agree for all purposes on a
fixed and finite and listed universe *a, b, . . . , h.*"

[58] Bertrand Russell, *An Inquiry into Meaning and Truth* (London: George
Allen & Unwin, 1940), p. 84.

[59] H. H. Price, *Thinking and Experience* (London: Hutchinson's University Library, 1953), chap. v.

words. A reply might be that this objection is self-defeating because it denies the physical or differentiating kind of descriptive significance to such mental descriptions as "shy," "hesitant," and "schizophrenic," which refer to physical states no more directly than "or" and "not," and it thus supports the other counterclaim by tacitly admitting that there are nonlogical words which have no more descriptive significance than logical words.

However, to say merely that "or" corresponds to a state of hesitation is inadequate, for then a difference could be mentioned between the ways in which "or" and "hesitant" correspond to the same mental state. "Hesitant," it could be said, denotes a property of the state, whereas the correspondence, whatever it may be, between "or" and the state is certainly not that of a word to part of its denotation, if only because "or" is a relational term and cannot denote a property. And it could be objected that the kind of descriptive significance that nonlogical words have but logical words haven't is *denotative* significance, and this is the basis of the distinction between logical and nonlogical words.[60] To counter the objection, however, it is sufficient simply to formulate more accurately this view of the nature of the descriptive significance of logical words. It might be said that what "or" denotes is, among other things, the rela-

[60] Reichenbach, in his *Elements of Symbolic Logic* (New York: Macmillan Co., 1947), pp. 319 ff., differentiates between logical and nonlogical signs on the basis of a distinction between "denotative" and "expressive" signs, a sign being denotative "when it stands in the place of an argument variable, a functional variable, or a propositional variable," and expressive when it is not denotative. When a sign is "merely expressive" (that is, when it has no denotative component) and also "indispensable" (that is, when its elimination would be accompanied by the appearance of another expressive sign), then it is a logical sign. (Thus, Reichenbach forestalls the objection raised by Pap in "Logic and the Concept of Entailment," pp. 381–82, that "or" could be used in such a way that it stands for a functional variable, as in "or (p, not-p)," and is therefore denotative and nonlogical, by pointing out that the nondenotative or expressive role is then taken over by the parentheses, so that "or" as an expressive sign is not really dispensable.) However, Reichenbach himself draws attention to the flaw in his argument. The word "indispensable," he says, "may be applied in various ways; what is regarded as indispensable will depend on the purpose for which a language is constructed" (p. 323). Hence, the distinction between denotative and nondenotative significance and ultimately the distinction between logical and nonlogical words is, as Reichenbach formulates it, relative to particular languages and not the basic kind of distinction demanded in the present context.

tion between two alternative courses of action which makes a person confronting them hesitant (or prepared to pursue either, as Price shows). "Or" is thus a relational term like "older" and "happier," and it not only has descriptive significance but has the same kind that these words have. The answer Russell and Price give to the question about the kind of descriptive significance logical words possess cannot be used, therefore, to support the argument that there is an unalterable distinction between logical and nonlogical words; moreover, their answer may be true.

The attempt to distinguish between logical and nonlogical words on the basis of descriptive significance has faltered, and some other basis for differentiation must be sought. But the only other basis seems to be one of generality, as when Lewis says that logical truths differ from other analytic statements "only by having a certain kind of generality making them specially useful for the critique of inference."[61] Should someone want to know *what* kind of generality makes some statements or words useful for the critique of inference, no answer is forthcoming. It is simply logical generality. Of course a big thing could be made out of this philosophically; one could maintain, I suppose, that logical generality, or better yet *logicality*, is unanalyzable and *sui generis*. But then, I could have stopped with synonymy, or with analyticity itself, and announced that I had stumbled onto an unanalyzable and *sui generis* notion—or property—namely, analyticity. This does not seem an especially fruitful way of doing philosophy, however, and I am no more inclined to rest with an unanalyzable "logicality" than with an unanalyzable "analyticity."

Carnap, in his *Introduction to Semantics*, makes a sharp distinction between logical and descriptive signs but is unable to give a "satisfactory precise definition" of them,[62] and refers to

---

61 *An Analysis of Knowledge and Valuation*, p. 97.

62 At least in general semantics, the problem being quite easy in special semantics (see below, pp. 58 f.). Carnap, *Introduction to Semantics* (Cambridge, Mass.: Harvard University Press, 1942), pp. 56 ff., 87. See Alfred

Tarski's doubt about whether the distinction "is objective or perhaps more or less arbitrary." In *Meaning and Necessity,* however, Carnap distinguishes among signs on the basis of their degree of independence of meaning. The linguistic elements which have the highest degree of independent meaning are sentences, and "other expressions derive what meaning they have from the way in which they contribute to the meaning of the sentences in which they occur." Thus, the sign "(", which contributes very little to the meaning of sentences in which it occurs, has a very low degree of independence of meaning; "v" has somewhat more, and "descriptive constants (that is, nonlogical constants)" have still more. Furthermore, Carnap professes uncertainty about where to draw the line between expressions with little or no independence of meaning and expressions, to be taken as designators, with a high degree of independence of meaning. Where the division should come, he states, "seems more or less a matter of convention."[63] And even Lewis, who is committed to a most sharp and radical distinction between analytic and synthetic statements,[64] says (incidentally clarifying the "certain kind of generality" statement quoted above) that the question of which analytic statements are to be logical statements "is one which can be settled only by some convention or pragmatic decision."[65]

It seems, indeed, that the conclusion to which I am inescapably driven is that no distinction that is not ultimately a matter of convention can be made between logical words and nonlogical words. And since the distinction between logical truths and

---

Tarski, "On the Concept of Logical Consequence," *Logic, Semantics, Metamathematics,* trans. J. H. Woodger (Oxford: Oxford University Press, 1956), pp. 418–20, and Gewirth, "The Distinction between Analytic and Synthetic Truths," p. 407.

[63] *Meaning and Necessity,* p. 7. Drawing the line in question is an important procedure for Carnap, for without it he cannot know which expressions to take as designators.

[64] *An Analysis of Knowledge and Valuation,* p. 165.

[65] *Ibid.,* p. 124. (For Lewis, only formal statements can be logical statements, so that the question for him is really which *formal* analytic statements are logical statements.)

nonlogical truths has been seen to be entirely a function of the distinction between logical and nonlogical words, the conclusion must be that the former distinction cannot be made in any philosophically significant sense either. But now, not only am I unable to gain any understanding of the analytic-synthetic distinction because of an inability to transform statements which are analyticity candidates, such as "no bachelor is married," into logical truths; I am unable even to draw a significant line between logical truths and any other truths.

Every distinction examined so far, in fact, has proved to be a *matter of convention*, and the only way open to a distinction between analytic and synthetic truths is to draw up a series of conventions about other distinctions. In other words, if we can agree where to draw the line between logical and nonlogical words, then we have a sure way of distinguishing between logical and nonlogical truths. And if we can agree on which pairs of similar expressions to call synonymous expressions, then we have a sure way to distinguish between those nonlogical truths which are analytic and those which are synthetic. And if—to carry the chain of wishful thinking back even further—we have that sure way to distinguish between analytic and synthetic, then we need not (on these grounds, at least) give up our reductionist empiricism. But note that already the empiricism has been radically altered. The whole structure of analyticity rests on conventions, and there is nothing about conventions in either empiricism or the analytic-synthetic distinction as traditionally conceived. But I am ahead of myself, and must wait before developing this theme.

One other result of the investigation may be briefly indicated here, though it too must wait for further development until proper conceptual tools are available. This is the *matter of degree*. The idea of degree of synonymy, arising from the seeming inaccessibility of any clear notion of synonymy other than greater or lesser likenesses of meaning, has been mentioned. And Carnap has been quoted as formulating the idea of degree of independence of meaning, on the basis of which relatively logical words can be distinguished from relatively nonlogical words. Moreover, the similarity in structure of all the concepts so far examined suggests the relevance to them all of the concept of degree. Thus, besides degree of synonymy, the concepts of what might be called degree of logicality (which would apply both to words and to statements) and degree of analyticity may be singled out as important to the present inquiry.

Finally—and this point is of crucial importance to the thesis I want to present—it may be noticed that the two results of the foregoing investigation of analyticity, far from resembling and re-enforcing one another, tend to be antithetic. For if the line is drawn between logical and nonlogical, synonymous and non-synonymous, or analytic and synthetic by agreement or convention, the concept of degree loses much of its significance. There is little need to be concerned with degree of logicality once it is decided that *these* words are to be logical words and all others nonlogical. Conversely, so long as the idea of degree of logicality is significant, the decision about where the line is to be drawn between the logical and the nonlogical has not been made.

I now find that the idea of *context*, an idea which is at the heart of my thesis, can no longer be avoided, for it is needed to qualify what was just said about degrees and conventions. It was said that when a convention has been arrived at there is no longer any significant question of degree, and that if the question of degree is significant then a convention has not been arrived at. What I want to say now is that when a convention has been arrived at, there is no longer any significant question of degree *within the context* determined by the scope (temporal, spatial, logical, causal, or any other) of the convention. What the convention accomplishes is the determination of what shall and what shall not be a question of degree, which is to say, the determination of a context. The converse also holds, of course: When, and to the extent that, a question of degree is significant, no context has as yet been determined, at least with respect to whatever it is that is conceived as a matter of degree.

Let me briefly introduce yet another pair of expressions, which will be considered at length later, but which may be seen here in the abstract. These are the terms *internal* and *external*, borrowed from Carnap.[66] In the vocabulary I seem suddenly to have acquired, a question of degree is an external question; once a decision about a convention has been made and a context determined, then—and within that context—any question about the context is an internal question. Furthermore, the answer to an internal question will have the form of a definite ("yes-no") assertion, and this answer is determined by the nature of the context which gives the question significance. The answer to an external question, however, will be a statement of degree, or a proposal about establishing a convention.

I am afraid that the last few paragraphs, which have introduced the new words "convention," "degree," "context," "internal," and "external," have been so abstract as perhaps to be meaningless. I hope not. At any rate I will try in the following chapter to make more concrete what has been left abstract, focusing on the key word of the five, "context."

[66] "Empiricism, Semantics, and Ontology," pp. 209 ff.; see also his "Testability and Meaning," *Philosophy of Science*, IV (1937), 2 ff.

CHAPTER II

The Analytic-Synthetic Distinction and the Method of Rational Reconstruction

1. ANALYTICITY AND ARTIFICIAL LANGUAGES

IT WAS SAID, in the discussion of Carnap's idea of explication, that an explication both sharpens its explicandum and replaces it within a certain context. Similarity of meaning between explicatum and explicandum is desirable, and there would be no point, of course, in explicating an established concept rather than inventing a new one unless some part of its meaning is carried over or, as Quine says, some favored context is preserved. But, given this modicum of correspondence, the explicatum may depart—and because of the vagueness of the explicandum, must depart—in any number of respects from the original meaning or meanings of the explicandum.

The relevance of explication at this juncture is that I now wish to present an explication of analyticity. It might be thought that this is what I have been doing all along, but this would be to misconceive the nature of explication. The aim in the previous chapter was neither precision (not, at least, in the sense of precision that will be aimed at now) nor the limitation of analyticity to a certain context. It was simply to examine the concept of analyticity within the entire range of its traditional significance —however vague that significance and however blurred the limits of that range—and to investigate recent claims that the concept rests on a shaky foundation.

The aim in this chapter, however, is to explicate analyticity in such a way that there can be no question of its validity. The concept will be precise, and it will be exhibited within a context where there can be no question of degree; every sentence will be either analytic or synthetic, and every analytic sentence will wear its analyticity on its syntactic (or semantic) sleeve. Once this has been done, moreover, the form as well as the content of the explication may be utilized, for not only will analyticity have been explicated, but the terms introduced at the end of the last chapter will have been clarified and illustrated.

The context within which analyticity will be explicated is an artificial language, call it L_1.[1] Thus, the explicandum is to be the concept of analyticity within artificial languages, and the explicatum to be proposed is "analytic in L_1." This is the representative, so to speak, in L_1 of the concept of analyticity within artificial languages. By calling L_1 artificial, I mean to point to its origin. It is a constructed language, consciously built on a primitive foundation designed to meet certain specifications. Because I have constructed it, I am able to control it, at least to the extent of being able to prevent the formation of sentences whose meanings are unclear or indistinct. And L_1 will be an extensional language, because an intensional language would involve the notions I was unable to clarify in connection with Lewis' theory of meaning.

In constructing L_1, its primitive vocabulary is first specified as consisting of logical and descriptive signs, or constants, every sign being easily recognizable as either logical or descriptive. Next, rules of formation are given, according to which certain formulas, or sequences of signs, are well-formed formulas, and only well-formed formulas are recognized as statements in L_1. The well-formed formulas of L_1 are the least class of formulas which satisfy the formation rules in L_1. If L_1 were meant to be used for deduction, its primitive basis would contain, besides rules of formation, rules of transformation, including specification of which statements are to be taken as axioms; however, deduction will not be required of L_1, so that it need not have such rules. In addition to specifying vocabulary and formation rules, it is required that L_1 be *effective*, in the sense that a meth-

---

[1] The concept of artificial language presented here is based partly on the work of Alonzo Church (*Introduction to Mathematical Logic*, Vol. I [Princeton: Princeton University Press, 1956]) and partly on that of Rudolf Carnap (*Introduction to Semantics* [Cambridge, Mass.: Harvard University Press, 1942]; *Meaning and Necessity* [Chicago: University of Chicago Press, 1947]).

od must exist by which we can tell whether any sign is a primitive sign in L_1 and whether any sequence of signs is a well-formed formula in L_1 (in the case of a language with rules of transformation, effectiveness would also require a method for recognizing valid inferences). L_1 is to be a semantic system in the sense of Carnap, and so, besides vocabulary and formation rules, it is equipped with rules of designation and with rules of truth, which respectively translate the primitive descriptive signs or designators of L_1 into English—that is, interpret them—and determine necessary and sufficient conditions for the truth of every statement in L_1.[2]

The equipment needed to explicate analyticity is now at hand. A statement in L_1 is *analytic in L_1* if and only if it can be transformed into a logical truth of L_1 by putting synonyms for synonyms. A statement in L_1 is *synthetic in L_1* if and only if it is not analytic in L_1.

Locating the analytic truths in L_1 is now child's play. Which statements are candidates for analyticity, that is, which statements are statements in L_1, is determined merely by observing which formulas in L_1 (or sequences of signs all of which are signs in L_1) are well formed according to the formation rules. Should there be doubt about any formula, a method exists for dispelling that doubt, thanks to the requirement of effectiveness. If the doubtful element is a sign, then the sign in doubt belongs to L_1 just in case it is either a primitive sign in L_1 (again, follow the effectiveness procedure) or can be eliminated in favor of a primitive sign. If there is any question about synonymy, there are any number of answers possible. An expression in the language is synonymous with another, for example, if it is explicitly introduced as an abbreviation for the other. And finally, if what is wanted is a way of distinguishing the logical truths in L_1 from other truths in L_1, nothing could be simpler. The logical truths in L_1 are all the statements in L_1 which are true solely by virtue of their logical components, or which are true and remain true however their nonlogical components be interpreted. All that is left is the question of logical components. A constant in L_1 is logical if and

---

[2] The specification, requirement, and rules all occur in the metalanguage.

only if it appears in a list headed "logical constants in L_1" or can be eliminated in favor of a sign which appears in that list. In most cases, not only will there be a list of logical constants but also a list of well-formed formulas; nor, for that matter, would it distort the picture to speak of a list of signs in L_1, primitive and derivative, or of a list of what Quine calls "synonympairs" in L_1, or of lists of logical truths in L_1, or even, though more figuratively, of analytic truths in L_1.

There are other ways of defining "analytic in L_1" than in terms of synonymy and logical truth. I could, for example, borrow Carnap's explication which involves the notion of "state-description"[3] and say that a statement is *analytic in L_1* if and only if it holds in every state-description in L_1. It will be noted that this definition also explicates the traditional requirement that an analytic truth be true in all possible worlds.

A difficulty with this method has been found, however, which centers about the requirement of independence[4] and is interesting in the present connection. The requirement of independence is the requirement that every atomic statement in a language be logically independent of every other atomic statement, and the purpose of the requirement is to avoid contradictions by means of logical isolationism. To maintain the requirement, certain kinds of predicates must be barred from the language. For example, the relational term "warmer than" might lead to the contradiction resulting from the conjunction of "x is warm," "y is not warm," and "y is warmer than x." Again, L_1 might contain synonym-pairs—for example, "bachelor" and "unmarried man" —that would lead to state-descriptions including both "x is a bachelor" and "x is married." The difficulty can be met either by maintaining the principle of independence and excluding

---

[3] "A class of sentences in S_1 which contains for every atomic sentence either this sentence or its negation, but not both, and no other sentences, is called a *state-description* in S_1, because it obviously gives a complete description of a possible state of the universe of individuals with respect to all properties and relations expressed by predicates of the system" (*Meaning and Necessity*, p. 9).

[4] See John G. Kemeny, "Extension of the Methods of Inductive Logic," *Philosophical Studies*, III (1952), 38–42, and Carnap, "Meaning Postulates," *Philosophical Studies*, III (1952), 65–73.

terms which have syntactic properties by virtue of their meanings, or else by allowing such terms, eliminating the principle, and modifying the notion of state-description. The former method is unsatisfactory because it results in a drastic curtailment of possible languages, allowing only those which are relatively weak. The latter is preferable, therefore; moreover, a device is readily available for allowing the terms in question: the device of meaning postulates, or semantic rules. Thus, a semantic rule may be added to L_1 stating that, for all x and y, if x is warm and y is not, then x is warmer than y; another asserting the asymmetry of "warmer than"; and a third rule stating that, for all x, if x is a bachelor, then x is not married. The notion of state-description must now be modified, however, since some state-descriptions are ruled out by the meaning postulates, and a statement is now *analytic in L_1* if and only if it is true in all *permissible* state-descriptions.

Now that the notion of meaning postulate is available, another definition may be given for "analytic in L_1," utilizing that notion directly, as well as what Carnap calls "L-implication." A statement p "L-implies" another statement q if and only if q holds in every state-description in which p holds. Now if p is taken to be the conjunction of the meaning postulates of L_1, the state-descriptions in which p holds will be just those state-descriptions permissible in L_1—that is, just those state-descriptions in which every analytic statement of L_1 must hold. A statement may now be said to be *analytic in L_1* with respect to p if and only if it is L-implied by p. Less precisely but more succinctly, a statement is analytic in L_1 if its truth follows from the semantic rules of L_1.

This last explication of analyticity is interesting because it provides a rather exact analogy between logical truth and analytic truth. For now there are semantic rules as well as syntactic rules, and just as logical truths may be said to be true by virtue of syntactic rules alone, so analytic truths may now be said to be true by virtue of semantic rules alone. And the distinction between logical truths and analytic truths is analogous to that between syntax and semantics. Both distinctions, in fact, are dependent ultimately on the distinction between logical and nonlogical constants, and both are absolute distinctions in L_1 because there is an absolute distinction in L_1 between logical and nonlogical constants.

Such, then, is the nature of the explication of analyticity that emerges from a consideration of artificial languages. Whether it is an appropriate explication is not at the moment an appropriate question. That it *is* an explication, however, cannot be doubted. What has happened is that one of the constituent concepts historically packed into the concept of analyticity has been unpacked and sharpened in such a way that it can perform a function within a certain context, the context of artificial languages.

Incidentally, it may be noted that this conceptual unpacking is exactly what, according to Kant, analytic statements do. These statements he called *explicative*, and said their sole function is to set forth and make intelligible the concept of the subject, which we already have, by "breaking it up into those constituent concepts that have all along been thought in it, although confusedly."[5] Now if Kant's notion of explication is accepted, any statement expressing an explication will be an analytic statement, its predicate-concept being a constituent of its subject-concept.

Suppose, however, that someone challenges the accuracy of the explication by asking whether the explicatum ever really was a constituent concept of the explicandum. In effect, what he would be challenging is the analyticity of the statement expressing the explication. If *p* is the latter statement, then to ask whether the explication involved is correct is to ask whether *p* is really analytic. But to answer such a question is to investigate whether an explicatum really is, or was, "contained" or "thought, although confusedly" in the explicandum, and this might require a historical, sociological, or even psychoanalytic investigation. In other words, the inspection of meanings in this case is an empirical inspection. A statement verified empirically, moreover, is a synthetic statement, so that the statement "*p* is ana-

[5] *Critique of Pure Reason*, trans. Norman Kemp Smith (London: Macmillan & Co., 1953), pp. 48 f.

lytic" is synthetic. And as if the situation were not complicated enough already, it could be asked, in turn, whether the statement " 'p is analytic' is synthetic" is analytic or synthetic.

The point, however, is not to produce a paralysis of this sort but to make clear the difference between the general question about the meaning of analyticity and the specific question of whether any given true statement is analytic—the difference, roughly, between the intension and part of the extension of "analytic statement." The general question involves not merely Kant's "unpacking" process but also—and this is the important consideration—theoretical judgments about extending the concept to new situations. And once this extension has occurred, the specific question of whether a given true statement is analytic is in a sense a factual question, to be answered by investigating whether the statement is or is not a member of the extension of "analytic statement" as the term has been explicated.

Thus, when "analytic in L_1" is taken to be an explication of "analytic," to say that a statement p is analytic is to make a factual assertion: that p belongs to L_1 in the sense that all its elements belong to L_1 and it is well formed, that either p is logically true or else there is a logically true statement q which differs from p only in containing synonyms of nonlogical elements of p, that not-p does not follow from the semantic rules of L_1, and so forth. In other words, the verification of a statement of the form "p is analytic" requires what Reichenbach calls logical evidence[6] and therefore involves investigation of the world in so far as the world contains systems like L_1. On the other hand, a statement of the form "any analytic statement is a statement which . . . ," when offered as an explication, is not subject to verification at all, being a proposal rather than an assertion, but is subject only to criteria of theoretical adequacy.

To return to the explication itself, it is not being maintained that an adequate definition of "analytic in L_1" solves the problem of analyticity but only that this explication of analyticity

---

6 Hans Reichenbach, *Elements of Symbolic Logic* (New York: Macmillan Co., 1947), pp. 182–91. As Reichenbach makes clear, his concept of logical evidence is a metalinguistic concept, and as I point out below, the question cannot be asked within the object language, L_1.

does clarify one of the senses in which the notion is used. And if just one of these senses can be made clear, something, at least, will have been learned about analyticity.

For the logician working in L_1 then, or for the man who "speaks" L_1, the explication given above is perfectly adequate. It cannot be objected that he is unable to tell whether the statements he calls analytic are really analytic or only true, on the grounds, for example, that he cannot know them to be true in *all* possible worlds, or that he has no way of *really* distinguishing between semantic and syntactic rules, or between logical and extralogical constants. He knows that they are true in *his* possible worlds, which are those state-descriptions in which the conjunction of the semantic rules holds, and he can distinguish between semantic and syntactic rules and between logical and extralogical constants because he can read the signs posted at the head of each list. How the rules and constants got there is not his concern, and in fact he is unable even to pose the question whether his analytic statements are really analytic statements. What all these terms mean is, for him, how they are to be used.

Suppose now that this user of L_1 suddenly finds himself bored with his language. He emerges from his linguistic cocoon and announces his intention of spinning an entirely new one, L_2. Aware that a language must have statements that are analytic, he now discovers that his previous source of knowledge about analyticity—the list of statements in L_1 labeled "analytic"—is no longer available to him because he wants a new list of such statements, and in order to compile such a list he must be able to characterize analytic statements independently of any particular list of statements in any particular language. We could offer to help him by telling him about the explication of analyticity as "analytic in L_1." But this only confuses him more, because we are using such terms as "logical constant," "well-formed formula," "synonym," and "meaning postulate" or "semantic rule," and he wants the expressions which fall under these headings in L_2 to be different from the corresponding expressions in L_1, so that now he requires independent information about these notions too.

In particular, since this is the first of the things we mentioned that he will need to know in constructing L_2, he wants to know how to distinguish between logical signs and nonlogical signs. We tell him that logical signs look like wedges, horseshoes, dots, and so on, but he says these are the signs that appeared under that heading in L_1, and if we try, say, to give him exclusive disjunction, he sees right away that it merely combines negation and equivalence. Were we to generalize, and announce that a logical sign is any sign definable by truth tables, the complaint—assuming our logician would not balk at the elimination of membership or at the reduction of quantification to conjunction and disjunction—would be that any logical sign he might choose is eliminable in favor of the signs in L_1, so that any shift in logical vocabulary is only apparent.

Trying a new tack, we tell him that logical constants are those signs which appear essentially in logically true statements, but this satisfies him only so long as it takes him to realize that he doesn't know how to separate logically true statements from other analytic statements; not only doesn't he know what an analytic statement is but also what a logically true statement is. Leaving logical constants in favor of analytic statements once more, we might try "true in all state-descriptions" or "true in virtue of the semantic rules," but these can be useful only after the language has been constructed. And, anyway, he might ask how a semantic rule is to be distinguished from an axiom, which is supposed to be purely syntactic. At this stage we both admit we have reached an impasse, and he crawls back into L_1, a wiser logician than when he left.

The impasse, I suggest, is due to failure to distinguish clearly between internal and external questions. The entire discussion was an attempt to answer certain external questions, but they were posed as internal questions. The answers demanded, therefore, were assertions, which could only have been arrived at by investigation, but there was nothing to investigate and hence no assertions to be made. Had the questions been asked properly, as external questions, it would have been seen that the proper answers are practical decisions arrived at by consideration of such factors as purpose, fruitfulness, and simplicity.[7]

Thus, no distinction can be made between logical and extralogical constants which will be applicable to all artificial languages;[8] that we seem to have a notion of which constants are logical constants testifies only to the pervasiveness of the ones we habitually use. And if this distinction cannot be made except with respect to a particular artificial language L_1 or (if we possessed it) L_2, the same is true for the distinctions between logically true statements and other analytic statements, between semantic rules and syntactic rules—for that matter, between syntax and semantics—, and finally, between analytic and synthetic statements. All these distinctions can be made as internal distinctions by investigating whatever language is in question, but it makes no sense to ask for a basis for making them independently of any particular language.

Certain aspects of the discussion may be thrown into relief by a consideration of explicanda of analyticity rather than explicata.

[7] Note the difference between (1) the internal-external distinction and (2) the object language-metalanguage distinction. The former is a distinction between two kinds of questions, the latter a distinction between two kinds of linguistic frameworks within which questions may be asked. Internal questions are framed within the metalanguage of the object language to which they refer. Thus, a question about the analyticity of a statement in L_1 is (1) an internal question, the answer to which is in the form of a definite assertion about the language L_1 and is verified by investigation of the relevant logical evidence in L_1, and it is (2) a question to be asked and answered in the metalanguage of L_1. Within the object language L_1 itself, no such question can be asked. The language within which external questions are posed and resolved might be considered to be a metalanguage; however, I have conceived the terms of external questions as broader in scope than those of the metalanguage of any particular object language, and I have given this medium within which external questions may be asked the neutral name of "antecedent framework." Within antecedent frameworks, alternative conventions may be weighed and decisions arrived at, and though decisions thus arrived at may be expressed in the appropriate metalanguage, I think it would be stretching the meaning of "metalanguage" to identify it with "antecedent framework" as I have conceived the latter.

[8] See Carnap, *Introduction to Semantics*, pp. 56 ff., in which he distinguishes between *special* semantics and *general* semantics, and comments on the logical-descriptive distinction in terms of the two kinds of semantics.

Though the examination of analyticity in the first chapter was not, strictly speaking, an explication of the concept, since the goal was neither precision nor fruitfulness of a systematic sort, it may nevertheless help to look on that examination as a crude or preliminary sort of explication. One of the factors distinguishing that early explication of analyticity from the one in this chapter is the absence from the former of what Carnap calls clarification of the explicandum. In effect, an attempt at explication was simply begun, with no self-conscious concern for what exactly was to be explicated. Thus, the discussion ran the gamut from Kant's notion of containment through Lewis' intensional theory of analyticity to a consideration of some linguistic aspects of the concept. In so far, then, as this relatively haphazard operation represented explication, the explicanda were, first, "analytic" in no definite sense of the term at all, and second, "analytic in L," where L is a variable ranging over all kinds of languages, natural and artificial, useful and decorative.

This chapter, on the other hand, did begin with the articulation of an explicandum representing a preliminary clarification, though there seemed at the time no special reason for formulating the explicandum any more exactly than as "analytic in artificial languages." A more explicit formulation would be "analytic in L_i," where L_i is a variable ranging over all artificial languages. The approach to an explicatum of "analytic in L_i" was to inquire into analyticity as viewed within a particular well-defined artificial language, L_1, so that the explicatum was represented by the expression "analytic in L_1."

However, once a clear understanding was reached of "analytic in L_1," it was found that there is no way of getting back to the explicandum, "analytic in L_i." In other words, while there is a perfectly clear and distinct meaning of "analytic" within any particular artificial language, as soon as the attempt is made to generalize—to take the variable L_i instead of the constant L_1— the clear and distinct meaning disintegrates. The explicandum involved, therefore, is not really "analytic in L_i" but "analytic in L_1."

The difference was pointed out above between the general and the specific questions of analyticity, or between the question about the meaning of analyticity and the question, with respect to any statement, whether or not it is analytic. The general question was seen to be a question of proper explication, subject to the canons not of truth but rather of theoretic adequacy. The specific question, on the other hand, is a question which presupposes an answer to the general question; before one can verify that a given statement is analytic he must know what "analytic" means. And once verification is possible, the specific question can receive a specific answer that will be true or false.

The question that must now be faced is not whether the explicata I have borrowed (true in every state-description, or true by virtue of semantic rules) are correct but whether my explicandum is adequate and appropriate. In other words, when an explicatum has been given for "analytic in L_1," do we have the kind of understanding of analyticity for the sake of which the inquiry was undertaken?

To answer this question requires consideration of the concept of artificial language, both as the context within which analyticity has been explicated and as related to the empiricism which, now given a linguistic twist, is the prime motivation of the concern for analyticity. Before this consideration is faced, it may be pointed out that if the analyticity principle, that is, the principle that there is a fundamental cleavage between truths which are about the world and are assured by investigation of the world and truths which say nothing about the world and are assured simply by inspecting the meanings involved[9]—if analyticity has any validity at all and the distinction really is a sharp distinction rather than one of degree, then it must be maintained as explicated, for it has become apparent that other forms of the distinction cannot be maintained in the same irrevocable way.

[9] To formulate the analyticity principle in this way is of course to bring in the a priori–a posteriori distinction as part of the analytic-synthetic distinction, since the assurance of truths refers to the former and the content to the latter. But I see no harm in this so long as it is recognized that in so doing I assume the validity of empiricism (in that I am then unable to express its denial, that synthetic a priori truths exist). Moreover, this formulation accords with most recent literature.

2. RATIONAL RECONSTRUCTION

It was suggested that the attempt to clarify the expression "derived from," as it appears in the empiricist principle that all empirically significant ideas are derived from experience, led to reductionism, according to which "derived from" is to be properly explicated as "reducible to," and to rational reconstructionism, which further clarifies empiricism by explicating "reducible to." "Rational reconstruction" is the name given by Carnap to a philosophic activity that takes place within what Reichenbach calls the *context of justification*, which is distinguished from the *context of discovery* by being concerned not with actual processes of thinking but, instead, with a reconstruction of those processes along logical lines. This reconstruction clarifies processes of thinking, "distinguishes meanings and the relations between meanings from the blurred background of psychological motives and intentions," and justifies the results of thinking by substituting an ordered (deductive) chain of thoughts for the processes intermediary between point of departure and point of arrival. Rational reconstruction, according to Reichenbach, is controlled by logic, and analysis of it reveals what we call logical laws.[10]

Rational reconstruction is engaged in for reasons other than justifying thought processes, however, chief among these being epistemological reasons. Epistemologists have been interested in reconstruction not so much for logical reasons as for those mentioned above in connection with empiricism, particularly the provision of a framework within which the relation held by empiricists to obtain between "ideas" and "experience" may be seen clearly—or explicated. In fact, Bergmann, whom I shall select as representative of recent practitioners and defenders of the faith in question—not because he is typical of rational reconstructionists (in many respects he carries rational reconstruction to far greater lengths than any of his colleagues) but because his

[10] Reichenbach, *Experience and Prediction* (Chicago: University of Chicago Press, 1938), pp. 6–7; *Elements of Symbolic Logic*, pp. 2–3. It is not clear which comes first, the reconstruction or the laws.

methodological excesses, besides having great heuristic value, seem to me to coincide most closely with the actual philosophic pronouncements of most reconstructionists—Bergmann would replace "justification" by "explication," saying "we are not obliged to justify anything," and I will speak hereafter of the contexts of discovery and of explication.[11] L_1, for example, is a language without rules of transformation and therefore useless for justifying thinking procedures; nevertheless, it has an epistemological use because of its explicative value, and in fact I have already used it for explicating analyticity.

For Bergmann rational reconstruction, or, as he calls it, philosophical analysis, "proceeds properly through the construction of an ideal language," or, "disregarding the problems of a possible plurality, the ideal language."[12] This language is, to begin with, a formal or syntactic language; upon interpretation it becomes "a picture or reconstruction of ordinary English," by which is meant those statements made or makable outside the philosopher's study;[13] and by discoursing about the language we can dissolve the philosophic puzzles and dissolve all of them simultaneously. Philosophy is, according to Bergmann, "the solution of the traditional philosophical problems, the simultaneous solution of all these problems, and nothing but the solution of these problems."[14]

For the primitive descriptive terms of his language, which I

[11] Gustav Bergmann, "Two Cornerstones of Empiricism," *The Metaphysics of Logical Positivism* (New York: Longmans, Green & Co., 1954), pp. 82–83.

[12] *Ibid.*, p. 84. Bergmann does not rule out the possibility of a plurality of ideal languages, though he apparently assumes that every language contained in such a plurality would share the structural features he builds into the language here discussed. See his "A Note on Ontology," *Philosophical Studies,* I (1950), 89–92; reprinted in his *The Metaphysics of Logical Positivism,* pp. 238–42.

[13] *All* such statements in ordinary English, moreover, must have their representatives within the ideal language. This is the requirement of completeness. See Bergmann, "Logical Positivism," *A History of Philosophical Systems,* ed. Vergilius Ferm (New York: Philosophical Library, 1950), pp. 471–82; reprinted in his *The Metaphysics of Logical Positivism,* pp. 1–16. Present reference is to p. 8 of the latter.

[14] "Two Cornerstones of Empiricism," pp. 79–80.

shall call L$_B$, Bergmann would be "willing to accept . . . a class of predicates referring to qualities of and some spatial and temporal relations among those particulars which it is customary to call sense data." Besides these constants, he would build up L$_B$ out of logical constants, individual and predicate variables, and quantifiers.[15]

In terms of L$_B$, analyticity can receive the same explication given above in terms of L$_1$, with the single difference that "analytic in L$_1$" must now be replaced by "analytic in L$_B$." Moreover, it is now easily seen how rational reconstruction can clarify empiricism through explicating the terms by which it is expressed. Reductionism represented an improvement over the original formulation of the empiricist principle in that "derived from" was sharpened into "reducible to." In terms of L$_B$ it can be seen that "reducible to" has as its explicatum "equivalent to some logical construct upon terms which refer to," a phrasing taken from Quine's characterization of reductionism, quoted earlier.

In different words, the primitive vocabulary of L$_B$ consists of logical constants, descriptive constants or designators referring to sense data and to their qualities and relations, individual and predicate variables corresponding to the latter, and quantifiers. Every descriptive constant in L$_B$ is either one of the primitive descriptive constants or else can be eliminated in favor of these. Therefore, every statement in L$_B$ contains, besides variables, quantifiers, and logical constants, nothing but the descriptive constants listed in L$_B$'s primitive vocabulary and other constants defined by means of these. Empiricism is now explicated in just these terms. "Significant statement" becomes "well-formed formula," "experience" or "immediate experience" becomes "primitive descriptive constant"—since this is Bergmann's intention in L$_B$—and the whole principle becomes simply the assertion that no statement contains any descriptive constant other than primitive descriptive constants and constants definable in terms of primitive descriptive constants.

15 *Ibid.*, pp. 88–89.

I mentioned, in connection with the relation between the principles of empiricism, the statement theory of significance[16] as the element common to both analyticity and reductionism, and the element by virtue of which both are rejected by Quine. Because the objections Quine brings against that common element are obviated when analyticity and reductionism are explicated within L_B, it will prove revealing to say more about the statement theory here.

The empiricist theory of meaning shines forth in all its simple splendor when seen within L_B or any other L_i. Every "idea" or term is either logical or else refers to experience, and every statement contains only these terms. Every statement, therefore, every formula that is well formed in accordance with the rules of formation, either definitely asserts something about experience or else just as definitely asserts nothing about experience. Statements cannot slide over from being experiential to being non-experiential or quasi-experiential, nor can terms slip into the vocabulary which are neither logical nor experiential, because any L_i, being an artificial language, is a language we have constructed and, having constructed, can control, at least with respect to membership and to intralinguistic associations. Thus, the kind of statement empiricists were originally motivated to expel from the class of significant statements is in fact liquidated through construction of an ideal language whose vocabulary is well specified and whose statements are formulated in accordance with equally well-specified formation rules.

As first articulated by Locke and Hume, empiricism, or the empiricist principle, referred to "ideas," an empirically significant idea being one derived from experience. Thus stated, the principle is, as Quine points out, "unnecessarily and intolerably restrictive in the term-by-term critique which it imposes,"[17] a defect that was mitigated when, with the concept of definition in

---

[16] The expression is Albert Hofstadter's; see his "The Myth of the Whole: A Consideration of Quine's View of Knowledge," *Journal of Philosophy*, LI (1954), 400.

[17] W. V. Quine, "Two Dogmas of Empiricism," *From a Logical Point of View* (Cambridge, Mass.: Harvard University Press, 1953), p. 38.

use and the verification theory of meaning, the statement rather than the term became the unit of empirical significance. Even so, however, the empiricist principle is still too restrictive, according to Quine, for much of the meaning any statement has is due to its place among a class of other statements.

This interrelatedness of statements with respect to meaning is especially apparent when viewed from a scientific vantage point. Duhem, whom Quine cites in support of his contention, had written that "physics is not a machine which may be taken apart; we may not try each piece in isolation . . . ; physical science is a system which we must take as a whole; it is an organism of which we cannot make one part function without the parts most distant from it entering into play, some more, some less, all to some degree."[18] In the same spirit, Quine believes that "the unit of empirical significance is the whole of science."

But whatever may be the general merit of Duhem's and Quine's opinions about quanta of significance, the objection to the statement as the unit of meaning cannot be sustained when statement and meaning are seen within an ideal and artificial language, L_1. For within such a language we are able to isolate its elements, whether terms or statements, without losing the significance accruing to them by virtue of belonging to a whole. It is precisely the opportunity offered for viewing statements in isolation without diminution of significance that constitutes a major advantage of artificial languages. The context is implicit in every element simply because neither context nor element has independent existence.

I do not, incidentally, say that Quine is wrong in pointing to the limitations of the statement theory of significance as militating for a holistic or contextualist theory of significance. I only say that, whether Quine is right or wrong, the consideration does not necessarily constitute an objection to the two dogmas of which the statement theory is a common element. It does not because, when analyticity and reductionism are explicated as they have been here, the statement theory and the contextualist

18 Pierre Duhem, *La théorie physique: son objet et sa structure* (Paris: Chevalier & Rivière, 1906), pp. 307–8.

theory coincide. Moreover, in the case of Bergmann's L_B, which is the ideal language in terms of which all the problems of philosophy are to be solved and solved simultaneously, the context, which endows statements with meaning and which is implicit in any statement in isolation, is universal (that is, the broadest context compatible with empiricism), so that there is no need to worry about relations between L_B and other values of L_i, or between Bergmann's ideal language and other artificial languages. Henceforth, I can concentrate on L_B.

In the Preface of his *Analysis of Knowledge and Valuation* Lewis remarks that "for contemporary empiricism, the theory of meaning has that same intimate connection with epistemology which earlier rationalistic and idealistic conceptions assigned to metaphysics." The reason for this, Lewis believes, is that a priori knowledge is now believed to be "certifiable by reference to meanings alone." I want to point out the significance of Lewis' remark with respect to artificial languages, focusing again on L_B.

The metaphysical—or ontological, to narrow it down a bit— question about L_B is the question of what the statements in L_B are about. And what the statements in any L_i are about are, as Quine has made so abundantly clear, the values of the bound variables belonging to the L_i in question. The variables of L_B take as their values particulars customarily called sense data, qualities of these, and relations among them. There is nothing else so far as L_B is concerned. Ontology thus finds its explication along with analyticity, logicality, synonymy, and so on, as ontology-with-respect-to-L_B. Ontology is what a language is committed to in the way of bound variables; and what a language is committed to in this way are those entities to which its bound variables must be capable of referring in order that its statements be true.[19]

[19] Quine, "On What There Is," *Review of Metaphysics*, II (1948), 21–38; reprinted in *Semantics and the Philosophy of Language*, ed. Leonard Linsky (Urbana: University of Illinois Press, 1952), pp. 189–206; reprinted in Quine's *From a Logical Point of View* (Cambridge, Mass.: Harvard University Press, 1953), pp. 1–19. Present reference is to the latter, pp. 12–14. Bergmann, by the way, thinks Quine evinces an unwarranted ontological fascination with the existential operator and the variable it binds, and is himself

For the inhabitant of L_B, of course, there is no problem about ontology, and he would find the concept itself puzzling. But for us who have known different ontologies, it is possible to characterize that of L_B, and we would characterize it with the expression "logical atomism." In so characterizing it, however, we encounter the problem that atomism must always face, the problem of connections among individuals, and in particular, necessary connections among individuals. In explicating analyticity as "analytic in L_1" I showed how empiricism, through rational reconstruction, accounts for logical necessity. It is now incumbent on me to do the same for causal necessity.[20]

What makes the problem of explicating causal necessity in an extensional language difficult is that causal necessity is well stated, and it should be possible to state it, in terms of counterfactual conditionals, which are "if . . . then" statements whose "if" clauses are false; but what makes a counterfactual conditional true in an extensional language is, because of the truth table for material implication, not at all like the necessity thought to reside in empirical laws and to account for their truth. The problem is the same one facing the rational reconstructionist who wants to allow disposition terms such as "soluble" into his language. A disposition term presumably refers to a property that is

---

interested chiefly in the undefined descriptive constants of the ideal language ("Two Cornerstones of Empiricism," pp. 102–4). I do not see that it is the operator and its variables that Quine is talking about, however, so much as the values of the variables. The difference between Quine and Bergmann, as the latter points out, is that whereas Quine countenances classes and higher abstractions in his ontology whether or not we are "acquainted with any of their exemplifications," Bergmann governs his ontology by the "principle of acquaintance," allowing only his undefined descriptive constants (which "we all agree to be acquainted with") and whatever is definable in terms of them. The difference, as it happens, is not pertinent in the present context, nor, since I do not agree that the primitive descriptive constants of Bergmann's ideal language are privileged under the principle of acquaintance, will the difference become pertinent in any imminent context—though, since it is Bergmann's ideal language I am discussing, it would perhaps be appropriate to consider his sense of "ontology" rather than Quine's.

20 These two—logical necessity and causal connection—appear to Morton G. White to be "the rocks on which every empiricism must break" ("Ontological Clarity and Semantic Obscurity," *Journal of Philosophy*, XLVIII [1951], 373–80).

present even when it has no sensory or other experiential manifestations. Such a term cannot qualify for membership in the primitive descriptive vocabulary of L_B, and therefore must, if it is to be in L_B at all, be defined explicitly in terms of that vocabulary. But the definiens will consist of a counterfactual conditional, and the latter is as much of a problem in this connection as it is in connection with causal necessity.[21]

Carnap attempts to get around the problem by means of what he calls "reduction sentences."[22] A pair of reduction sentences specifies a necessary condition and a sufficient one for the presence of the definiendum and does so using as descriptive terms only those found in the primitive vocabulary or definable in terms of that vocabulary. But, as Carnap points out, such a pair of sentences has as its consequence a third sentence which asserts the impossibility of a state of affairs to which both the definiendum and its contradictory would be applicable, and this third sentence is a synthetic one. Thus, the strange—and, so far as L_B is concerned, intolerable—circumstance comes about that two logical statements have as their consequence a nonlogical statement. Moreover, a reduction pair does not define a term so much as it "introduces" it, and the addition of more reduction pairs will further specify the meaning of the term, or as Carnap says, "diminish" its "region of indeterminateness." The idea of indeterminateness, however, strikes as jarring a note in relation to L_B as does the idea that a synthetic statement can be a consequence of logical statements. The meaning of a term for the user of L_B is exhausted within the language; either the term appears in L_B, in which case its meaning is its use in the language, or else it does not, in which case it is meaningless, but in neither case is its meaning indeterminate.

It may be pointed out that if "soluble" were allowed as an undefined, or primitive, descriptive constant, as L_1 would allow and

21 See Nelson Goodman, "The Problem of Counterfactual Conditionals," *Journal of Philosophy*, XLIV (1947), 113–28; reprinted in *Semantics and the Philosophy of Language*, ed. Linsky, pp. 231–46; reprinted with minor changes in Goodman's *Fact, Fiction, and Forecast* (Cambridge, Mass.: Harvard University Press, 1955), pp. 13–34.

22 "Testability and Meaning," *Philosophy of Science*, III (1936), 440 ff.

L_B would not, then it could be handled without use of reduction sentences. For just as I was able to rule out state-descriptions containing the conjunction of "x is a bachelor" and "x is married" by means of a semantic rule, I can also rule out state-descriptions containing the conjunction: "x is soluble," "x is immersed in water," and "x doesn't dissolve."

But even in L_B the solubility of any given material could be handled, so long as the unnecessary demand were not made that "soluble" have a synonym in L_B.[23] Once a term designating the material in question—say, "sugar"—is defined, then by the method of semantic rules, or of meaning postulates, any state-description containing the conjunction of the three statements, "x is sugar," "x is immersed in water," and "x doesn't dissolve" could be banned from the language. And by the same method, empirical lawfulness and causal necessity may be explicated within L_B—in fact, what has just been explicated is the law that sugar is soluble.

It might be objected that the only accomplishment of this method is to rule out state-descriptions in which the counterfactual "if x is sugar and is immersed in water, then it dissolves" is false, whereas what is wanted is a way of ruling out state-descriptions in which the counterfactual is true but vacuous. Such state-descriptions are those containing the statement "x is not immersed in water." However, not only would such a demand be unfair; it would also be inconsistent for anyone who has accepted the explication given above for analyticity. It will be remembered that for the man who "speaks" L_B (it was L_1 then, but the substitution makes no difference), there is no question about analyticity; analytic statements are either those listed under "analytic statements" (if there is such a list) or those that can be turned into logical truths by putting synonyms for synonyms. The explicatum given for "analytic in L_B" is "true in all (permissible) state-descriptions," or—to bring out more force-

[23] See Bergmann, "Comments on Professor Hempel's 'The Concept of Cognitive Significance,'" *Proceedings of the American Academy of Arts and Sciences*, LXXX (1951–54), 78–86; reprinted in his *The Metaphysics of Logical Positivism*, pp. 255–67. Present reference is to pp. 260–63 of the latter.

fully the parenthetical term—"true by virtue of the semantic
rules." What is being done now for causal connection is precisely analogous. From within state-descriptions containing "x is
sugar" and "x is not immersed in water," there is no way of
knowing whether the vacuously true statement "if x is sugar and
is immersed in water, then it dissolves" is any "truer" than the
vacuously true statement "if x is sugar and is immersed in water,
then it doesn't dissolve." But by the same token, there is no way
of knowing, within a given state-description, whether "no bachelor is married" is true not only in this state-description but also
in every permissible state-description. Like analyticity and logical
necessity, lawfulness and causal necessity are concepts that cannot be entertained from "within" an artificial language of the
sort under investigation. There are in L_B what I shall call *nomological statements*; some of these are analytic, others are synthetic,[24] and everything there is to say about them can be conveyed simply by pointing them out.

Enough has now been said, I think, to give an indication of
the sort of philosophic position empiricism becomes when confined within the context of an artificial language, or in other
words, when thought of as the thoroughgoing kind of rational
reconstruction Bergmann wants to engage in for the purpose of
dissolving all philosophic puzzles simultaneously. The discussion
of rational reconstruction, it will be remembered, was undertaken in an effort to deepen the understanding of the explication
given for analyticity. Not the correctness of the explicatum but
the appropriateness of the explicandum is at issue here, and, toward the clarification of that issue, I now turn briefly to some
limitations of rational reconstruction.

3. LIMITATIONS OF RATIONAL RECONSTRUCTION

The philosophy whose method is rational reconstruction is one of those philosophic standpoints that may be
likened to the emperor's new clothes: so long as the illusion is

[24] See Reichenbach, *Elements of Symbolic Logic*, pp. 360 ff.

sustained the clothes are quite dazzling, but once the illusion subsides the emperor is not merely ill-clothed, he is naked.

The success of rational reconstruction in explicating the reduction underlying empiricism depends heavily on the adequacy of the empirical or experiential basis of the primitive descriptive vocabulary of the ideal language. Until now I have assumed without question the empirical propriety of the primitive descriptive constants in L_B. If these constants really do designate elements in our primitive or immediate experience, then every well-formed formula in L_B really will accord with the intent behind empiricism, and empiricism may properly be formulated by the principle that every empirically meaningful statement is a well-formed formula in L_B and every well-formed formula in L_B is either analytic or an empirically meaningful statement. Although the question of primitive descriptive constants, as well as its extralinguistic parent question involving the nature of primitive or immediate human experience, will occupy a central position in Part II, it may be raised briefly here.

The question, more precisely, is whether our most intimate and indubitable experience—the kind to which empiricists have wanted to relate all nonanalytic knowledge—is accurately designated by the primitive descriptive vocabulary of L_B. What the terms of this vocabulary designate, once more, when interpreted by means of the designation rules that come with the language, are sense data, qualities of sense data, and "some spatial and temporal relations" among sense data. And what must be answered sooner or later are, first, whether these are in fact what we experience when we have the kind of experience that is often called "direct," and second, whether this (or any other) direct experience is "indubitable" in any sense of indubitability that could have epistemological utility and empirical significance. A third question to be considered is whether, provided we can appropriately characterize a certain kind of experience as "direct" and can appropriately describe this direct experience as "indubitable," we can, without distorting the nature of human knowledge, get from this indubitable direct experience to the kind of knowledge that, as epistemologists, we are investigating.

72

If the question about the objects of direct experience is a psychological question—that is, if what is wanted is a factual answer—then, of course, it is not for the epistemologist to say out of hand whether the designata of L_B's primitive descriptive constants are or are not directly experienced. Recourse must be had to empirical psychology, for even though I might conclude on the basis of introspection that *I* directly experience sense data, still I would have no right to extend the conclusion to other people's direct experience.

However, some epistemologists who take sense data seriously do not think any question of psychological fact is involved, and some even say explicitly that whatever the opinion of psychologists may be on the subject—even if it be the view that "direct" experience does not contain such elements—their opinion has no epistemological significance. It is epistemology rather than psychology that is looked to for guidance in the case of sense data, and accordingly sense data must be examined in a purely epistemological light. What this means is that whether or not sense data have real existence, all that a "sense-datum philosopher" need claim for them is logical or epistemological or what might be called "analytic" existence; as Russell put it, "the atoms that I wish to arrive at as the sort of last residue in analysis are logical atoms and not physical atoms."[25]

What I wish to question is whether the issue of real or empirical existence can be so easily dismissed. For sense data are defined—or if not defined, described—as the objects of direct experience

[25] Bertrand Russell, "The Philosophy of Logical Atomism," *Monist*, XXVIII (1918), 497. H. H. Price has said that psychological explanations are vitiated, so far as epistemology is concerned, by their reliance on the principle of induction (which itself involves perception) as a presupposition (*Perception* [2d ed.; London: Methuen & Co., 1950], p. 171 n.). C. I. Lewis, though resting his epistemology on the given as an "ingredient" or "aspect" of experience, and asserting that "it would be absurd to deny" the "direct apprehension of the immediate," nevertheless doubts whether there are any experiences of the given unadulterated by elements supplied by interpretation or construction; given data are, in Jacob Loewenberg's phrase, "postanalytic," and one may doubt whether such data are empirically inspectable (see *Mind and the World-Order* [New York: Charles Scribner's Sons, 1929], pp. 54, 120 f.). Again, C. D. Broad speaks of pure sensation as "an ideal limit rather than an observable fact," in *The Mind and Its Place in Nature* (London: Kegan Paul, Trench, Trubner & Co., 1925), p. 216.

or of direct awareness, and must therefore be described also as existing in the full-bodied or empirical sense of existence. The experience of empirically nonexistent objects would be a strange kind of experience indeed for empiricists to invoke in connection with empirical meaning, whatever nonempirical kind of existence the objects were said to have. Bergmann puts up a long and valiant struggle against Ayer's view that part of what is meant by saying something is directly experienced is that it exists, or that "x is directly apprehended" entails "x exists."[26] But I need not consider Bergmann's arguments in order to point out that if sense data are considered not to exist, then the concept of sense datum is not providing what it is supposed to provide, and we had better find ourselves another concept that will.

What the concept of sense datum is supposed to provide is a device whereby we can say that there is a sense in which what we perceive is always exactly as it is perceived. In the case of visual perception, for example, visual sense data really exist and really have the properties they appear to have, entirely apart from anything we may discover later about the material objects of our perception. Should anyone believe that there is no sense whatever in which any objects of perception always have the properties they are perceived to have—that in no sense whatever is perception always veridical—he would have no reason for believing that sense data exist, and in fact he would have no use for the concept of sense datum; from the appearance of sense data in his ontology it could be inferred that he had not made judicious use of Occam's razor. Conversely, and as I said above, one who requires the concept of an object of direct experience, but who believes that sense data do not exist, cannot use sense data to provide the concept he requires. And once more, the kind of existence that sense data must have, if they have any, is the customary kind we attribute to things, and not a special "analytic" or "epistemic" kind. Price has said that though sense data exist they do not

---

[26] Bergmann, "Sense Data, Linguistic Conventions, and Existence," *Philosophy of Science*, XIV (1947), 152–63; reprinted in his *The Metaphysics of Logical Positivism*, pp. 176–96.

persist the way substances do.[27] But if existence-without-persist-
ence is an extraordinary, epistemic kind of existence, then it is
not the kind that sense data must have in order to discharge their
responsibilities; and if it is not an extraordinary kind of existence,
then its inability to persist makes it a queer kind of ordinary
existent entity for empiricists to be talking about. Pending a
fuller investigation of perception in Part II, there is little that
can be added concerning sense data and existence.

Within L_B, of course, the issue could not arise, and in so far as
Bergmann is talking about L_B he is talking about something entirely different. It seems, moreover, that Bergmann's argument
consists mainly in showing that the question whether "x is directly apprehended" entails "x exists" is vacuous so far as the
ideal language is concerned; much of his argument is given over
to the status of the word "exist" in L_B. What must be done here,
however, is to step outside the ideal language in order to evaluate
both its contribution to the empiricist cause and its fitness as a
context in which analyticity may be explicated.

The evaluation will be facilitated by use of the terminology I
developed at the end of the first chapter. To make clear the difference between the present field of discourse and Bergmann's,
and to distinguish the present approach from that of the last
section, it need only be said that external questions are now at
issue, whereas previously the concern was for internal questions,
which are what Bergmann is dealing with. I am now outside L_B
looking in, not in the sense that I am carrying on a metalinguistic discussion about an object language—this, after all, is what
Bergmann is doing, and it is all he can ever do so long as he tries
to say what he means instead of showing it—but in the much
stronger sense that I am looking at L_B with a view to justifying
or criticizing the epistemological technique it exemplifies.

The question involving the primitive descriptive vocabulary of
any ideal language purporting to exhibit empiricism as per-
manently built into it may be said now to be at least partly a

[27] *Op. cit.*, p. 103. Any persistence that sense data may have, Price thinks,
is entirely dependent on external conditions, and it is because of this dependence that the persistence of sense data differs in kind from that of substances.

question of psychological fact. And if this is correct, then much needs to be said about L_B which has so far been left unsaid. In particular, its primitive nonlogical constants require empirical justification, and until such justification is provided, the empirical fitness of the language can be nothing but an assumption.

Bergmann, it is true, seems occasionally to admit a possible plurality of ideal languages, each possessing certain structural "invariants."[28] It might be argued that, whether or not the primitive vocabulary of L_B is empirically accurate, at least it is one of a very few vocabularies which might contend for the title, and therefore a few ideal languages may be constructed, each incorporating one of these vocabularies. The class of these ideal languages (most likely there would be only two or three) could then be utilized as I have been utilizing L_B alone; explication would be slightly more complicated, but the present objection would be obviated.

This counterargument might have been valid if Bergmann, in his eagerness to solve all the problems and solve them simultaneously, had not gone too far. Whether or not a plurality of languages could permit that simultaneity, all other factors ignored, is questionable, but I will let it pass. What I cannot let pass is the even more questionable procedure of both asserting categorically that there is an experiential datum-element in our knowledge which is indubitable, and suggesting as methodologically sound a plurality of ideal languages, each with its own primitive vocabulary vying for empiricist recognition. Bergmann does make the categorical assertion: "Some things, such as that we have at the moment a chair percept, we know, whenever we do know them, so that it makes absolutely no sense to say that we may doubt them."[29] Believing this, it would be strange if he were to go to all the trouble of constructing alternate languages with

[28] See n. 12 above.

[29] "Two Cornerstones of Empiricism," pp. 80–81. Though Bergmann speaks of "percepts" here, instead of "sense data," the distinction does not seem to be the radical one Roderick Firth calls attention to in his "Sense-Data and the Percept Theory" (Mind, LVIII [1949], 434–65; LIX [1950], 35–56). Whether sense datum or percept, however, the present argument is not affected.

alternate primitive descriptive vocabularies; with such objects of direct awareness as chair percepts already known by him to be indubitable datum-elements, Bergmann has an appreciable head-start on the road to a rational reconstruction that compels the assent of empiricists. I conclude that if Bergmann were to tolerate a plurality of ideal languages, the primitive empirical constants of L_B would comprise one of the structural invariants shared by all of them, and that, therefore, the counterargument that there are a number of possible primitive vocabularies is not valid. The argument stands that, with respect to its empirical vocabulary, L_B—or any ideal language considered to be sufficient for rational reconstruction—involves assumptions without empirical justification.

Moreover, if the choice of any empiricist vocabulary as primitive has not been justified empirically—if, in other words, we do not know what direct or immediate experience is—then the assertion of the presence of an indubitable datum-element in human knowledge is without empirical justification. And since it is by virtue of his assumption of an indubitable datum-element that Bergmann is able to talk about the simultaneous solution of all philosophic problems by means of the rational reconstruction of knowledge within an ideal language, this is one more reflection on the empiricist integrity of rational reconstruction and of artificial languages.

Finally, if there is in knowledge no empirically available datum-element that is indubitable, my third question—how rational reconstructionists justify the method by which they get from this datum-element to the higher reaches of human knowledge—need not be asked.

Though these arguments, of course, cannot be expected to effect an about-face on the part of the reconstructionists, it might seem to many nonreconstructionists that I have not gone far enough. Whereas, it might be said, I have pointed out a limitation (and not even a limitation "in principle," since empirical psychology could conceivably provide what I have found wanting), what is begging to be said is that no philosophic consideration whatever militates for rational reconstruction as a way of doing philosophy. It is not a matter of being ill-clothed but of being unclothed.

There is something to be said for the view prompting this objection, and I will try to say it in terms of my vocabulary. In these terms, what rational reconstructionists are doing is, first, providing themselves with a rigorously defined *context*, and second, formulating and answering the classic philosophic questions as *internal* questions within this context. Internal questions, it may be remembered, are answered by definite assertions found by inspecting the context by virtue of which the questions are internal. So treated, it is not unreasonable to expect that all the problems of philosophy can be solved and can be solved simultaneously.

Still using my vocabulary, I may point out that rational reconstruction is able to occupy the philosophic stage only because it ignores that, in effect, it is proposing a *convention* enabling it to avoid the relativity accompanying the philosophic approach that treats every question as one of *degree*. There is, of course, no harm in agreeing to conventions by which philosophic questions become internal questions and philosophic answers become definite assertions, and at times it is essential to proceed in this way; herein lies the philosophic merit artificial languages have. But there is harm, at least from an empiricist viewpoint, in obliterating the *external* questions that must come first—questions about which conventions to make, which contexts to determine, which questions to ask as internal questions.

Surely no one could legitimately claim that the maxim, "to be is to be the value of a variable," is a solution of the problems Plato and Aristotle were working on when they were doing what is called ontology. Such a claim would be an example, *as* exact as it is egregious, of the confusion of internal and external questions. What the formula defines, of course, is "being in L_1"— L_1 again being any particular artificial language—and it would be better formulated as "to be, relative to L_1, is to be the value of a variable in L_1." This formulation would at least indicate that so far as ontology is in question, ontology is given the sense of "commitment by some particular language." But it is the external questions that are, properly speaking, questions of ontology. Quine's formula is incomplete so long as it is not accompanied by specification of which language provides an appropriate framework for employing the formula.[30] Though it is entirely adequate for the semanticist, the formula is useless, or worse, for the ontologist.

The impression grows that, for a way of philosophizing that professes to be empirical, this one has a cavalier way of treating empiricism. Empiricism, remember, is the philosophic position that meaningful discourse must be somehow "derived from" experience, that the genuine elements of human knowledge must in some way be "tied down" to human experience. Rational reconstruction does undeniably provide a picture of how our knowledge can be connected with our experience—connected in a manner unmatched for detailed precision. But the price is great. A whole area of human knowledge is left without the remotest attachment to experience; moreover, it is the area of philosophic knowledge, precisely the knowledge which early empiricists were most anxious to bring into contact with experience. To explicate analyticity as "analytic in L_B" without attempting an empirical justification of L_B as a proper context for explication seems not so different—or different only in degree—from explicating analyticity as "analytic in S_R," where S_R is any one of the rationalist systems of philosophy from which Locke and Hume were trying to get away. In neither case does there seem to be any special empiricist reason why a particular system or language should be chosen over any other available context. And what is true of the problem of analyticity is equally true of any of the other philosophic problems coming within the orbit of rational reconstructionists.

So far as philosophic knowledge is concerned, therefore, rational reconstruction, or the method of the ideal language, does not appear to have any valid claims on empiricists. But do ra-

[30] Quine, it should be pointed out, is well aware of the pitfalls in his formulation of the ontological problem (see "On What There Is," pp. 15 f.).

EXPERIENCE AND THE ANALYTIC

tional reconstructionists give an adequate account of scientific knowledge?[31] Many empiricists, after all, have wanted to hold scientific knowledge up before philosophers, if not as the only kind of knowledge worthy of the name, then at least as the prototype of all knowledge. And even though rational reconstruction cannot account empirically for philosophic knowledge, it might be forgiven and embraced if it could account empirically for scientific knowledge.

I mentioned, in connection with causal necessity and disposition terms, two circumstances, inimical to rational reconstruction, which would result from employment of reduction sentences. These were the entailment of empirical statements by logical statements, and the suggestion—by the concept of indeterminateness of meaning—that everything there is to be said has not been said in L_B. For the scientist who must try to fit everything into L_B, either the explication given of "nomologicality" must be accepted as the only way of dealing with causality, or else partial defeat in the attempt to stay within L_B must be admitted. But acceptance of "nomologicality in L_B" as the explication of causal connection forces a scientist to admit that, when he thought he was discovering and demonstrating the law that sugar is soluble, all he was doing was proposing a convention about admissible state-descriptions.

Nor, so far as the scientist is concerned, is this the end of his disenchantment with L_B. For the ontological atomism that is required of him would, if rigorously adhered to, put an end to all discovery and prediction and, in effect, bring about that purely descriptive science which so many have desiderated for so long. What the scientist is asked to do by the rational reconstructionist is, in the words of Russell's principle, to substitute constructions out of known entities for inferences to unknown entities—and, moreover, to forget that the substitution has been made. But what constructions out of known entities amount to (ignoring questions about which entities are known entities) are summaries and organizations of known entities, and these are, ex

[31] Assuming—wrongly, as I will contend—that the implied distinction can be drawn between philosophic and scientific knowledge.

hypothesi, all that exist. And if everything that exists is known, then nothing remains to be predicted.[32]

To put it still another way: Any descriptive term which may form a component of a well-formed formula in L_B either belongs to the primitive vocabulary of L_B or else is definable in terms of that vocabulary. Bergmann thinks that no limitations on existent entities are indicated by the structure of the ideal language; to conclude, according to him, that, because any descriptive term that is not a charter member of L_B is eliminable in favor of terms that are, therefore only such charter members designate existent entities, is to make a wholly unwarranted conclusion and to be "a traditional phenomenalist rather than a Logical Positivist."[33] But whether or not Bergmann contracts phenomenalism from his affair with the ideal language, it is more usual than not for rational reconstruction to lead its exponents into such ontological depopulation. And whatever function the scientist may be given by the rational reconstructionist, it will, in view of the paucity of kinds of empirical entities he will usually be given to work with, bear little resemblance to the empiricism rational reconstruction was designed to explicate.

Empirical science, to make the point clearer, is helpless when confined to a context of justification or explication because such a context is a *closed system* and lacks the openness and indeterminacy essential to empirical science. The openness and indeterminacy are to be found in contexts of discovery, but rational reconstruction is, by its own admission, unequipped to inquire into such contexts. All that rational reconstruction can accomplish is a "clipping [of] the wings of speculation and dogmatism after experimental discoveries have been made."[34] I do not want to minimize the importance of this activity or of the sanction it rightly receives from philosophic empiricism. Within a rationally

---

[32] For a clarification of the terms "construction" and "inferred entity," as well as a lucid discussion of the questions of existence and prediction, see Lewis White Beck, "Constructions and Inferred Entities," *Philosophy of Science,* XVII (1950), 74–86; reprinted in *Readings in the Philosophy of Science,* ed. Herbert Feigl and May Brodbeck (New York: Appleton-Century-Crofts, 1953), pp. 368–81.

[33] "Logical Positivism," p. 11.

[34] Beck, *op. cit.,* p. 381.

reconstructed framework, moreover, relations among concepts and among propositions may become crystal clear, and this is a great boon to the empiricist. But I do want to suggest that the empiricist philosopher of science should be at least as concerned with scientific discovery, and that, with regard to such discovery, rational reconstruction as described by Bergmann has no value whatever. The conclusion is that rational reconstruction not only cannot account empirically for philosophic knowledge but cannot even account empirically for scientific knowledge, and it therefore has but a meager claim on the philosophic empiricist.

It should in all fairness be added that rational reconstruction *is* able to account empirically for mathematical knowledge, or that at least its account of mathematical knowledge need cause empiricists no embarrassment. The reason its account of mathematics need not embarrass empiricists is that mathematical knowledge is exempted from the empiricist principle. But note that rational reconstruction is entirely adequate only so long as questions about mathematics are internal and are recognized to be such, as by the mathematical formalists. No irrevocable harm is done to empiricism by rational reconstruction when the logicists consider mathematical questions to be external, because actually the questions are still internal, to be answered by assertions based on "logical evidence."[35] When mathematical questions not only are considered to be external but are in fact external, however, as are those formulated by intuitionists or finitists, then they are not exempt from the empiricist principle. From the viewpoint of the intuitionist, no extensional artificial language can be an adequate context for mathematics, and rational reconstruction is unable to account for mathematical knowledge.

4. CONSEQUENCES FOR ANALYTICITY AND EMPIRICISM

The apparatus is at hand for tying up some loose ends and severing others. Let me recapitulate the discussion so

[35] What does result from the logicist viewpoint is failure to take logical or mathematical contexts to be either transient enough or limited enough, with consequent confusion over the philosophic significance that ought to be attached to such work as Gödel's and Church's on undecidability.

far. After briefly describing the historical background of the principles of empiricism (or reductionism) and analyticity, I inquired into the relations between the two principles and found that, though one need not maintain the principle of empiricism in order to defend a sharp and rigid distinction between analytic and synthetic truths, nevertheless one cannot maintain the principle of empiricism in any pragmatically justifiable sense if he simultaneously denies the analytic-synthetic distinction. This result enabled me to map strategy, since a demonstration that no sharp and permanent distinction can be maintained between analytic and synthetic truths would require empiricists to reject the empiricist principle, and a demonstration that the applicability of the analyticity principle is in certain ways limited would imply the existence of the same limitations on the applicability of the empiricist principle. Accordingly, I turned to an investigation of the analyticity principle as it has been attacked and defended in recent years.

Taking a cue from Kant's formulation of the distinction in terms of "containment," a similar and less metaphorical formulation was found in Lewis' treatment of meaning and analyticity, in which the notion of inclusion plays an important role. As illustrated by his distinction between implicitly and explicitly analytic statements, Lewis analyzes analyticity in terms of certain intensional adverbs, such as "necessarily" and "by definition." These in turn are claimed by Lewis to rest on relations among "sense meanings," or more accurately, on the relations of inclusion and exclusion among "sense recognizable characters," as indicated by our willingness or refusal to apply some terms to the same characters to which we apply others. My objection to all this—an objection which forced me to reject Lewis' entire treatment of meaning and analyticity—was that any empirical assurance about Lewis' analysis must rest on the reliability of relations among terms, or "linguistic meanings," as an index to relations among sense-recognizable characters, or sense meanings, and that there is no way of gauging this reliability because there is no way of getting back and forth between sense meanings and linguistic meanings except perhaps by means of scientific induction, which cannot provide the necessity on which analyticity is said to rest.

An investigation of the extensional concepts of definition, synonymy, and the distinction between logical and nonlogical terms and statements yielded no positive results so far as a basis for distinguishing between analytic and synthetic truths is concerned, and the conclusion seemed inescapable that this distinction, as well as the concepts that might otherwise have supported it, must either be defined on the basis of a convention, or else must be said to be a matter of degree. The relations among these concepts of convention and degree I was able to delineate roughly by means of two other concepts: context and the distinction between internal and external questions. Within a well-defined context established by means of conventions, the distinctions between analytic and synthetic and between logical and nonlogical, as well as the collateral ideas of definition and synonymy, are precise concepts, and questions about them are internal questions. Without such a context the concepts are all vague unless entertained as matters of degree, and questions about them are external questions.

In this chapter I sought a clear and distinct conception of analyticity by looking in the only place where one might be available, a context of the sort just mentioned. Such a context is provided by an artificial language which may be rigidly controlled by means of strict rules governing the selection and the interpretation of its vocabulary, and the formation, the transformation, and the truth of all statements allowed in it. Analyticity in this context gains a precision which is a model for philosophic analysis.

This contextual analysis—or explication—of analyticity has its drawbacks, however. For one thing, the artificial language chosen must be an extensional language, since the objections found against Lewis' theory of meaning would militate also against any intensional language as a suitable context for a precise concept of analyticity. Moreover, it was found that, while analyticity is easily understood within any *specific* extensional language, this explication of it does not admit of generalization. That is, if L_1

is a constant designating a particular extensional artificial language, and if L_i is a variable ranging over all extensional artificial languages, then, whereas "analytic in L_1" is an adequate explication of analyticity, "analytic in L_i" is not.

The major drawback of "analytic in L_1" as an explication of analyticity, however, is seen when the philosophic significance of artificial languages is sought. Such significance is exemplified by the kind of philosophy which is a function of it: rational reconstruction. The inability of rational reconstruction to account empirically for knowledge was pointed out, and the appropriate conclusion with respect to philosophic empiricism was drawn. Empiricism does not retain its original intent when interpreted as rational reconstruction. Far from it, the concepts of logical clarity and syntactical precision dominating rational reconstruction—in practice, at least—are uncomfortably close to the concepts of self-evidence and natural reason characteristic of the rationalist philosophies which empiricism was originally designed to avoid.[36]

However, my examination of rational reconstruction was undertaken in order to gain a direct insight not into empiricism but into analyticity. Specifically, it was undertaken in order to see whether, when an explication has been given of "analytic in L_1" or "analytic within a particular artificial language," analyticity has been understood. And for reasons stated—involving what might be called disguised conventions—it must be concluded that when an explicatum is reached for "analytic in L_1," an understanding has been gained of nothing more significant than analyticity in L_1. In other words, while a correct explicatum has been given for "analytic in L_1," the latter expression is not an appropriate explicandum for analyticity. It may be added that L_1

---

[36] It is interesting to note, in this connection, how often reconstructionists, formalists, and related analytic philosophers speak of a *feeling* (sometimes of an "undeniable feeling") of analyticity or of synonymy or of logicality. What is interesting is not that philosophers should *have* such feelings but that they should so confidently build their feelings into their philosophic frameworks. See, e.g., Bergmann, "Two Cornerstones of Empiricism," pp. 90–91; Hilary Putnam, "Synonymity, and the Analysis of Belief Sentences," *Analysis*, XIV (1953–54), 117–18; Arthur Pap, *Elements of Analytic Philosophy* (New York: Macmillan Co., 1949), pp. 474–75.

itself depends on the analytic-synthetic distinction; there must be a sharp and available distinction in L_1 between statements dependent for their truth values solely on the meanings of their constituent terms, and statements whose truth values may involve rules of designation and must involve rules of truth—between, in Carnap's terms, L-true and F-true statements.[37] Hence, the reason "analytic in L_1" is such a clear-cut notion is that, if it were not, L_1 could not have been conceived to begin with.

Since, however, the principle of analyticity—the principle that there is a sharp and fundamental cleavage between analytic and synthetic truths—can be maintained only within a particular extensional artificial language such as L_1, I am driven also to the conclusion, on the basis of my investigation of the connection between the two principles, that the same is true of the empiricist principle. The empiricist principle can be said to be valid only within some particular language such as L_1. And since rational reconstruction, as exemplified by Bergmann's unique ideal language, is in accord with the above conclusion, the nod must be given to it, and empiricism must be explicated as "empiricism within or with respect to L_B."

"Empiricism within L_B" is no more acceptable than "analytic in L_B," of course, and so there are two alternatives: either empiricism must be given up, or else a different interpretation must be found for it. And since I find the first alternative intolerable, I choose the second. Not to give up empiricism, in face of the difficulties found with the only acceptable form of it, must be equivocating on the word "empiricism"; I must be talking really about two philosophic positions, not one. However, there is an affinity between the position I am forced to relinquish and the one I hope will emerge from the present work, and this affinity is of such a kind that I feel justified in naming both positions empiricism. Again, I am ahead of myself.

I think it would not be a misstatement to say that, of the problems discussed so far, the root problem is that of the relation

---

[37] The class of analytic statements may of course be coextensive with that of logical truths.

of the formal elements in experience and in discourse to the factual or the empirical elements, part of this problem being to distinguish the two kinds of elements. With respect to empiricism,
the problem takes the form of the relation between experiences
and the "meanings" by which experiences can be conceptualized,
articulated, and communicated. With respect to analyticity, the
problem is one about meaning itself and deals with the relation
between statements whose truth depends on the elements in experience represented by the meanings involved and statements
whose truth depends solely on the meanings themselves.

So far I have been unable to discover any satisfactory account
of this root problem. To the extent that the formal-factual distinction may be formulated with precision, its range of significance seems to diminish almost to the point of triviality. And
when its range of significance is preserved, it is of such a vague
sort that it seems not to be the kind of significance empiricists
would like to place their faith in. If I may speak of "internal"
and "external" significance: When the formal-factual distinction
is seen within a sufficiently well-defined context, its internal significance has the kind of precision that empiricists, particularly
analysis-minded empiricists, aim for. But then its external significance, which is a function of the significance of the context itself, is at a minimum, because the context is the result of a more
or less arbitrary convention and hence has only the significance
invested in it by us. When, on the other hand, the distinction is
viewed independently of any particular context, it is wholly a
matter of degree, and not even of degree as susceptible to any
objective mode of determination, but of degree as determined by
such nonobjective considerations as purpose and point of view—
and as far as that goes, psychosomatic state—of whoever is doing
the determining. The conflict between matters of convention
and matters of degree, mentioned at the end of the last chapter,
is evident here. Either a context is delineated by means of a convention, and precision is achieved, or else whatever is at issue is
treated, if at all, as a matter of degree, preserving breadth of
significance at the cost of precision. It could be said, with but
minor historical inaccuracy, that in the latter case the concept in

question is clear but confused, whereas in the former it is distinct but obscure.[38]

The problem to be investigated now, at any rate, is whether a sharp distinction can be drawn between the formal and the empirical aspects of experience and of discourse, or—since this question has already been answered and I am still in the dark—what sort of relation obtains between these formal and nonformal aspects. This is the problem to which the rest of the inquiry will be devoted, beginning with an examination of human experience itself in an effort to see whether the problem extends into our primitive experiences or whether it arises at some more advanced stage of experience. The examination of experience, which will touch on some problems about perceiving and thinking, with a few side glances at the primitive stages of meaning—partly in connection with human values—will occupy the next part of the work. Utilizing the results of this experiential inquiry, in the third and last part I will return to some of the considerations already discussed, especially the matter of context as it enters or ought to enter into the methods practiced by empiricist philosophers, and I will talk about a philosophic method, to be called *pragmatic reconstruction*, which seems to me to embody what is of philosophic importance about rational reconstruction without losing the empiricist significance for the sake of which the inquiry is being undertaken. The emperor will remain clothed, and, moreover, about as well clothed as men have a right to expect.

[38] See below, pp. 205 ff.

PART II

EMPIRICISM

AND

EXPERIENCE

CHAPTER III

A Critique of Some Theories about Perception

1. ATOMISM AND ANALYSES OF THE GIVEN

I CONCLUDED the first part of my inquiry by viewing the problems that had arisen so far as clustering about the basic problem of relations between the formal and nonformal aspects of experience and of discourse. And I said that I would begin investigating this basic problem by examining human experience in order to see how primitive a level of experience the problem could be traced to. What I want to know is whether the formal-nonformal distinction arises at some relatively sophisticated stage of experience or whether it is present from the very beginning. If the distinction is not present from the very beginning, I want to know whether the kind of experiences that do not contain it can be called cognitive in any sense of the word.

The expression "from the very beginning" is apt to cause trouble. It may or may not be intended to have a temporal significance. If it is intended to have a temporal significance, it could refer to the historical beginnings of human experience, in which case the investigation would be anthropological in character, or it could refer to the biographical beginnings of the individual, in which case the investigation would be psychological in character, construing "anthropology" and "psychology" quite broadly. If the expression is not intended to have a temporal significance, it must involve priority either of a logical or of a nomological sort, and since the question is not a logical one, nomological priority must be what is meant. By nomological priority here, I mean priority according to some kind of extra-logical law.[1] If physical or causal law were in question, the investigation called for would be of a psychological or anthropological kind, or in other words, the kind called for if "from the

[1] See above, p. 71.

very beginning" had a temporal significance. The priority might be due, however, not to physical law but to some sort of epistemological law. The inquiry needed to answer questions about the level of experience at which the formal-nonformal distinction manifests itself might be, in particular, the peculiarly epistemological one to which most sense-datum theorists have wanted to confine questions about experience.

The ambiguity of "from the very beginning" forces me, therefore, to decide whether my inquiry into the experiential significance of the formal-nonformal distinction is to be scientific, or factual, or whether it is to be "epistemological" in that virgin manner which scorns the testimony of fact and which many philosophers have said is the sole way of solving philosophic problems about human knowledge. However, though I cannot avoid the decision, I can postpone it and proceed, for the time being, in the latter or epistemological way, since so many philosophers have done the same and I want to be able to discuss them on their own terms. And the first question that must be answered is: What is the nature of the primitive experience to which one must look for symptoms of the formal-nonformal distinction?

Many philosophers have said that perception comes about through a combination of two different kinds of mental operations or states of mind. The first they have called direct or immediate awareness, and the second, interpretation or inference or construction. Corresponding to the perception resulting from this second mental operation or state of mind are the objects we are familiar with—dogs, trees, and airplanes. But corresponding to direct awareness is another kind of object, the given, and in relation to this kind, the second is called the supplied, or mind-supplied.[2]

[2] See, e.g., C. I. Lewis, Mind and the World-Order (New York: Charles Scribner's Sons, 1929), pp. 38 ff.; Lewis, An Analysis of Knowledge and Valuation (2d printing; La Salle, Ill.: Open Court Publishing Co., 1950), p. 188; H. H. Price, Perception (2d ed.; London: Methuen & Co., 1950), chap. i; Price, Thinking and Experience (London: Hutchinson's University Library, 1953), pp. 44 ff., 78 ff.; W. T. Stace, The Theory of Knowledge and Existence (Oxford: Clarendon Press, 1932), p. 28; Ledger Wood, The Analysis of Knowledge (London: George Allen & Unwin, 1940), pp. 36 ff.; Roderick Firth, "Sense-Data and the Percept Theory," Part II, Mind, LIX (1950), 35 ff.

If this explanation of perception is correct as far as it goes, the present question has an answer. There is an element in experience, the given element, and a corresponding state of mind, direct awareness, and nothing about either of them supports or even suggests a distinction between the formal and the nonformal in experience. The kind of experience in which that difference first manifests itself is perception, because perception consists in two kinds of mental operations or states of mind, one of which has formal elements and one of which has not.

Of the philosophers who explain perception by means of the distinction between the given and nongiven, moreover, many attach cognitive significance to the given or to the state of being directly aware of it. They find in the given the foundations of empirical knowledge, describing awareness of it as indubitable (whether or not they call it "knowledge") and making it a presupposition for empirical knowledge.

The question about the nature of primitive experience now becomes one about the nature of the given and of awareness of it. If corroborating evidence can be found for the view just sketched, its consequences for the formal-nonformal distinction may be accepted; if such evidence cannot be found, this too will have its consequences. The question at issue is not a new one to the present inquiry, for the given has already been discussed in terms of sense data.[3] It was said that only on the basis of psychological investigation can sense data be declared to be the objects of that direct experience to which empiricists have wanted to connect all meaningful nonanalytic statements.

However, even if the existence of sense data were said to be epistemic or analytic rather than empirical—even if they were said to belong to the "epistemic given" rather than to the "psychological given"[4]—there are, nevertheless, competing *epistemo-*

[3] See above, pp. 72 ff. The term "sense datum," incidentally, will be used here in a sense broad enough to include what other philosophers have traditionally meant by "impression," "idea," "quale," "image," "sensum," "phenomenon," and in some respects, though not all, "percept." See Firth, *op. cit.*, Part I, *Mind*, LVIII (1949), 434.

[4] See John W. Yolton, "Linguistic and Epistemological Dualism," *Mind*, LXII (1953), 20–42.

logical views about what the elements of direct experience are, so that sense data could not be awarded the decision until these other views were considered. Assuming that sense data do have a special, epistemic, kind of existence, the question now is whether, even if the criterion for this existence is of the sort indicated by Russell in describing the logical atoms he was looking for as "the sort of last residue in analysis," this "last residue" consists necessarily in sense data. In effect, the criterion for the epistemic given has become "being the end result of analysis," and a consideration that immediately presents itself is that not everyone's end results will be the same; an analysis of experience may be imagined quite easily whose end results are not sense data.

Suppose I were to analyze visual perception by (1) thinking of the visual field as having the shape and consistency of a wedge of semihard cheese, say, port du salut, and (2) slicing off layers from this visual field, perpendicular to my line of sight, of the thickness of soap film. These layers may be likened, if one simile may be clarified by another, to very thin kodachrome slides which match when superimposed. Now, are these layers the end result of my analysis? Or should I proceed (3) to slice each layer into strips of diminishing width and then finish up by (4) cross-carving each strip into squares? If I am an atomist, of course, I must carry the analysis as far as possible, for if the result of my analysis is itself analyzable I have not yet reached the atoms I am after. Analysis, however, need not be atomistic; I might stop at any stage and argue that, while it is true that I might go further—say, toward strip-elements or square-elements—nevertheless I have gone as far as I intend to go. To push the analysis any further would be to push it beyond the limits of significance; it would be to give up genuine elements of perception in favor of arbitrary and artificial subelements. I am doing philosophy, not mathematics. A molecular analysis is preferable, for these reasons, to an atomistic one—or at least so this argument might run.

The atomist is certainly entitled to object that, once an analysis is undertaken, its executor is bound to push it as far as he can. Only in this way, he might add, can there be the sort of control that ought to be the aim of analysis. If the analytic process could be terminated anywhere, at the discretion of the analyst, the purpose of analysis would be lost; everyone would have his own theory about the point at which analysis should end, and we might just as well return to preanalytic methods. Moreover, if the objector is a sense-datum theorist as well as an atomist, he may point out that the atoms I have arrived at, or would arrive at if I gave in to his views about analysis—the squares out of strips out of layers—are none other than the very sense data I was trying to get away from.

However, even if the atomistic argument about the limits of analysis were to be granted, a countercomplaint could be brought against the sense-datum theorist. The countercomplaint is that he himself has failed to pursue his analysis of visual perception to the bitter end; he has no right to end his analysis with colors, because color is analyzable into hue, saturation, and brilliance, and perhaps the latter should be further analyzed into tint and shade.[5] Qua atomist, the sense-datum theorist stands convicted of gross dereliction of duty. But atomism aside, the atoms resulting from my sliced-layer analysis are not identical with sense data in any sense of the latter I know of. Supposing visual sense data to be color patches, they are certainly not the same as squares carved out of kodachrome slides. Either the latter are geometric points (as they will be if I accede with a vengeance to the "bitter end" criterion), in which event they are infinitely smaller than the color patches of which we are immediately aware according to the sense-datum theorists, or else they are finite in area, in which event not only might they be multicolored, unlike sense data, but also squares (rectangles with all sides equal, with maximum area per given perimeter, and so on), and therefore much too complex to be atoms. If it be objected that I have introduced this complexity myself for no good reason, that the layers needn't be sliced into squares but only sliced haphazardly, my reply is that, however the visual layers be cut up,

[5] See "color," *Webster's New International Dictionary* (2d ed., unabridged; Springfield, Mass.: G. & C. Merriam, 1951), pp. 528–29.

the final elements will be either geometric points or else areas of some determinate shape. Nor can I allow the complaint that this determinacy, by virtue of which my analytic elements are complex, is not essential and hence should be ignored. In terms of my analysis the determinacy is essential; my analysis essentially involves cutting up visual layers into pieces of visual layers, and however I do this the pieces will have some determinate shape. This determinacy and complexity are, in fact, a major difference between my analysis and a sense-datum analysis, and it is a difference sufficient to reject the charge that the two end results are identical. And if there is a priority of some sort attaching to sense data but not to bits of sliced layers of visual fields, this is exactly the information I am looking for with such conspicuous lack of success.

Perhaps sense data will be said to have a priority that my koda-chrome squares do not have because the analysis which arrives at sense data as its end results is no such indiscriminate process as chopping up visual layers into squares or other polygons. Philosophic analysis, it might be said, is a much more complex and difficult method; it is more like unfolding a head of cabbage than carving it into slices with no regard for its natural folds. But again, precisely what I would like to know is where these natural folds lie in the case of perception. Why do sense data, but not kodachrome squares, follow the folds? If the sense-datum theorist should point to *facts* of perception, such as, for example, that the sense-datum vocabulary does apply to our experience, then he is invoking the psychological elements he claimed to be able to dispense with in his analysis, and "being the end result of analysis" is by itself no longer his criterion for epistemic existence.

A reply the sense-datum philosopher might make to the last criticism is that simply to claim the objects of direct or immediate visual experience to be correctly described by the words "red" and "green" isn't necessarily to invoke psychology. "Red" and "green" are in this instance members of a sense-datum vocabulary and serve to give sense data an empirical reference, but their use does not entail that their designata have empirical existence. It is an undeniable fact, moreover, that we all can describe things accurately to a certain extent when limited to a sense-datum vocabulary, and herein lies the efficacy of the sense-datum theory.

However, to admit this fact is not to concede anything to the sense-datum theorist. Such a concession would follow if he could show that when I point and pronounce the word "red," what I am pointing to, and hence what I mean by "red," is a sense datum rather than a physical object or a geometric square. But unless this can be proved, it might just as well be the case that by "red" I mean "the red of that chair" and not "the red color patch" or "red here now." The mere fact that I can use a sense-datum terminology to describe my perceptions does not, it is true, turn the sense-datum theory into a psychological theory, but neither does it insure its correctness.

Furthermore, the utility of the sense-datum terminology in describing our experiences does not grant a unique status to the sense-datum theory, because there are other terminologies which are not physical-object ones but which have experiential reference. For example, "helicoid" and "torus" can be used to describe thing as accurately as "red" and "green" do; this experiential reference could be used to support the theory that the objects of our direct visual experiences are geometric shapes and to support it as firmly as the experiential reference of "red" and "green" supports the analogous theory involving color patches. By "geometric shapes," moreover, I do not mean simply the rough shapes color patches may have according to the sense-datum theorists—shapes describable by "roundish" and "squarish"—but on the contrary, precise and complicated geometric shapes, accurately described by "torus" and "helicoid" or, even better, by mathematical equations. It cannot be objected that "helicoid" is a sophisticated word and "red" a familiar one, because the intended meaning of "red" is not "the red of that chair," which *is* a more familiar expression than "helicoid," but "the red color patch" or "red here now," which to me are no less sophisticated than the geometric term—if indeed the notions of sophistication and familiarity are relevant here, which I doubt. Nor can the objection be allowed that the concepts designated by "helicoid" and "torus" are ideal concepts, no more realizable than perfect circles; this consideration must prompt the retaliatory question, which shade of red is the color designated by the sense-datum theorists' "red," and is it ever realized exactly? And if the answer is that a more correct designation is "reddish" rather than "red," I can change my designation from "helicoid" to "helicoid-like." Furthermore, deviations from the geometric norms could presumably be described by more complicated equations.

Perhaps it will be remarked at this juncture that, though it is true that the criterion for inquiries into perception indicated by such writers as Russell seems to be well stated as "being the end result of analysis," nevertheless this is an oversimplification of the nature of epistemological analysis, occasioned historically by the need to govern perceptual inquiries by more rigorous controls than had hitherto been customary. Perception is not analyzed, it may be said, for the sake of analysis; rather, analysis is instituted as a means to an end.

The end toward which analysis is designed to lead epistemologists may be indicated in the following way.[6] A theory of knowledge should contain two stages. The first of these is the stage of Cartesian doubt. In this stage, human knowledge is analyzed by means of a progression from more dubitable to less dubitable elements, ultimately reaching a level of indubitable elements. This first stage is over when the analysis arrives at these indubitables. The second stage of epistemology is that of reconstruction. Starting with the indubitable elements reached by the method of Cartesian doubt, epistemologists build up the structure of human knowledge, which now can be known to rest on a foundation of indubitability. The method of construction may be any of several; it may consist in logical construction, in inductive inference, or it may attempt to utilize psychological laws of association, interpretation, or mental (fictitious) construction. The important consideration, so far as epistemology is concerned, is that all

[6] I am indebted to Professor Yolton for this way of stating the nature of epistemological analysis.

have in common the construction, or reconstruction, of human knowledge out of elements thought to be indubitable. And the present objection is that I have distorted the nature of episte- mological analysis by reducing all this to a criterion of "being the end result of analysis."

However, though it is interesting and historically important to recognize the motivation underlying epistemological analysis, it is not apparent that this elaboration on the nature of analysis constitutes an objection to the foregoing treatment of the prob- lem. The subject of discussion has been the first or Cartesian stage of epistemology, the analyzing of human knowledge into primitive and indubitable elements, and though the *criterion for* primitiveness and indubitability must not be mistaken for the epistemological *significance of* these concepts, the criterion re- mains, so far as I am aware, "being the end result of analysis."

The burden of these epistemological difficulties must now be shouldered, as indicated, by the concept of analysis. The end results of one analysis may be never even suggested by another, and though certain analyses seem natural and others artificial, the difference between them is exactly what needs to be discovered. What is the significance of "natural" and "artificial," and when does analysis conform to the natural folds of perceptual experi- ence instead of slicing indiscriminately through them? It might be said that the analysis to be performed should be dictated by the nature of the indubitability to be arrived at, or, as it has also been called, epistemological priority. But how is epistemological priority to be determined if not by means of analysis? Certainly preanalytic opinions about priority are no indication, for how is one to choose from among Descartes' *cogito*, Hume's impres- sions, Russell's sense data, and Reichenbach's tables and horses?[7] The analysis cannot be slanted to arrive at elements already known to be indubitable, not only because this is cheating, but also because it is a fact that we do not know, prior to analysis, which elements are indubitable.

[7] See Irving M. Copi, "Analytical Philosophy and Analytical Propositions," *Philosophical Studies*, IV (1953), 87–93.

It may be, however, that the first, or analytic, stage in epistemology is determined by the second, or reconstructionist, stage.
It may be, in other words, that "being the end result of analysis"
is surreptitiously augmented by "and also a convenient starting-
point for reconstruction." As a control for inquiry, however,
something is still lacking. It was mentioned that there are various
methods of reconstruction—as many, it is tempting to add, as
there are methods of analysis. And "being a convenient starting-
point for reconstruction" is just as much a function of the particular kind of reconstruction chosen as "being the end result of
analysis" is a function of the particular kind of analysis chosen.
Considerations of convenience for reconstruction seem no more
helpful than those of indubitability or of analytic results, and
since, if we are starting with the full-bodied experience that we
usually do start with, the analysis comes before the reconstruction, "being the end result of analysis" must remain the criterion
for perceptual inquiry. I conclude that the charge of oversimplification is ill-founded.

2. ADMISSIBLE SENSE DATA, AND PRICE'S THEORY OF COMPLICATION

Most of the preceding discussion of sense data has
been designed to show that even if an adequate characterization
of the given could be framed by means of sense data, nevertheless there are other analyses and other "end results," and sense
data have no priority over these alternative constituent elements.
So long as "being the end result of analysis" is taken to be the
sole criterion, the nature of the given will depend on which
analysis you perform. I have tried so far to keep the discussion
away from the boundaries of empirical psychology, but this
seems to be increasingly difficult. One argument already has
come up utilizing the experiential reference of words that designate sense data; in an argument professing to be entirely epistemological and not at all psychological, I was forced to assent to a
view citing experiential reference. And most epistemologists,
after all, even if they are adamant about keeping epistemology
free from psychologizing, nevertheless find it impossible to get

very far without some kind of appeal to experience.[8] Often this appeal takes the form of introspection, which of course is a neat way of smuggling in an enormous psychological law, the law of the uniformity of human nature. Many sense-datum theorists, for example, define "sense datum" as the "object of direct awareness" and then proceed to judge statements about sense data on the basis of introspective evidence about direct awareness. And not all such illicit appeals to experience are introspective in character; often descriptions of observed human behavior are offered as epistemological evidence by philosophers who appear to be shocked at the unexamined acceptance by their colleagues of the validity of the induction underlying scientific inquiry.

To characterize the methodology practiced by these theorists as being either scientific or analytic is a distortion. In view of their own reluctance either to avail themselves of the rights of, or to assume the obligations of, scientific investigation, it certainly is inaccurate to describe the activities of such epistemologists as scientific. And in light of the empirical element infiltrating into their epistemology, it would be a misuse to apply the word "analytic" in this connection. It may be helpful to glance at a specimen of epistemological inquiry which is obviously neither scientific nor analytic, such as this well-known passage from Price's *Perception:* "When I see a tomato there is much that I can doubt. I can doubt whether it is a tomato that I am seeing, and not a cleverly painted piece of wax. I can doubt whether there is any material thing there at all. Perhaps what I took for a tomato was really a reflection; perhaps I am even the victim of some hallucination. One thing however I cannot doubt: that there exists a red patch of a round and somewhat bulgy shape, standing out from a background of other colour-patches, and having a certain visual depth, and that this whole field of colour is directly present to my consciousness."[9] Now, leaving aside the difficulties centering about Price's "end results" (why does he stop with red, round and bulgy patches, if not from his own convictions

---

[8] "Thus if we press our eyeball out of place, everything is doubled"; "Consider, for instance, the sound 'tick-tock'" (Price, *Perception,* pp. 79, 115).

[9] P. 3.

101

about indubitability or epistemological priority, and how can he support these convictions?), how should the activity he is engaged in be characterized? The phrase, "directly present to my consciousness," suggests that Price might be introspecting. Introspection, however, is an operation presupposing an introspecting self, of which "my consciousness" is a property, and presumably Price has the same doubts about an introspecting self that he has about a material tomato. Or if Price hasn't, I have.

A better term, suggested by Wood,[10] is "inspection," which "represents the phenomenological level of experience, and as such involves a minimum of interpretation." To engage in this phenomenological activity requires, according to Wood, an "innocence of mind" that only the sophisticated psychologist or epistemologist can recapture; it demands on the one hand a "passive receptiveness" and on the other an "alertness of attention," and this combination is "by no means easy to cultivate." This description of inspection and the phenomenological attitude comes close to describing what most epistemologists really believe they are doing when they investigate perception. But the difficulties Wood mentions as necessary to overcome before the phenomenological attitude can be reached are insuperable so far as the desire for some sort of empirical control on perceptual inquiries is concerned.

Since the inspectionist may be presumed to begin with the unsophisticated experience of a world of material objects and to peel off layers of interpretation, construction, inference, and so on until just the right innocence of mind is attained, the phenomenological attitude may be said to depend on the degree of innocence at which inspection operates. "Degree of innocence," however, leads right back to "indubitability" and "epistemological priority." Every epistemologist who engages in inspection will have his own conception of the degree of innocence required for that activity. And if it be said that there is no matter of degree involved here, that one simply peels off layers of interpretation until the given is reached, the reply is that this is tanta-

[10] *Op. cit.*, pp. 44–51, 89. Wood credits Titchener with having distinguished between inspection and introspection.

mount to what I have been talking about under the heading of "analysis," and once more the criterion for investigating perception is that of being the end result of analysis.

It seems that any attempt to pin down exactly what epistemologists do when they talk about perception is preordained not to succeed. Science, analysis, introspection, inspection, phenomenology—none of these uniquely designates the nature of investigations into perception, and most are invoked at one point or another by almost every epistemologist who examines the subject. In the present inquiry into theories of perception the discussion will be kept, for the time being at any rate, on a level as untainted by "scientific" considerations as possible, in order that certain theories may be discussed on their own terms. If occasionally I essay a psychological gambit, I will know that I cannot be justly accused by the anti-psychologists of violating their own standards of epistemic purity—at least if their efforts to adhere to standards may be said to reveal the nature of them.

What I want to do now is take a closer look at the sense-datum theory itself, apart from the other theories and would-be theories I have been looking at in conjunction with it. Should it be thought that too much space is being devoted to combating a theory which is moribund as it is, I can only plead that the distinction under discussion, between the given element in experience and the elements supplied by interpretation or construction, is most often maintained with the help of the concept of sense data. Moreover, the sense-datum theory is instructive and ought to be discussed because it manifests other important philosophic tendencies, certain aspects of analysis and atomism being among them.

Judging from examples given by sense-datum epistemologists of sense data present to any single sense, the number of such data, as Firth points out, are limited.[11] Among visual data colors predominate, and after shape (roundness, bulginess, and so on) has been mentioned, it is difficult to find universal agreement

11 Op. cit., Part I, pp. 438, 446 ff.

among sense-datum theorists about other kinds of visual data. Bergmann, as seen in the last chapter, allows spatial and temporal relations among sense data as part of his primitive descriptive vocabulary, and, while not all sense-datum epistemologists have mentioned them, it may be assumed that all would, if pressed, admit relations of external contiguity into their ontology of immediacy—relations which, in the case of visual perception, are spatial. Such spatial relations, however, are two-dimensional only and leave open the more questionable matter of depth. Whereas Stace adopts Berkeley's opinion that "sight by itself gives only a flat plane,"[12] Price includes visual depth among his given elements.[13] Thus depth may be either given, as Price believes, or constructed, as Stace believes.[14]

How is the question to be decided? The reasons given by Price and Stace for their respective beliefs are instructive as specimens of epistemological debate, but not helpful in choosing between them. "It is obvious," Price writes, "that all visual sense-data have the characteristic of *depth* or 'outness.' This characteristic of them is just as much 'given' as colour or shape, whether we can explain it or not."[15] This is an interesting bit of information but, in the absence of evidential support, not enlightening with respect to the decision under consideration. Stace too, in commenting on a statement of Broad's about depth, which parallels Price's even in the use of "obvious," finds it "perfectly obvious" that he himself does not "sense patches of colour at different visual distances." Stace's comment on Broad is sufficient as a counterargument (it being sufficient to counter "it is obvious that *p*" with "it is obvious [to me] that not-*p*"), but of course carries no general conviction. His criticism of James on

12 *Op. cit.*, p. 35.

13 *Perception*, p. 3; *Thinking and Experience*, p. 50, n. 1.

14 Stace distinguishes between inference and construction, so that inference represents for him a third possibility (*op. cit.*, p. 214). However, this is a finer distinction than the present context requires, and I will continue to lump together construction and inference under the head of "supplied" as opposed to "given."

15 *Perception*, p. 218. He adds in a footnote, "it seems to me *no more* in need of explanation than colour or shape—and no more likely to get it." I entirely agree.

the issue of whether or not depth is given—the criticism that
James confounds the direct awareness ("aboriginal perception")
of depth with the experienced feeling of the construction of
depth—does no more than explain what is assumed to be an incorrect theory in terms of a yet-to-be-proved alternative theory;
in particular it would be helpful to be furnished support for the
distinction James fails to make. And the only other argument
adduced by Stace for his view that depth is constructed is that we
are often deceived about it: we see the stars as equidistant from
us though "we know that enormous differences of distance
exist," and a flat disk can be painted so that it will be mistaken
for a sphere.[16] The force in this argument is not apparent either,
for if the argument were valid, any illusory perception would depend on supplied rather than given elements. It would, for example, have to be concluded that because I see my living-room wall
as blue in daylight and as gray under artificial light, color is constructed rather than given. The impression grows that there are
no decent arguments available—outside the psychologist's laboratory at any rate—that would incline one either toward the view
that depth is a given element in perception or toward the view
that depth is perceived only because the mind supplies it, and
the question must be left in suspension.

Though we perceive visually the snow-capped mountain as
"distant," therefore, we are unable to say whether or not this
perception occurs on a level characterized by the presence of the
formal-nonformal distinction. We also perceive visually the
snow-capped mountain as "cold," a phenomenon for whose description Price utilizes the psychological term *complication*.[17]
Complication cannot be explained in terms of inference, be-

[16] *Op. cit.*, pp. 216–19.

[17] *Thinking and Experience*, pp. 98–100. Price, it should be noted, is concerned here to defend his view against philosophers who cannot see coldness
as entering into visual perception at all, or who see it only as associated with
other elements of visual perception. His points of emphasis are thus not what
one would expect them to be were he defending his view against philosophers
who cannot see any elements of visual perception as being more "direct" than
coldness. And incidentally, I am paraphrasing him, because his example is ice
rather than a snow-capped mountain (see Firth, *op. cit.*, Part I, pp. 438–39).

cause the idea of coldness does not simply "follow upon" sensation of the elements given in the situation. Nor can the laws of association account for complication, because it is not a matter of an idea associating with sensations; in fact it is not a question of an idea accompanying sensations at all, so that Russell's notion of "condensed induction," for example, intended as an explanation of the "habitual concomitants" of a stimulus, is not helpful either.[18] The idea is, as Price puts it, "blended" with the perception of the given.

Now, what is to be said about complication? Price, despite his reluctance to classify complication under any of the familiar psychological and epistemological categories, sees it as a case of elements in perception that are mind-supplied rather than given (in his recent terminology, as a case of secondary recognition rather than of primary recognition). On what grounds? Some persons, he thinks, who have never experienced the coldness of snow or of high altitudes will not perceive the snow-capped mountain as being cold. But a relativity argument doesn't prove the point, at least not without proving it also about depth, which some persons do and others do not perceive in the same situations, and about color, which some persons are able to discriminate to a much greater degree than others.

Price has a much stronger argument for asserting that, though the complicating idea in cases of this kind is "so closely tied to sensation" as to be blended right in with it, nevertheless the idea is not a given or directly sensed quality. It differs from given or directly sensed qualities, he thinks, in being a determinable, whereas the objects of direct sensation are determinates. In the case of the snow-capped mountain, whiteness and perhaps jaggedness are determinates, coldness is a determinable. Price gives two other examples of complication, these being "non-visual ones." The first example is hearing the notes of the college choir, practicing in the distance, as "multi-vocal," and the second is hearing a knock at the door as "human and visitatorial." As in the example of coldness, the multi-vocal and the human and

[18] Bertrand Russell, *An Inquiry into Meaning and Truth* (London: George Allen & Unwin, 1940), pp. 81, 120.

visitatorial qualities really are perceived, and they blend with the
directly sensed qualities which are elements in the same perceptual situations. But nevertheless, according to Price, the complicating ideas are not themselves to be considered sense data, because they are determinable rather than determinate.

Price's argument unfortunately is marred by a confusion about
the nature of the distinction between determinate and determinable, or at least about the nature of the distinction he is taking as his criterion for differentiating between direct sensation
and complicating idea. In the example of coldness he thinks that,
though perhaps the thing perceived may look "very cold" or
"rather cold," usually even this degree of determinateness is
missing; "the object just looks cold," and the complicating idea
is the idea of cold in general. By "determinable" here, Price
seems to mean "not at all determinate." The same is true of the
knock at the door. With visual perception entirely obstructed,
the human and visitatorial quality heard in the knock is presumably in no degree determinate. On the other hand, when "multi-
vocal" is taken as his example, Price must mean "not completely
determinate" rather than "not at all determinate," because he
does find a degree of determinateness in the complicating idea,
being able, up to a point, to specify the degree of multi-vocality:
there are perhaps more than three and less than twenty voices.

An amendment of some sort is needed for Price's criterion;
either "determinable" must be taken to mean "not completely
determinate," or else a distinction must be made between the
two kinds of complication exemplified on the one hand by
"cold" and "human and visitatorial" and on the other by "multi-
vocal." Before deciding this question, though, let me point out
an accidental linguistic feature of the situation involving coldness. In saying that a mountain peak looks cold we are ruling out
such thermal possibilities as that it looks hot or very hot or luke-
warm; in other words, coldness is not the appropriate determinable in this example. It is a distortion of the situation to discuss
the possibility of seeing thermal qualities without recognizing
that they range in degree from very hot to very cold. "Cold" is

just as determinate as "old," which for Price is a determinate of the determinable "human and visitatorial."[19] Though I will still discuss the complicating idea of "coldness," I will use the term loosely, in the more inclusive sense of what physicists ordinarily call "heat," and I will link "cold" with "multi-vocal" as having a degree of determinateness.

Furthermore, there is no reason why a degree of determinateness should not be applied to "human and visitatorial." Though I cannot be certain who is at the door, I nevertheless feel confident that some persons, like Aristotle Socrates Onassis and the Imam of Yemen, are not there; probably I will even have narrowed down the possibilities to colleagues, friends, and relatives, and the expectation of these may be as much a quality of the sound as the less determinate human and visitatorial quality. Even with respect to the qualities Price mentions, there is a determinateness about the human and visitatorial sound of the knock. The age of the visitor can be specified with the same accuracy as the number of voices in the choir—say, between ten and ninety years; outside these limits, there is a hesitancy or a lack of firmness that is as much a "heard" quality as the quality which differentiates a duet from a multi-vocal choir. The same can be said about color and size: I no more expect a man eight feet tall than I expect one whose face is solidly tattooed. It may, of course, turn out that I am deceived—it may be a four-year-old knocking with a stick, or the circus may be in town—but this is not to the point. It may not have been a knock on the door that I heard *as* a knock, as far as that goes, but whatever it was, I would be inaccurate if I did not describe the sound I heard as the sound of a knock on the door.

[19] Of course, one could squirm out of this situation by means of an *ad hoc* qualification: One could say that the quality in question is not the quality ranging from very hot to very cold but an entirely different one ranging from cool to very cold and accurately designated as the quality of coldness. But then why not do the same for multi-vocality and preserve uniformity? The quality in question, one might say, is not accurately designated by "multi-vocal" but rather by "multi-vocal 3/20?" which is defined as "having perhaps more than three and less than twenty voices," and which is not determinate in the perceptual situation under discussion. All this, however, amounts to no more than a warning to pay closer attention to the difference between philosophic arguments and linguistic accidents.

"Cold," "multi-vocal," and "human and visitatorial" all will be taken to be determinate to some degree, and Price's criterion amended accordingly; what distinguishes complicating ideas like these from directly sensed elements in perception will now be said to be their incomplete determinateness as opposed to the complete determinateness of the latter. What I want to suggest now is that the elements in perception which are thought by Price and by the most uncompromising of sense-datum philosophers to be directly sensed are not completely determinate, and in fact are often no more determinate than the elements said to be mind-supplied in the mode called complication. And that directly sensed qualities are like complicating ideas in being incompletely determinate is sufficient reason for rejecting the distinction Price uses to support his view that the complicating ideas in perception are not directly sensed.

In the perceptual situation containing the complicating idea of coldness, an element directly sensed is whiteness. I mentioned, in connection with perception of depth, my wall which is blue by daylight and gray under artificial light. But it is not always an open and shut case. Sometimes I cannot tell whether I am seeing it as blue or as gray; in fact, some time and effort was required when it was first painted to learn as much about its color as I know now. A similar situation exists when I look at a snowy mountain peak in the late afternoon sun: is the mountain peak white or is it blue? In neither case am I concerned with, or even conscious of, the question of color. And in both cases, it seems to me, the color *as sensed* is to a certain degree indeterminate. It is a matter, not of either sensing white or else of sensing blue, but instead, of sensing white-or-blue.[20]

Take the "multi-vocal" sound of the practicing choir. What elements of this auditory perception are given and can be said to be completely determinate? If by chance a single part were being sung, and if by chance every chorister's intonation were the same as every other chorister's intonation, then—at least within the

[20] See the discussion of the descriptive significance of "or" above, pp. 43–45.

limits of musical as opposed to acoustic theory—the sensation of pitch could be said to be completely determinate. But if, as is more probable, more than one part were being sung, and if, more probable still, a variation in intonation prevailed, the sensation of pitch could hardly be said to be more than crudely determinate, much less completely determinate, and certainly little more determinate than "multi-vocal" is for Price.

Nor can the direct auditory sensation of the choir be said to be completely determinate with respect to timbre, because timbre is what I take Price to be referring to when he speaks of multi-vocality, so that if timbre is completely determinate, so is multi-vocality. Intensity, finally, seems to be characterized by what has been said about pitch. It is no more determinate than multi-vocality. I can perceive the choir as having perhaps between three and twenty voices but not whether it has seventeen or eighteen, and by the same token I can recognize a crescendo and distinguish between piano and forte but am unable to recognize piano directly, as distinct from both a heavy pianissimo and a light mezzo forte (the designations being too inexact to be of much help here). True, the choir director can recognize what I cannot, and it is even conceivable that he has such discriminating auditory sensations that the group literally sounds "seventeen-voiced" or "eighteen-voiced" to him depending on whether there are seventeen or eighteen members present, but in any case this is the sort of relativity argument that is best avoided.

The examples of color, pitch, timbre, and intensity all show that the attempt to mark off given elements in perception from these complicating elements on the basis of complete versus incomplete determinateness is sure to fail. Even in the third example, the case of the knock at the door, though the given elements seem to be more determinate than in the previous examples, one still may raise difficult (and perhaps otherwise trivial) questions. Can the sound of the knock be said to have recognizable pitch or is it simply a noise? What sensed elements distinguish it from the sound of someone descending the stairs outside the door?

Sharpness, perhaps, but something else is needed to differentiate it from a book slammed shut in despair down the hallway, or from a baseball striking a catcher's mitt outside the window. One might mention a certain distinctive oaken quality, but if there are scruples against allowing "human and visitatorial" as a sensed quality, there will be as many against allowing "oaken." More to the point, even if these qualities were allowable and sufficient, could they be said to be completely determinate? The fact is that we often hear such sounds either as other sounds (the slam of a book, a step on the stairs) or as what might, analogously to the sensation of blue-or-white, be called "disjunctive sounds" (the sound of a step-on-the-stairs-or-knock-on-the-door) which evoke disjunctive expectations.

The issue is further confused because Price appears to believe that subjective relativity, which I have tried to steer clear of except by way of anticipating objections, is relevant to the question of degree of determinateness.[21] Thus he says that the hardness of a wall would have been "nearer to complete determinateness" in the experience of a general accustomed to storming walls than it is in his own experience, though still a determinable. With such a relativity criterion of determinateness available, the task of showing the futility involved in trying to distinguish between complicating idea and sensed quality would have been immeasurably simplified. In the case of color, for example, it would then be sufficient to point out that my capacity for distinguishing color is not nearly as fine as a painter's, whose discrimination, in turn, would seem defective from the physicist's viewpoint. The same sort of thing could be said in the case of tactual sensations, where mention of safecrackers and of readers of braille would be

[21] There is, of course, a kind of relativity that is important to the question of degree of determinateness: the relativity of determinateness to determinability. In any question involving degree of determinateness, a clear conception of what determinable is being determined is required. It has been seen that "cold" is indeterminate for Price because he takes it to be the determinable in question, whereas if "heat," in the physicist's broad sense, is taken as the determinable, "cold" is relatively determinate. Again, Price takes "old" to be a determinate of the determinable "human and visitatorial," and "old" itself can be a determinable of which "80 years" is a determinate.

relevant; in fact, every perceptual element said to be given could be shown to be no more determinate than certain perceptual elements said not to be given.

At any rate, with or without the relativity criterion of determinateness, the conclusion seems justified that neither the complicating ideas cited by Price nor the directly sensed qualities themselves are ever completely determinate. But it is only his ability to distinguish between the kinds of determinateness belonging to sensed qualities and to complicating ideas, respectively, that enables Price to deny complicating ideas entrance into the class of given perceptual elements. It would do no good to talk about the idea of sensuousness—to suggest, say, that complicating ideas are distinguishable from sensed qualities because the latter are sensuous and the former are nonsensuous. Sensuousness is simply another way of expressing what is common and peculiar to sensed qualities, and what is at issue is precisely whether complicating ideas have sensuousness or not. Price has claimed that the issue may be settled in terms of determinateness and determinability, and his claim has been challenged, I think successfully. And I know of no other way to settle the issue, short of reintroducing such concepts as association, inference, and induction, which Price dismissed as inadequate to account for the thoroughness with which complicating ideas and sensed qualities are blended. The proposition must be taken seriously that whiteness, jaggedness, coldness, multi-vocality, humanness, visitatorialness, and sensations of pitch, timbre, and intensity may well be on a par so far as their givenness is concerned.

3. ATOMS, MOLECULES, AND SENSORY BLOCKS

Let me retrace the argument. I began this chapter by asking whether the distinction between formal and nonformal is present in experience from the beginning or whether it arises at some later or less primitive stage. If the distinction many philosophers have made between given and nongiven elements in perception is correct, it follows that there is indeed a primitive stage of experience unsullied by the presence of any formal ingredients. By "correct" in the previous sentence is not meant "factually accurate," because an epistemological inquiry into perception cannot itself rely on the perception needed to garner the facts—or so epistemologists have said. By "correct" can only be meant, therefore, "supported by good epistemological arguments." The immediate question to be answered is about the nature of the given, and a frequently offered answer involves sense data, in a broad sense of the term.

The "correctness" of the sense-datum answer has to lie in its "epistemological" rather than its factual support, and a criterion that might carry epistemological sanction is "being the end result of analysis." It was seen, however, that other answers about the nature of the given also meet this criterion, and that the sense-datum answer has no priority over these. There followed an examination of sense-datum theories, centering on the limitation thought by most sense-datum philosophers to characterize the number of kinds of data present to any single sense. Colors and shapes are the most frequently mentioned visual data, though doubtless few, if any, philosophers would deny that relations of two-dimensional spatial contiguity are also directly sensed. There are disagreements about whether relations involving a third spatial dimension are given, however, and no criterion for deciding one way or the other. Moreover, no available criteria for deciding whether or not such complicating ideas as coldness (seen) and multi-vocality (heard) are given stand up on analysis.

If coldness as a visual datum and multi-vocality as an auditory one are allowed to be given, however, or at least are allowed to be perceptual elements whose givenness is no less problematic than that of elements of color, shape, and depth, then what perceptual elements are endowed with any less direct status? The argument seems to have opened the way for all sorts of direct sensations—in fact, any perceptual element said to be a contribution of the mind, through inference, interpretation, or construction.

Note, though, that I have not said there is no difference between elements given to the perceiver and those supplied by him. All I have said is that any attempt I know of to draw a hard and fast distinction between the two ends in failure. As a matter of fact, I have no difficulty whatever in understanding philosophers who say there is a basic difference between the two elements of our perception. Like some of the distinctions discussed in Part I, it is one the student of philosophy intuitively feels must exist. An empiricist cannot ignore intuitive feelings people actually do have, even when only students of philosophy have them, but neither can he accept such feelings as any sort of criterion for anything said to transcend them. It is worthwhile on occasion to explain intuitive feelings in terms of other features of the world, but it is never worthwhile to explain other features of the world in terms of intuitive feelings.

So far I have concerned myself with the nature and variety of data which may present themselves to the senses, assuming that whatever presents itself does so as a sensory atom. It is this atomistic view of perception that I want to glance at now.

A matter has already been mentioned about which discrepant opinions may understandably exist—that of the limits of analysis. The merit of the atomists' demand that every analysis be pushed to the farthest extremity until unanalyzable elements are reached is not apparent. Among other things, analyzability is a function of who is doing the analysis and for what purpose. Sense-datum theorists end their analysis with colors, shapes, sounds, and so on, but these elements certainly are not unanalyzable; color, as was mentioned, may be analyzed into hue, saturation, and brilliance. Hue may be analyzed into its "primaries," but what these are will depend on whether it is pigment or light that the analyzer is interested in. For purposes of perceptual analysis light is presumably paramount. But why stop with red, yellow, and green? The physicist is able to analyze all these into wave lengths, and on the "sheer doggedness" criterion of analysis this physical analyzability may not be ignored.

It will be objected that I am attacking a straw man, a grotesque caricature of philosophic analysis. No analyst, it will be said, pushes his analysis on indiscriminately, borrowing from the psychologist here, from the physicist there, and depending the rest of the time on logic and his own imagination. The force of

the objection, moreover, may be acknowledged, though sometimes it seems to the uninitiated that this is the way much analysis is done. The point, in fact, is precisely that other criteria
operate in philosophic analysis besides the "bitter end" criterion,
but that they are not made explicit. Some of these will be dealt
with in Part III, but it is quite apparent that *relevance* is at the
root of the matter. The wave-length analysis of the physicist is
no more relevant to certain perceptual analyses than psychological analysis, according to many "pure" epistemologists, is relevant to their inquiries. In both cases the determination of relevance involves purpose, so that the question about the limits of
analysis is at least as much a matter of the aims of the analyst as
it is of his endurance. The decision about when an analysis has
yielded the minimal or simplest elements consonant with the
purposes of the analyst demands as much deliberation as the
decision where to begin the analysis.

The point of this discussion is that I want to question the
viewpoint according to which the given elements of perception,
whatever be their precise characteristics, are such relatively discrete ones as those usually cited by sense-datum theorists.
Whether or not coldness (seen) and multi-vocality (heard) are
allowed along with whiteness and loudness, all these are what I
am calling relatively discrete; though not discrete from the
physicist's viewpoint, they are discrete from the viewpoint I
want to take now.

If the analyzandum of a perceptual analysis is the full-bodied
perception of material objects, there is a stage in the analysis that
occurs about midway between the psychologically prior thing-per-
cept and the epistemologically prior sense datum. This midway
stage is occupied by what have been called "sensory blocks,"
which would be viewed by the sense-datum theorist as a collection of sense data, but which from the present point of view
provide the raw material out of which sense data are abstracted.
As conceived by Wood,[22] sensory blocks are "fluid, sensory
wholes" carved out of experience by "the most rudimentary of

[22] *Op. cit.*, chaps. ii–iii, esp. pp. 55 ff.

the interpretative processes of perception." Thus, the distinction between given and supplied elements comes at a higher perceptual level than yet considered, the level at which sensed qualities are fused or blended not because they have been combined out of more discrete elements but because they have not yet been separated into more discrete elements.

As intended by Wood, however, sensory blocks are more discrete than either the facts or "epistemic" considerations warrant, and the unwarranted discreteness has two facets. First, sensory blocks are "qualitative," which is to say that with respect to the sensory qualities of color, pitch, and so on, they are "homogeneous." A prerequisite of perception is "the recognition of lines of demarcation" separating qualitatively heterogeneous areas. On what basis, however, can my perception of the snow-topped mountain be said to depend on my recognition of a line marking off the white of the snow from the blue of the sky? It may be true that "a differentiation of colour is the first clue to the boundary of objects in the visual field," but the perception of such boundaries is not a prerequisite for the perception of objects. I can take in the mountain-top perception in an instant, but only caprice would lead from this to the statement that recognition of the boundary in question is any more fundamental than, say, recognition of the brilliance of the white or of the blue. To separate out the white and the blue is, as a matter of fact, as much a question of abstraction or of analysis as the separation of any of the atomic elements over which "sensory blocks" are intended to be an improvement. And if the boundary line is recognized at all, it is more apt to be for its own sake, as having the quality of jaggedness, than for the sake of the areas it demarcates. All this supports the view that sensory blocks need not be qualitatively homogeneous.

4. INTERSENSORY PERCEPTION

The second facet of the unwarranted discreteness of sensory blocks lies in their confinement to a single sense. They are not intersensory, and the reason is what Wood terms "the principle of the heterogeneity of the senses," the principle

that "there are wide qualitative gulfs between the different
senses and, at least in the present state of our psychological
knowledge, there is no indication that sensations of the several
senses admit of arrangement in a single unbroken series as do, in
certain cases, the qualities of a single sense."[23]

With respect to the several senses, I want to argue two points.
First, a comparative investigation of the senses lays bare great
differences among them, and second, the "given" can no more
be said to present itself already broken down into single sensory
blocks than into single sense data or qualitatively homogeneous
sensory areas. These points might appear to conflict, but they
only appear to. For it is only after perception has been analyzed
and the various senses or modalities prescinded that the differences among them are noticed; they are not directly noticed as
functioning within perception. I will argue my second point first.

It will be remembered that in cases of complication the distinction could not be maintained, with respect to givenness, between the complicating idea and the elements said to be directly
sensed. It now may be noted that in many cases the complicating
element is a quality thought to be proper to another sense. Coldness is ordinarily thought to be proper to the thermal sense, not
to the visual; hardness is a tactual quality, not a visual one. But
if, in the case of the snow-topped mountain, coldness and whiteness are on a par so far as the given is concerned, then either of
two conditions must hold. It may be that the quality of coldness
visually sensed is different from the quality of coldness thermally
sensed. Or it may be that the quality sensed visually from the
distant heated room is the same as that sensed thermally on the
mountain top.

In the latter case the concept of sensory propriety breaks
down: a quality can be sensed just as "directly"—that is, "properly"—visually as thermally; and as the other example shows, the
same can be said for the tactual sense. Furthermore, examples
can be constructed to demonstrate that, on this alternative, any
so-called proper sensible can be sensed in at least one additional
mode. In the case of there being two qualities—coldness visual-

[23] *Ibid.,* p. 52.

ly sensed and thermally sensed—the same examples would serve to demonstrate that, for every so-called proper sensible, there is at least one duplicate sensible proper to a different sense. And since every sensible is thought to be proper to some sense, the result would be the duplication, if not the triplication or worse, of the sensory world. This circumstance seems a terrible price to pay for the preservation of the integrity of the several senses, but if anyone is willing to pay it I will not quarrel with him. For since, on this view, two senses might have as their objects qualities as intimate with one another as coldness seen and coldness felt, the gaps among the senses would still be diminished. My own choice is the circumstance in which sensibles may be proper to more than one sense, but the grounds for my choice are solely dialectical. In either case it can no longer be maintained that the different senses, so far as they function in perception, are separated by "wide qualitative gulfs"; certainly the words used to designate sensory characteristics—"blue," "loud," "cold," "soft," "sharp"—tend to throw suspicion on the theory of rigid sensory propriety; in fact, there is a strong probability that the given, if there is a given, is not characterized by any intersensory differentiation whatever.

On the face of it, what I am saying sounds insane. Surely we hear sounds, and hearing is auditory, not visual or thermal; surely we smell odors, and smelling is olfactory, not auditory or tactual. Moreover, we know when we are using our various sense organs. When "I visually apprehend a distant landscape but receive no other sensory stimulation from it or hear a locomotive whistle before the train has rounded the curve and become visible,"[24] I know I am using my eyes alone in the first instance and my ears alone in the second; I could, for example, close my eyes and yet hear the whistle, and deafness would not prevent me from seeing the landscape.

But there are one or two features of this traditional view worth noticing. In the first place, the atomist is always under obligation to explain how things get connected, and though the "molecular"

[24] Ibid., pp. 36–37.

view under consideration—it might be called "sensory block atomism"—avoids some difficulties about the connectedness of data of a single sense, it does not avoid any about the connectedness of data of the several senses. Sensory correlation is explained by Wood in terms of correspondences arrived at inductively, the induction being facilitated by "the fact that the organs of one sense are in the field of other senses and can be apprehended at the very time when they are performing their sensory function."[25] It may be, however, that this latter fact is cited here to support the wrong view. That we have various sense organs, that they are variously located in our bodies, that they can be observed to function in different ways and at different times, and that these physiological facts can be correlated with physical facts about perceptual stimuli—all this is interesting and important, but that it always emerges from our ordinary, nonphilosophic perceptual activity (as it would have to in order to explain our ordinary, nonphilosophic sensory correlations) is anything but obvious. It is more likely to be the fruit of a sophisticated "phenomenological" or even scientific inquiry; furthermore, the same physical and physiological facts could be cited— were it assumed that intersensory connections are already built into the given—to explain why the customary, even intuitive, view is that the given presents itself already broken down into different objects of the different senses. If these physiological facts are allowable, moreover, it may be legitimately insisted that the objects of perception thus explained are wave lengths, quanta, and so on. But the perception at issue at the moment is that of trees and houses, colors and sounds, and this must be divorced from the "perception" of physical stimuli.

The possibility that the given is broken down into its sensory components not for us but by us, on the basis of intuitive correlations among physical and physiological facts, leads me back to the first point I wanted to make: that great differences are revealed by a comparative inquiry into the senses. For once we fix our minds on such physiological and physical facts, none but

[25] *Ibid.*, p. 60.

the very mildest analogies among the senses seems justified, and any perceptual inquiry attempting to account for all phases of all the senses is most apt to bog down in a hopeless morass of major and minor sensory differences. This is why most epistemologists content themselves with an analysis of one or two or sometimes three senses, often brushing aside the others with the unexamined remark that "what is true of the sense(s) here considered is true also of the others." But even when an inquiry is restricted to a particular sense, the truth is that next to nothing is known of the senses of smell and taste, little more of hearing, a bit more of touching, and most of seeing; yet, as the examples in the previous discussion have shown, hardly anything is known even about seeing.

Most often discussed is the sense of vision, perhaps because light is "a corner-stone of physical theory,"[26] perhaps because the eye is "not only the most important of sense organs [but] the most complicated."[27] At any rate, epistemologists concerned to construct the physical world out of sensory data almost always begin with visual data, and their second move is often the correlation of visual with tactual data. Thus Ayer finds four principles of grouping by which visual sense data are related to one another; he believes that these principles apply also (though less clearly) to tactual data and account for the correlation of the two kinds of data. And though tactual data play the lesser role in our construction of the external world, they have, according to Ayer, a "greater sensible constancy," evident in the predictive value which measurement possesses.[28] These remarks, moreover,

[26] Russell, *The Analysis of Matter* (New York: Harcourt, Brace & Co., 1927), p. 317. Russell believes that "vision is much the most important and least misleading of the senses, when considered as a source of the fundamental notions of physics" (*ibid.*, p. 260). See also *ibid.*, pp. 163–67.

[27] "Man is predominantly eye-minded. Most of his information of the world about him comes by way of his two eyes, each of which is connected to his brain by as many axons (about a million) as all the rest of his sense organs combined" (Warren McCulloch, "Information in the Head," *Synthèse*, IX [1953], 233, 235).

[28] A. J. Ayer, *The Foundations of Empirical Knowledge* (New York: Macmillan Co., 1940), sec. 23. Rudolf Carnap, in *Der Logische Aufbau der Welt* (Berlin: Weltkreis-verlag, 1928), assigns to the visual sense a greater "dimensionality" than any other sense; see Nelson Goodman, *The Structure of*

gain support from considerations of verifiability and scientific confirmation, because it is usually in terms of visual and tactual data that verifiability is conceived and confirmation carried out.

The literature is teeming with statements about relations among the senses. In a recent article, Broad confines his discussion to seeing, hearing, and touching; for human beings these are the "most important" sensory experiences. Moreover, seeing is a "very peculiar form of sense-perception," since normally the physical and phenomenological accounts of seeing do not always agree, while those of hearing and feeling do.[29] Russell distinguishes, on a physical basis, between the public senses—sight, hearing, and smell—which depend on radiations, and the bodily senses, which "travel along nerves, but not through air or empty space."[30] On a nonphysical level, Price finds that sounds, smells, and thermal data, unlike visual and tactual data, do not "have shapes"; that tastes, unlike sounds, smells, and thermal data, have no connection with sight; and moreover that tactual data, unlike visual data, "belong to two objects at once."[31] Nor are such comparative observations to be confined to contemporary accounts. Heraclitus noticed that "the eyes are more exact witnesses than the ears,"[32] and Bergson added an awful metaphysical dimension to the issue by suggesting that reality or *la durée réelle* is better apprehended through the ear (as when hearing a melody) than through the eye.[33] But perhaps the peak of intersensory

Appearance (Cambridge, Mass.: Harvard University Press, 1951), pp. 138–39. In "Testability and Meaning," *Philosophy of Science*, IV (1937), 7–9, Carnap discusses visual and tactual data as sufficient primitive bases for the language of science.

[29] C. D. Broad, "Some Elementary Reflexions on Sense-Perception," *Philosophy*, XXVII (1952), 3–17.

[30] *The Analysis of Matter*, p. 316.

[31] *Perception*, pp. 229, 231.

[32] John Burnet, *Early Greek Philosophy* (4th ed.; London: Adam & Charles Black, 1930), p. 134. This may be a condemnation of hearsay evidence.

[33] Henri Bergson, "The Perception of Change," *The Creative Mind*, trans. M. L. Andison (New York: Philosophical Library, 1946), pp. 173, 176. However, Bergson says in *Durée et simultanéité* (Paris: Félix Alcan, 1923) that what is given to us in perception is "a continuity of visual extension, and therefore of color," and that "we have no reason to suppose that we are not here in the presence of reality itself" (p. 45).

differentiation and its consequences is reached when it is said, apropos of space and the given, that "the first thing to notice is that different senses have different spaces."[34]

It is small wonder, in view of the vivid impression most writers have of deep cleavages among the senses, that beliefs on the subject should find their way into epistemology, resulting in such statements as "that the fields of the several senses are so many virtually water-tight compartments is an inescapable truth of epistemology,"[35] and perpetuating themselves in a "principle of the heterogeneity of the senses." But it is equally clear that the facts of perception do not warrant either the principle or the beliefs, any more than they warrant their denials.

Some of the facts of intersensory perception customarily embarrassing to epistemologists may now be exposed to view without seeming "curious" or "accidental." Most of these facts are usually filed under the category of *synesthesia*, which is an adequate name so long as it is not taken too literally, as implying only association or accompaniment. Cases of synesthesia have already been encountered under the heading of complication, being those instances in which complicating elements may be directly sensed in other perceptual situations. I have suggested that no criterion for distinguishing some perceptual elements as less directly sensed than others entering into the same situations emerges from an inquiry into perception.

To return to synesthesia, we often instinctively apply, both to sensory qualities and to perceived objects, descriptions more "directly" applicable to qualities sensed through other modalities or to objects thought to present themselves mainly to other senses. We predicate thermal qualities of colors and tastes, gustatory qualities of smells and sounds, olfactory qualities of sounds and

[34] Russell, *Our Knowledge of the External World* (London: George Allen & Unwin, 1952), p. 118. Italic not in original. See also Stace, *op. cit.*, pp. 201 ff.

[35] Wood, *op. cit.*, p. 57.

colors; and material objects characterized by certain of these
qualities are for this reason also characterized by others of different modalities.

From the molecular point of view involving sensory blocks—
not to mention more atomistic points of view—such synesthetic
phenomena are simply coincidences, and the qualities thus predicted are "associational" and of metaphorical significance only.
But from the alternative point of view just mentioned and tentatively adopted, such an opinion is entirely unwarranted. "Coin-
cidence" and "association" are invoked simply to help epistemologists out of the artificial situation they create at the start by
splitting sensation into separate compartments. In a recent ballet
whose choreography and staging provide visual complements to
a musical theme with variations—these variations in turn being
based upon variations among the instruments of the orchestra—
the costumes corresponding to the string section are in red, and
those corresponding to the woodwinds are in blue. Moreover,
costumes corresponding to various instruments of each section
are colored in varying degrees of brilliance, violins and piccolo
being the most brilliant, and contrabasses and bassoons the
least.[36] In terms of this example, there is no more reason for saying that the color scheme merely caters to certain accidents or
coincidences of perception than that it reflects the underlying
structure of the sensible world. Certainly, if the predictable
shock or perplexity occasioned by correlating the bassoon with a
pastel tint and the piccolo with a deep shade of blue were any
sort of index, there would be more reason for the "underlying
structure" interpretation.[37] Almost as dramatic is the correlation
of red and blue with strings and woodwinds. Both the visual and

[36] Fanfare, choreographed by Jerome Robbins to Benjamin Britten's The
Young Person's Guide to the Orchestra (variations and fugue on a theme of
Purcell), op. 34.

[37] This might be called, after W. V. Quine ("The Problem of Meaning
in Linguistics," From a Logical Point of View [Cambridge, Mass.: Harvard
University Press, 1953], p. 53), the "bizarreness reaction" index to the given.
See F. A. Hayek, The Sensory Order: An Inquiry into the Foundations of
Theoretical Psychology (Chicago: University of Chicago Press, 1952), pp.
19–23.

the auditory qualities involved, moreover, are allied with thermal qualities, as evidenced by a habitual designation of red as a warm color and blue as a cool one and—though there are "thermal" differences among members of each section—by the designation of strings and woodwinds as warm and cool respectively.

However, these habitual designations of qualities are not to be taken as an index to their "real" interrelationships; they serve rather as a warning that the theory of perception which views the given as broken down into units of sensory homogeneity without allowing for other possibilities is making assumptions wholly unwarranted by the facts of perception. A more balanced interpretation, one that seems to be supported by those facts, is the view, as Hayek expresses it, that "though in some respects one particular colour or one particular tone may be most closely related to other colours or other tones respectively, yet in other respects they may be closer to qualities belonging to different modalities."[38] Thus, to say, for example, that any two colors naturally "belong" together, even though one is bright and one dark, whereas a bright color and a high-pitched sound are only metaphorically or synesthetically related, is a distortion of the nature of perception; this is so, not because the opposite is true, but because perception by itself offers no basis for asserting that either pair of qualities is more closely related than the other.[39] Perception by itself does not justify the assertion that qualities are directly sensed in units that are a function of modality, and once more I am unable to distinguish between the given and the supplied elements in perception.

[38] *Ibid.*, p. 20. See also Charles Hartshorne, *The Philosophy and Psychology of Sensation* (Chicago: University of Chicago Press, 1934).

[39] Some of these same considerations support the view that such "affective tones" as "pleasant," "unpleasant," "good," and "bad" are as much given as qualities more usually thought of as sensory. See Hayek, *op. cit.*, p. 22, and Lewis, *An Analysis of Knowledge and Valuation*, pp. 400 ff. Dewitt H. Parker suggests a "direct effect of the sensory light stimulus upon the feelings. Rays of light affect not only the sensory apparatus, causing sensations of color; their influence is prolonged into motor channels, causing a total attitude of the organism, the correlate of a feeling" (*The Principles of Aesthetics* [2d ed.; New York: F. S. Crofts, 1947], p. 207). However, this is not mentioned as a matter of breaking down intersensory barriers, since on the customary view values are not sensory at all.

5. THE PSYCHOSOMATIC SENSE AND TOTAL ORGANIC AWARENESS

Before concluding this purely destructive phase of the present inquiry, I would like to try to shatter one remaining vestige of atomism. Though, as indicated, we cannot maintain unquestioningly that the immediately given is broken down modally into sensory blocks, it might still be assumed that the sensory units attributable to the given on the basis of perception are limited in so far as they may be adequately characterized as combinations (disjunctive or conjunctive) of the familiar five modalities. In other words, it might be thought that the given may be described as "auditory-gustatory-olfactory-tactual-visual," and that when hearing, taste, smell, touch, and sight have been enumerated, we have exhausted our ways of sensing the world.

Even this, however, does not seem in accord with the facts. Throughout this chapter I have referred both to thermal and to tactual qualities and sensitivities; customary interpretations of the latter require a differentiation between the two. Besides thermal sensations, though, there are muscular and kinesthetic ones, and there are sensations of such other internal bodily conditions as hunger and visceral pressures.[40] If all these are to be neatly wrapped and deposited along with the traditional five, they might be collectively designated, following Price, as the *somatic* or *corporeal* sense.[41]

But merely to add another sense to the usual five is not enough. It still implies a tidiness about perception and about the theory of perception that does not exist. For the fact is that we perceive our world in ways so numerous, so varied, and so complex that, as epistemologists, we have barely scratched the surface. We have not been able to forge conceptual tools sharp enough and delicate enough to dissect the perceptual process

[40] See Wood, op. cit., p. 40, and William H. Ittelson and Hadley Cantril, Perception: A Transactional Approach (Garden City, N.Y.: Doubleday & Co., 1954), pp. 1–2.

[41] Perception, p. 231. I am not sure whether, as Price intends this expression, it designates a sense receptive to somatic qualities originating either inside or outside the body, or a sense receptive only to those originating inside the body. Since I find the distinction unclear, I will use the broader designation.

without mutilating it. Consider the following passage from a recent work of fiction:

... rather gradually, she realized without turning about that she was not alone in the room.

In an inhabited room there are refracting objects only half noticed: varnished wood, more or less polished brass, silver and ivory, and beyond these a thousand conveyors of light and shadow so mild that one scarcely thinks of them as that, the tops of picture-frames, the edges of pencils or ash-trays, of crystal or china ornaments; the totality of this refraction—appealing to equally subtle reflexes of the vision as well as to those associational fragments in the subconscious that we seem to hang on to, as a glass-fitter keeps the irregularly shaped pieces that may do some time—this fact might account for what Rosemary afterward mystically described as "realizing" that there was some one in the room, before she could determine it. But when she did realize it she turned swift in a sort of ballet step and saw that a dead Negro was stretched upon her bed.[42]

The "realizing" of the presence of a foreign object is a familiar fact of perception, and it has not only been captured here in words, but elements in the perceptual situation that could be of explanatory value have been noticed and mentioned. Lest the artistic sensitivity manifest in the passage be exploited, though, in an effort to show that there is a clear distinction between the given and its interpretation, it may be pointed out that the distinction may be granted only if an adequate description and explanation is provided for the expressions "half noticed," "subtle reflexes of the vision," and "those associational fragments in the subconscious that we seem to hang on to." This done, one may still wonder whether there are not other given elements present in the situation, appealing to such other "subtle reflexes" as the auditory, olfactory, and even somatic, as well as to "mental" or psychological factors.

Mention of psychological factors raises another issue, for psychological elements certainly seem to afford a clear example of

[42] F. Scott Fitzgerald, *Tender Is the Night* (New York: Charles Scribner's Sons, 1934), pp. 143 f. I am indebted to Professor Alfred Schütz, of The New School for Social Research, for citing this passage in the present connection.

perceptual elements that are not given but are supplied by the mind. It may be noted, incidentally, that the possibility of pointing out nongiven elements of perception has not been doubted; the problem is rather to point out elements which are not nongiven, and to do so in a way that clearly distinguishes them from others we know are not given. But even so, one may question whether and how psychological elements in perception can be said definitely to be not given. What differences are there between these elements and those involving, say, the somatic sense, on the basis of which it could be asserted with confidence that only the former are not given?

It cannot be said that the differences between the two kinds of "senses" are grounded in differences of "degree of immediacy" between the kinds of qualities sensed, because there is no reason to think that the psychic state of the organism (which presumably is the object of the psychological "sense") is not as immediately given as the somatic state. In fact, because the elements in perception said not to be given are precisely those supposed to be contributed by the mind, the given-nongiven distinction is an important one for the dualistic viewpoint which gives rise to the pair of terms "mental" and "physical," or "mind" and "body." That viewpoint, moreover, is compromised by an inability to locate a boundary between perceptual elements that are given and those that are not. At any rate, even the addition of a sixth, corporeal or somatic, sense may not be sufficient to account for the facts of perception, and the possibility had better be entertained of an *organic* or *psychosomatic* sense,[43] a sense attuned both to the bodily and to the mental conditions of the perceiving organism.

Still another sensory distinction that might have been made seems on the point of collapse now. Whereas previously the traditional five senses could be ranged—singly or collectively—along with the somatic sense and opposed to the "psychic" elements in

[43] ". . . the whole of the Subject's psychosomatic energy functions in the perceiving. It is his personal singularity, body and mind together, that perceives" (Horace M. Kallen, "Human Beings and Psychological Systems," remarks at the dedication of the Perception Demonstration Center, Princeton University, March 6, 1954).

perception, whatever these might be, now even this opposition is blurred by the possibility that the psychic and the somatic are less clearly distinguishable and should be considered jointly as the psychosomatic. But any inclination to differentiate sharply between sensations of "outer" and of "inner" data can no longer find support, for the so-called somatic sense, even when it was thought to be clearly defined and existing apart from any kind of "mental" sense, preserved neutrality between "inner" and "outer" elements. A somatic sensation of pressure, for example, might be traced to internal visceral pressure, to external atmospheric pressure, or to both. The distinction between inner and outer, therefore, seems inapplicable to somatic sensation, and since the merger of "somatic" into "psychosomatic" has become a strong possibility, while no perceptual characteristics warrant a differentiation between "somatic" and "auditory-gustatory-olfactory-tactual-visual," the conclusion is that the facts of perception may sanction only the concept of a single undifferentiated sense, which could be called, with a broader meaning than before, the psychosomatic sense.

Doubtless it will still be maintained that only perversity could bar recognition of at least the gross and essential differences separating "intradermal" and "extradermal" perception. But all such essential differences seem to emerge from psychological, physiological, and physical considerations of a kind so familiar that common sense, permeated by them, is unable to entertain alternatives.[44] What I take to be a phenomenological inspection of the perceptual process reveals no intradermal-extradermal differentiation or any of the other alleged differences which have played such an important role in theories of perception.

A brief recapitulation may be in order. Having pointed out[45] in the first two sections of the present chapter that no unique distinction can be drawn by means of atomistic analyses be-

[44] See Arthur F. Bentley, "The Human Skin: Philosophy's Last Line of Defense," *Philosophy of Science*, VIII (1941), 1–19; reprinted in *Inquiry into Inquiries*, ed. Sidney Ratner (Boston: Beacon Press, 1954), pp. 195–211.

[45] By arguments summarized on pp. 112–13 above.

tween elements in perception which are given and those furnished by the mind, I proceeded in the next three sections to
examine the distinction from what might be called the molecular point of view. One analysis from this point of view is given
by Wood, whose perceptual molecules are "sensory blocks." Two
limitations involved in the "qualitative homogeneity" of sensory
blocks, I suggested, are not supported by the facts of perception.
One of these limitations consists in the "qualitative homogeneity" of the presentations of the various senses taken one by one;
the other is the limitation of sensory blocks, to begin with, to
qualities of the same sense. The latter limitation appears to be
justified by the great differences noticeable among the functions
of the various sense organs; but these differences, like the sense
organs of which they are functions, need have no part in the
purely phenomenological inquiry which most perceptual philosophers have wanted to conduct. On the basis of such an inquiry,
we cannot be said to perceive our sense organs in any more fundamental way than we perceive other material objects, and sense
organs are thus no more to be taken for granted than other material objects. Finally, I suggested that it is not enough to question
the traditional differentiation of the five senses, together with
the concomitant fivefold differentiation of the given. Not only
might these "senses" function as one, but they might function
together with what can be called the "somatic" sense; and, since
differences between "inner" and "outer" tend in turn to become
fuzzy, the possibility must be reckoned with of expanding this al-
ready-expanded sensory "organ" into a single "psychosomatic"
sense.

Thus, one of the pictures of human perception which may
emerge from a phenomenological examination of the perceptual
process is that of the *total human organism* reacting in no very
clear-cut way to the surrounding world. It is not a very precise
picture, because it is prior to every distinction that could sharpen
perception enough to be seen precisely. Mental-physical, intradermal-extradermal, proper-synesthetic, direct-complicating, given-nongiven—none of these can be said with assurance to be a

distinction discoverable in the perceptual process, and yet every one marks a "felt difference" for the epistemologist.

So, besides the classic philosophic portrayal of our world as given to us broken down into discrete colors, sounds, and so on, an alternative portrayal now emerges of "the given" as something much more amorphous and indistinct than sense data as ordinarily conceived, a given which comes to us by way of a blurred, undifferentiated, psychosomatic awareness, and one which requires to be broken down by us into manageable bits and snatches. Furthermore, there seems to be no method outside of sheer speculation (barring—for as long as I can—the scientific, factual approach that has been held to be outside the province of philosophy) for deciding among these two extreme presentations of the way the world is given to us and all the possibilities that fall in between.

The upshot of the discussion is that no basis that empiricists might accept with an easy conscience can be discovered for the kind of distinction between the given and the nongiven in perception that could provide a clue to the level of human experience at which the formal-factual distinction first arises. The most promising avenue of inquiry has to be rejected, consequently, and other paths explored.

There is, nevertheless, one final possibility for salvaging the given-nongiven distinction, though in a slightly different form than that just examined. For if a basis for the kind of distinction needed can be supplied by the differences between elements actually present at the time of perception and others only remembered from the past, then a kind of given-nongiven distinction will have been discerned, and part of the answer will have been found for the question where to locate the formal and the nonformal in experience. To this possibility I now turn.

6. MEMORY AND THE EPISTEMOLOGICAL PRESENT

The perceptual elements dealt with until now might be said to be all contemporaneous or even simultaneous, in some unprecise—though nonetheless physical—sense of simultaneity. Even epistemologists who will view my approach as blurring the distinction between immediate awareness and mediate, or inferred or interpretational, knowledge, do not try to maintain the distinction on temporal lines. All these elements belong to the phenomenon of perceiving what is present, regardless of whether what is present is given or originates "in the mind," and what I have been doing, after eliminating the idea that the given can be reached simply by analyzing, is trying to track down—or to understand other people who try to track down—a kind of perceiving characterized by what could be called "ultimate pre-analyticity."

But apart from the levels of immediacy detectable within the activity of noticing what is present, there is another operation entering into perception, the remembering of what is past, and it may be held that here is an unassailable distinction between the given and the nongiven, whether our most immediate experience is of sense data in the classic sense or of an amorphous, undifferentiated, psychosomatic totality. Even if, with Price, perception is carried down to the rock-bottom level of primary recognition, still, primary recognition has two components, a noticing component and a memory component,[46] and whatever view be taken of the mental activities of noticing and remembering, the objects of the activities—the perceptual elements for which they are the vehicles—are clearly and distinctly two kinds of elements, the kind that is present and the kind that is past. And this, it may be said, furnishes a stable ground for maintaining, at the very least, the distinction between what may be given in perception and what cannot.

To ignore the memory component in perception is to ignore the temporal nature of all cognition, and when this done epistemological puzzles crop up corresponding to the classic philosophic puzzles about time. Just as philosophers used to be puzzled about how, if time is a series of discrete temporal atoms or "nows," anyone can get from anywhere to anywhere else, since there isn't enough time in a "now" for motion to occur, so

[46] *Thinking and Experience*, pp. 58 ff., 78 ff.

philosophers have managed to be puzzled also about how anyone can know *now* about *then*, since there isn't enough time *now* for knowing about anything else. This latter puzzle is part of the problem of memory, and this way of putting it shows that the apparent straightforwardness of the problem is only a blind for all the messiness associated with attempts, from Zeno's to Russell's, to grapple analytically with time. But in fact, the problem of how we can know *now* about *then* is as general as any problem about knowledge can be, because, by the same line of reasoning, there isn't enough time in a "now" for knowing at all, if knowing about an experience be different from having the experience.[47]

The trouble with all this, as such modern philosophers as Bergson have shown if they have shown nothing else, is that so far as experience is concerned time does not have the metronomic characteristics traditionally assigned it; rather, time is experienced as fluid and continuous, in an irregular sense of continuity associated with the expressions "real duration" and "stream of consciousness," and what is supposed to be at the bottom of the experience of time is memory. There is an epistemological side to this modern insight, and it is well expressed by Lewis. "Knowing is itself a temporal process, like hearing a tune or guiding a car round a corner. It is not the time-extended cognition but the chopping of it up into unextended instants which is fictitious."[48] Any fears about the possibility of knowing, on the ground that to know requires more time than is now available, are seen to be ill-founded. Any question about how much time is available for a process that *actually occurs* must be answered by "long enough," and when the process in question is the cognitive process, the "long enough" is the *epistemological present*—"a present in which what is sensuously given is surrounded by or embedded in a mass of epistemically pertinent surrogates of past experience, in the form of memories or of the sense of past experience as having been so and so; and . . . such present-as-past items are capable of being elicited by attention and reflection

[47] See Russell, *An Inquiry into Meaning and Truth*, pp. 48 ff.
[48] *An Analysis of Knowledge and Valuation*, p. 330.

and brought into relation with one another and with the sensuously given—all without going beyond the bounds of what is genuinely present now."[49]

Lewis' prescinding of the sensuously given from the mass of "pertinent" epistemic proxies of the past must not be taken to provide the basis for the kind of distinction between given and nongiven that has been in question, however. For one thing, there is no reason to think the sensuously given ever exists in an unalloyed state. But even if there were, one cannot measure the temporal duration required for an epistemological present and then talk about a cognitive process requiring only half the time, in hope of catching the sensuously given before it has had a chance to mingle with the present-as-past; to attach epistemological significance to the shorter process would be to destroy the longer or original process by violating what Collingwood has called "the principle of minimum time."[50] To talk about anything which does not require as much time as the epistemological present is to talk about something so entirely different from the epistemological present that it could not be said even to be a part of it or, therefore, to have epistemological significance.

In fact, no basis for the dichotomy between elements in perception which are sensuously given, or present-as-present, and elements which are present-as-past is provided by a phenomenological inspection of perception. Elements in perception are not perceived differently according to whether they are present by virtue of our capacity for noticing or by virtue of our capacity for remembering. They bear no witness to their medium of arrival. Nor is any other conceivable criterion for telling what is given now from what is carried over from (or otherwise represents) the past—vivacity, independence of the will, unmistakability, coherence—of such a nature that it both applies solely to the given and might serve as a workable criterion for human beings. This is, in fact, what I take to be the significance of Lewis' description of the epistemological present. Knowing requires two kinds of

[49] *Ibid.*, pp. 331–32.

[50] R. G. Collingwood, *The Idea of Nature* (Oxford: Clarendon Press, 1945), pp. 19–27.

elements in a certain relation to one another, and if one kind is missing or if the relation is disturbed, knowing cannot occur.

The objection might be made at this point that I am failing to recognize another distinction, the distinction between two kinds of knowledge, or, if a narrower view be taken of knowledge, the distinction between knowledge and a more primitive state of consciousness that must precede it. In an older vocabulary, the distinction I might be accused of overlooking is between knowledge by acquaintance and knowledge by description or knowledge about. The epistemological present that Lewis talks about is a necessary condition for knowledge in the second sense, it might be said, but acquaintance is a process that occurs without it, and in fact is an element in it, the element, namely, that is present-as-present and that could be isolated from the present-as-past if not for my prejudicial invocation of the principle of minimum time. The object of acquaintance, finally, is the given, pure and simple.

For Price, the distinction in question is between primary and secondary recognition.[51] Secondary recognition is recognition by means of signs, and it is primary recognition that enables us to recognize the signs by means of which secondary recognition can occur. Primary recognition is not subject to verification, but secondary recognition is; in fact it is in terms of primary recognition that secondary recognition may be verified (or at least confirmed). Secondary recognition is learned, and primary recognition is the learning medium. However, according to Price, the relation of secondary to primary recognition, though it is the relation of nongiven to given, is not the relation of inferred to uninferred, or of interpreted to immediate. To identify it with this latter relation would be to distort it, because we have no experience of inferring or interpreting; what we perceive, whether by means of primary or of secondary recognition, is perceived as immediate and direct, so that experience offers no clue to the distinction between the two kinds of recognition.

But—at least on Price's analysis—even if the distinction did

51 *Thinking and Experience*, pp. 44 ff.

have an experiential basis, not everything recognized by means of primary recognition could be given, because primary recognition has its epistemological present also, within which its "noticing" component and its "memory" component are inextricably interwoven. "In primary recognition a characteristic is not only noticed; it is also *familiar* in some degree."[52] This familiarity, or present-as-pastness, would appear to be Price's reason for calling the phenomenon "recognition." But, by definition, what is familiar, or present-as-past, cannot be given in the sense of present-as-present, and as long as it is the given and the nongiven that are in question, Price's concept of primary recognition must be rejected as a basis for distinguishing between them.

Moreover, if this distinction cannot be made between elements of primary recognition that are given and those that are not, the force of the distinction between primary and secondary recognition seems considerably diminished. Knowledge in the full-fledged secondary sense uses signs, and Price's only reason, apparently, for bringing in primary recognition is in order to provide a more primitive kind of knowledge by which we can recognize signs without using other signs. This, by the way, is an example of a familiar argument in epistemology, which may be called the "can't get started" argument and which may be identified as a pillar of the kind of philosophic thinking against which the present work is directed. The can't-get-started argument will be further considered, and a counterargument developed, in the next chapter. Other specimens are Russell's arguments that there must be a language of lowest type, since if there were not, the hierarchy of languages would extend downward indefinitely and "language could never get started,"[53] and that inferential knowledge requires as an "indispensable minimum" epistemological premises or data which are the most nearly certain beliefs we have and for which no reason can be given.[54] In the present case it is secondary recognition that can't get started, and Price is

[52] *Ibid.*, p. 58.

[53] *An Inquiry into Meaning and Truth*, p. 63.

[54] *Human Knowledge: Its Scope and Limits* (New York: Simon & Schuster, 1948), pp. 166, 171.

using primary recognition as his epistemological self-starter. However, primary recognition operates only in the case of characteristics already familiar to us, so that, if the motivation is unchanged, a still more primitive kind of knowledge (it need not be called "knowledge") is required to explain how we recognize (it ought not be called "recognize") unfamiliar characteristics. Primary recognition, in other words, is not really a self-starter, so that it can be of little assistance in getting secondary recognition started, at least without a starting device of its own.[55] (Such a device might, if left to the imagination, turn out to be what has been called in another connection a "Judas eye notion of double-perception,"[56] a device by which sense data or percepts would receive a preliminary screening by the superego, which would then allow only familiar ones to confront the primary recognition.)

Similar considerations may be brought against Lewis' distinction between perceptual elements that are present-as-present and those that are present-as-past. There is no way of picking elements out of the epistemological present that are present as pres-

[55] Price does have a rather ingenious way out: he could say that we become familiar with characteristics previously unfamiliar to us by means of the *déjà vu* illusion (*op. cit.*, pp. 83–84). But this explanation, at least as Price would use it, is unsatisfactory because the *déjà vu* illusion can deceive just as effectively about individuals as about characteristics and, hence, could be invoked to explain secondary recognition directly rather than through the offices of primary recognition. Thus, instead of learning to (secondary) recognize a piece of lead at sight by inferring other characteristics from its "peculiar dull-grey colour," which I (primary) recognize through the illusion of having seen it before, I might learn to (secondary) recognize a piece of lead at sight through the illusion of having seen the same individual object before. As an approach toward an explanation of learning secondary recognition, I think this use of the *déjà vu* illusion has something to recommend it even apart from obviating the need for primary recognition to explain the learning of secondary recognition (see below, p. 163).

[56] The concept of "perceptual defense" suggests to Jerome S. Bruner and Leo Postman an image of "the superego peering through a Judas eye, scanning incoming percepts in order to decide which shall be permitted into consciousness" ("Perception, Cognition, and Behavior," *Journal of Personality*, XVIII [1949–50], 14–31; reprinted in *Perception and Personality: A Symposium*, ed. Bruner and David Krech [Durham, N.C.: Duke University Press, 1949], pp. 14–31; present reference is to p. 25 of each).

ent. It is not so simple a matter as pointing to what we notice rather than to what we remember, because we only notice what we recognize, we only recognize what is familiar, and whatever is familiar is present-as-past.

What follows from this is that no conceivable empirical difference could lay bare the distinction between present-as-present and present-as-past. And I have already complained that even to separate intellectually these two elements of the epistemological present is to destroy the concept of epistemological present, which is to destroy the only useful concept I know of for getting around certain classic obstacles to the possibility of knowledge. But what sort of distinction is it that not only does not lead to any empirical difference, but cannot even be conceived without causing more intellectual damage than results from its inconceivability? I suggest that it is a distincton that cannot be significantly blurred because it is so obscure as to be without significance to begin with.

Once the concept of epistemological present is grasped, however, there should be no great shock at this inability to distinguish between what is present in it and what is past. This is, in fact, what I take to be the significance of the word "present"— the timelessness of anything occurring within what it applies to. Once allow a distinction to be drawn between present and past, and it follows that not everything distinguished is present. Conversely, within anything that we decide to call the present, nothing can be said to be past.

But I do not want to rest this argument on the words which happen to be involved. I am definitely committing myself to what these words, taken in their strictest sense, say. Perception takes place within the epistemological, or it might be called perceptual, present, which is merely what results when perception is examined from a certain point of view. Looked at from this point of view, all elements within the perceptual situation are contemporaneous, and all are "genuinely present now." There is no distinction of earlier and later, nor of past and present, unless we get outside the perceptual situation.

Before we get outside the perceptual situation, I want to see what has happened to memory. Memory entered the picture a few paragraphs back in connection with the temporal character of cognition, when it was pointed out that this temporal character must be given recognition in order to avoid certain difficulties in the theory of knowledge engendered by some classic puzzles about time. One of these difficulties involves memory, because when the temporal dimension of cognition is ignored or denied, there doesn't seem to be enough time just now for knowing anything that was earlier than now, if indeed there is time enough for knowing anything that is right here just now. The artificiality of this puzzle is seen when temporality is restored to cognition and one realizes that cognition takes place within an epistemological present, some elements of which are present-as-past. But when the epistemological present is spotlighted, the problem of memory seems to disappear, along with memory itself—at least so far as perception is concerned. For what might ordinarily be taken to be memory operating in perception can hardly be said to be memory when it does not refer "beyond the bounds of what is genuinely present now."

Let me state the situation in slightly different terms. The minimal cognitive operation, according to Price, is primary recognition. Primary recognition is more than just noticing something, though, because it is noticing something familiar, so that familiarity is always operative in perception. And if familiarity is always operative, then memory is never absent. But if memory is never absent, then where is the problem of memory? The problem involved seems now to be not the problem of memory but the problem of direct awareness: How can there be direct awareness of anything if there is never perception of any sort, including the sort called awareness, within which memory is not operating?

It will be noticed that in this restatement of the situation, the puzzle, though remaining, is reversed. Whereas the conclusion in the previous paragraph was that there is no reference beyond the present, so that memory must be said to be wholly inoperative, now the conclusion is that there is no direct awareness at all, but only memory, which is solely operative. The antithesis, of course, is due to equivocacy over the word "present," which can be understood as a mathematical instant or as a "greater now." Though I seem to have contradicted myself, actually I have only reinforced the conclusion I really want to come to, the conclusion not that perception is entirely a matter of memory or not at all a matter of memory, but that within perception memory and awareness, or remembering and noticing, are indistinguishable. We notice what is familiar, which is to say we recognize, and to maintain that there are two different operations involved is to distort the situation. To hold that two different operations are involved is to import explanatory devices from other disciplines. A careful study of the perceptual situation, without theoretic commitments other than the bare minimum necessary to study anything at all, discloses one and only one operation, noticing-the-familiar or, as it is aptly called, recognizing.

From outside the epistemological present, of course, failure to distinguish between awareness and memory, between noticing what is present and remembering what is past, is at first blush so counterintuitive as to seem to verge on madness. But the kind of philosophic stultification that results from glorification of the intuitive must be guarded against. Why is the fusion of awareness and memory counterintuitive? One important reason probably is that the distinction between the two is felt to be a function of the distinction between the present and the past and of the irreversibility of time. It is important to keep in mind the difference between psychological or "felt" time and physical or measured time, however; part of the justification for the concept of the epistemological present is that it enables us to overcome difficulties created by the relation between cognition and clock time. The present, so far as cognition is concerned, must be taken to be a fluid, stretchable sort of present, more like James's saddle-backed present than like the durationless point-instant that physicists find convenient, and within this saddle-backed present there is no past, nor any duration whose irreversibility could be violated.

Again, it may be objected that there is an ineluctable difference between awareness and memory because no one can deny the intuitive difference between perception brought about by present stimuli and perception brought about by stimuli now past. Nevertheless, from every point of view except the intuitive the difference *is* denied—and so far as the intuitive point of view is concerned, it is a question of whose intuition is considered. In the case of visual perception said to be brought about by present stimuli, the physicist is aware of the time required for light to travel to the retina from the object perceived, the physiologist is aware of the time lag between retinal impingement and excitation or stimulation, and the psychologist knows that time elapses between stimulation and awareness. And even if physics, physiology, and psychology are ruled out as "beside the philosophic point," still, the elements of perception, as already suggested, bear no witness to their medium of arrival. What the intuitionist must decide in the face of all this is exactly where he wants to draw the line between perceptual present and perceptual past, or between awareness and memory; the present claim is simply that the decision will be tantamount to a convention, and until the convention is made, the difference between the two is a matter of degree.

Consider, moreover, such perceptual situations as the following. From shipboard one may perceive land approaching, even though poor visibility, curvature of the earth, and sheer distance conspire to produce the scientific opinion that the land is beyond one's field of vision. (It may be thought that anticipation rather than memory is at issue here, but, though anticipation might be the occasion for the perception, memory would normally be thought to account for the nature of it.) Or, while at his desk, in any of several positions, one may throw wastepaper into the basket behind him without turning round; is memory operative along with awareness in this case? These are instances of what Ames calls "ultra stimulus perception," in which there is no impingement of light rays on the retina.[57] Wherein lie the time differences betwen stimulus perception and ultrastimulus perception? It cannot be said that the stimulus is past at the time of perceiving the land or the wastebasket and that this lapse of time accounts for the difference between the two kinds of perception, because, as just pointed out, there is also a lapse of time in stimulus perception. So far as time lapse is concerned, there is only a difference in degree, and the distinction must be marked by a convention.

Furthermore, where is the line to be drawn between stimulus and ultrastimulus perception at all, quite apart from the question of time and the awareness-memory distinction? The answer might be thought obvious in the case of the wastebasket behind one's back, but as Ames points out, there is a gradual blurring of the retinal image as it gets farther from the fovea and approaches the periphery, until at the extreme periphery there is almost no visual differentiation whatever.[58] Where is one to say that one kind of perception terminates and the other begins? There is, in fact, as much reason for distinguishing between foveal and peripheral (or nonfoveal) perception as between stimulus and ultrastimulus perception. And, apart from boundary-line difficulties, who is to say that intersensory considerations, as well as such subtle factors as those suggested in the passage quoted earlier from Fitzgerald, are not operative also in the case of the wastebasket?

In any case, the clear and distinct idea of memory as operating perceptually in a manner sharply differentiated from awareness, or noticing, has been replaced by a view of perception according to which no such differentiation can be made. Present-as-present and present-as-past, noticing what is present and remembering

[57] Adelbert Ames, Jr., "Reconsideration of the Origin and Nature of Perception in Situations Involving Only Inorganic Phenomena," *Vision and Action: Essays in Honor of Horace M. Kallen*, ed. Sidney Ratner (New Brunswick, N.J.: Rutgers University Press, 1953), pp. 251–74.

[58] *Ibid.*, pp. 255, 265. See also Bentley, "The Fiction of 'Retinal Image,' " *Inquiry into Inquiries*, ed. Sidney Ratner (Boston: Beacon Press, 1954), p. 284.

what is past, perceptual awareness and perceptual memory, stimulus and ultrastimulus perception—all these distinctions disappear within the epistemological present, and without the epistemological present they can be maintained only as distinctions of degree, or else on the basis of conventions about where the dividing line is to be drawn. And as these distinctions go, so, once more, goes the distinction between the given and the nongiven in perception. Not only can the given not be differentiated from the nongiven when the latter is thought to originate in the mind, but the distinction can be upheld only by a more or less arbitrary convention even when "nongiven" is simply taken to mean "not given at the time of perception." And it might be that the concept of the given is itself one of those concepts whose drastic alteration, if not abandonment, would be of immeasurably greater benefit to philosophy than their continued and unmodified existence.

The concept of the given, though epistemological rather than ontological in character, aids and abets, at the same time that it camouflages, the desire to penetrate to the ontological realities of the world. By reversing the processes of knowledge, it has been thought, we can learn what is given to us as the raw material of knowledge, and then, whether what is given is the reality philosophers have been seeking these many centuries or is a secondary reality interposing itself between us and the first, we have nevertheless finally gained knowledge about something that is really there.

Unfortunately, though, the problems that rise in connection with "the given" are no less difficult or intrinsic than those that prevent us from getting to know reality through a more direct channel, so that for empiricists the concept of the given is just as suspect as the more obviously metaphysical concepts they have discarded in the past. A more useful epistemological concept is that of "the taken," for it permits the investigation of the more interesting questions about perception and knowledge without unwarranted assumptions about the objects of perception and knowledge and without wrongly encouraging the concept of a sharp and rigid formal-factual difference at the perceptual level.

Meanwhile, though, a solution is needed by empiricists for the problem of how there can be cognitive experience at all without some such experiential distinction as the given-nongiven or factual-formal distinction. The attempt to locate the earliest experiential traces of such a distinction seems now to have bogged down altogether. More knowledge about the low or "early" levels of cognition is needed, and this requirement will necessitate a closer examination of the arguments customarily advanced against the view that epistemology can utilize scientific methods and evidence in the solution of its major problems.

CHAPTER IV

A Situational Approach to Cognitive Experience

1. FACTUAL EVIDENCE AND PERCEPTUAL THEORY

IN POINTING OUT the oversimplification indulged in by certain empiricist theories of perception, I seem to have made a deep and dark secret of the ordinary process of perceiving, a secret as far removed from the bright conceptual clarity of the sense-datum theory as, say, Bergson and Whitehead are removed from Russell and Moore. But, while I do want to maintain that perception is a deeper and darker phenomenon than empiricists have made out, I do not want to declare the sense-datum theory to be false or the "total organic awareness" theory to be true. All I am saying is that an adequate case has not yet been presented for any theory of perception, and that the resulting epistemological lacuna has serious implications for empiricism.

The aim of modern empiricism has been to allow the nature of direct perceptual experience to dictate the manner in which statements are to be tied down to that experience, and hence the manner in which empirical significance is to be attributed to statements. When direct experience of the world is thought to consist in impressions or sensations, statements are tied down when they are "carried back" to the impressions from which they are derived. If, on the other hand, direct experience were not made up of impressions or sensations but consisted in some such vague and amorphous initial awareness of things as sketched in the previous chapter, the problem of empirical significance would be just as troublesome as the problem of anchoring statements to so ambiguous a kind of experience. And if it is not known which, if any, of these theories of perceptual experience, or of the possible theories in between, is the correct one, then empiricism is in even greater difficulties, because it has not

yet reached the stage where it is entitled to begin to attack the
problem of anchoring statements to experience. The present task
is to examine more carefully the consequences for empiricism
when the concept of perception and direct experience is as obscure as it seems suddenly to have become. Before beginning this
task, however, a methodological stumbling block needs remov-
ing.

Throughout these chapters I have been skirting the question
of science and its pertinence to epistemological problems, but
any further prolongation of the irksome question could be justi-
fiably interpreted as shirking the burdens imposed by my own
setting of the issues. Let me examine the pros and cons of a
scientific approach to epistemology. It may be pointed out once
more that a wide gulf exists between any epistemology discussed
in chapter iii and the ideal of an epistemology which makes no
appeal, frank or furtive, to the facts. Whether called introspection, inspection, or simply and vaguely "experience," some sort
of factual appeal is used at one point or another by every epistemologist considered (though usually the empirical techniques so
employed would not pass muster in a sophomore psychology
lab). In the face of this disregard in practice for methodological
theory, it is hypocritical to insist that psychology has no place in
epistemological inquiry—and not merely hypocritical, for what
the insistence amounts to is a demand that uncontrolled inquiry
be substituted for controlled inquiry.

What reasons are given by epistemological purists for maintaining the sanctity of perceptual investigation against the in-
roads of science? One reason cited is that any empirical science
stands or falls with the validity of induction, and since the justification of induction is itself an epistemological question, epistemology must not be placed in a position of dependence on or
even of obligation to science. Otherwise epistemology would be
contaminated, if not vitiated, by a patent circularity.[1] There is
a measure of credibility in this argument, but there would be a

[1] See H. H. Price, *Perception* (2d ed.; London: Methuen & Co., 1950),
p. 171 n.

much greater measure if, as I just mentioned, epistemologists did not ignore their own stricture by smuggling in empirical observations of their own. Perhaps it will be said that the off-the-record fact-mongering indulged in by epistemological investigators of perception is not touched by the prohibition of induction because of the difference between the "private" nature of introspectional, inspectional, and phenomenological evidence and the "public" nature of psychological evidence. However, it has been remarked that the validity of an appeal to private data, no less than to public data, depends on induction—or, if it be insisted that induction plays no part in the reliability of inspectional evidence, the latter then depends directly on a law of the uniformity of human nature and experience. For surely the tacit premise in arguments from inspection or from introspection is that "my private perceptual experiences are a reliable index to other private perceptual experiences." Without this premise such arguments about perception would be no more than epistemological diaries and ad hoc attempts at their organization.

The argument that scientific findings are epistemologically disreputable because tainted by induction would be acceptable only if epistemology itself were untainted by induction. The question of circularity, of course, remains, and is involved, moreover, in another argument against contaminating epistemology by the introduction of psychological evidence. This is the argument that, induction aside, psychology, like any empirical science, depends on observation for its evidence, but observation, being itself perception, cannot be appealed to for knowledge about itself.

This argument, like its predecessor, involves methodological principles honored more in the breach than the observance, though an attempt at observance is made, usually along lines dictated, as Quine describes it, by the desire "to posit a realm of sense data, situated somehow just me-ward of the physical stimulus, for fear of circularity."[2] The desire to differentiate between objects of perception and objects epistemologically prior to these,

2 W. V. Quine, "On Mental Entities," *Proceedings of the American Academy of Arts and Sciences,* LXXX (1951–54), 202.

in order to avoid circularity without leaving epistemology wholly nonobjective, is a legitimate one inviting the sympathy of empiricists. In view of the shaky foundations on which the concepts of sense data and other denizens of the perceptual underworld have been seen to rest, however, it seems doomed to remain nothing but a desire. Whatever foundation the epistemologist may provide for his own investigation, it will be no less in need of justification than the perception he is investigating. Moreover, if the absence of a criterion does not preclude the investigation it would otherwise be governing, it is certain that some other criterion, however camouflaged or repressed, is at work, and the important question for empiricists is whether this other criterion is observationally grounded or has an intuitive or speculative basis. If the latter, the whole procedure is beyond the pale. But if the former, if epistemological inquiry is governed by an observationally grounded criterion, scientific evidence can hardly be ignored by the epistemologist on the ground that it depends on observation.

A further argument for segregating science and epistemology in the manner described is that science, psychology in particular, is concerned with *how* we perceive, whereas the epistemological problem is *what* we perceive.[3] However, many epistemologists, for instance those who have had dealings of one sort or another with a causal theory of perception, have been concerned both with what we perceive and with how we perceive it; to restrict the adjective "epistemological" to only part of this concern is provincial at best.[4] Moreover, psychological approaches to perception, especially in recent years,[5] have been of such a kind that a sharp distinction between the questions of what and how would either distort the nature of the psychological inquiry or else lead to a hopelessly unempirical interpretation of the question about what we perceive—the kind of interpretation, it is to

[3] Price, *op. cit.*, p. 2. See also A. D. Woozley, *Theory of Knowledge* (London: Hutchinson's University Library, 1949), p. 15.

[4] See C. D. Broad, *Perception, Physics, and Reality* (Cambridge: Cambridge University Press, 1914).

[5] See below, pp. 154–55.

be feared, that provides the main support for this argument involving a radical distinction between what and how.

There is one argument left. The philosophic inquirer into perception may claim that, unlike the scientist, he is exempt from the demands of empiricism, being engaged in a totally different kind of discipline. Either of two reasons may be given in support of this claim of exemption. The philosopher might maintain, as Ayer once did,[6] that epistemological theories about perception are really only alternative languages in which to describe perception. If this claim is correct—if what others have naïvely supposed to be different theories about the nature of perception are really only alternative ways of talking about perception—then the adequacy of the claim for supporting the argument about science and epistemology depends on whether criteria for choosing among alternative languages are entirely nonfactual or not. But there is, as Ayer himself admitted,[7] at least some factual component in these criteria, and therefore the argument based on there being none must be rejected.

The other reason likely to be invoked by the epistemologist claiming to be engaged in an activity wholly unlike science and therefore exempt from empiricist requirements is that, whereas the scientist is engaged in an investigation of the world, he, the philosopher, is engaged in an analysis of concepts.[8] Or at least he is engaged in explication, which, unlike explanation, involves eliciting meanings already present and, sometimes, conventions about meanings not already present, but never involves empirical fact. Put differently, the findings of the epistemologist can be expressed wholly by means of analytic statements, whereas synthetic statements are required to express the findings of the

[6] A. J. Ayer, *The Foundations of Empirical Knowledge* (New York: Macmillan Co., 1940), pp. 27 f., 46 ff.

[7] "It is a contingent fact that any domain of sense-experience possesses the structure that makes it convenient for us to apply to it the language that we do" (*ibid.*, pp. 255–56). See Price's review of the latter in *Mind*, L (1941), 291–92, and Ayer's "The Terminology of Sense-Data," *Mind*, LIV (1945), 289–312, reprinted in his *Philosophical Essays* (London: Macmillan & Co., 1954), pp. 66–104 (esp. pp. 103–4).

[8] Ayer, *Language, Truth and Logic* (2d ed.; London: Victor Gollancz, 1948), pp. 50 f., 151–52, chap. iii.

scientist, and this constitutes a difference so radical and unalterable as to preclude any fruitful interaction between the two.

This reasoning depends on a cluster of distinctions (investigation of the world versus analysis of concepts, explanation versus
explication, synthetic versus analytic), and must share the vul-
nerability of these distinctions. Analytic and synthetic statements
are adequately distinguishable, as suggested in chapter ii, only
within a rigid and particular artificial language framework. If this
is the case, then so long as conceptual analysis (which issues in
analytic statements but not synthetic ones) and factual investigation (which issues in both) are to be sharply differentiated,
they must be confined within frameworks of the same kind;
otherwise, the epistemologist might become factually engaged
despite himself. But to confine factual or scientific investigation
within a rigid framework of any kind is, as also suggested, to
deprive it of its customary openness and thus inhibit, if not ter-
minate, its most distinctive function, that of prediction.

It might be thought that the separation of conceptual analysis
and factual investigation would be accomplished if conceptual
analysis alone were confined within a rigid framework. But if the
analytic-synthetic distinction is drawn along fluid lines by the
scientist and along rigid ones by the epistemologist, as will be
the case if the latter alone utilizes the kind of context in question, there may easily be statements which function as synthetic
for the scientist but as analytic for the epistemologist, and such
statements might very well play a crucial role in an analysis of
concepts. In these circumstances, either the epistemologist is
more directly interested in empirical fact than the present argument allows him to be, or else his concepts are so far removed
from those of experience that he has transgressed the bounds of
empirical propriety. The argument under consideration requires
that both conceptual analysis and factual investigation be carried on within a kind of context characterized mainly by its
inflexibility.

At the very least, then, this argument involves the inhibition
of the predictive function of science. It is an argument against
the epistemological relevance of scientific activity, therefore, only

if and because it is really an argument against scientific activity. The epistemologist, if he is to grant scientific evidence and theories any sort of significance at all, must grant them epistemological significance.

I know of no further arguments against allowing scientific evidence to confirm and disconfirm epistemological hypotheses, and on the assumption that it is wrong for the philosopher to cut himself off without sufficient reason from any source of knowledge, I will feel free to consult empirical sciences for evidence about perception as well as about other elements of human knowledge. Relevant sciences are not confined to psychologies. Physics may be consulted regarding the perceptual environment, and physiology and neurology regarding the organic processes involved. But even to limit relevant sciences to psychology, physiology, neurology, and physics is to construe human knowledge too narrowly. As the previous examination of perceptual theories shows, it cannot be assumed that past theories of knowledge provide the only terms adequate for perceptual inquiry. In particular, mention of the possibility of a total organic sense suggests that something might be learned from biology, and biology leads into anthropology and sociology. From any of these sciences, whatever seems relevant to our immediate inquiry may be borrowed without violating the boundaries of epistemology. For many purposes a helpful general orientation is the biological, not because biology is the only framework within which human beings can be profitably viewed, but because in many inquiries a biological view of men seems to assume about as little as can be assumed. It may be questioned whether the most important thing about men is their intelligence, history, social behavior, chemical make-up, early influences, modes of producing economic goods, or the beliefs they hold, but it can scarcely be questioned for most purposes that men are biological organisms with certain common requirements for sustenance and self-perpetuation.

The problem of circularity is still outstanding. I am convinced that the proper attitude to take toward circularity is that it is something empiricist philosophers must learn to live with. Un-

less unquestioned assumptions are to be made somewhere along
the line, or unless some problems are to be solved by fiat, circularity is unavoidable. But nevertheless, as I will suggest in some
detail, there is a way of dealing with circularity which is compatible with empiricism, a way that will be called pragmatic
reconstruction. Essentially, it consists in treating problems of
philosophy within limited and provisional domains. Because they
are limited domains, it can be told exactly where the circularity
is located; and because they are provisional domains, the circularity can be located wherever it matters least for the purpose at
hand. Pragmatic reconstruction furnishes everything except certainty, which is as much as any method of philosophizing can
legitimately claim—though many have declined to be inhibited
by illegitimacy. All this, however, will be developed more leisure-
ly in the third part. The immediate problem is to examine human cognition at every level, partly in the light of whatever
available scientific evidence is found relevant and helpful, in an
effort to deepen our understanding of empiricism by discovering
the role played in cognition by the distinction between the formal and the nonformal.

2. THE PERCEPTUAL SITUATION

A striking fact of intellectual history emerges from
even a cursory consideration of a scientific approach to the epistemological problems of perception. This is the fact that, whereas the perceptual theories of the early philosophic empiricists
were in agreement with the best-informed psychological opinion
of the day (not a startling phenomenon in view of the virtual
identity of the two), the recent and present-day theories examined in the previous chapter are in sharp conflict with contemporary psychological theories of perception. Were one to work
out the kind of psychology that would support these present-day
epistemological views, in fact, the result would be something
very like the psychological atomism and associationism which
were respectable in the eighteenth century and which formed
the backbone of eighteenth-century empiricist epistemologies.
What is so striking about this fact is the complacency with

which it is regarded by most contemporary epistemologists, even though these same epistemologists would greet with ridicule the appearance of a philosophic position drawing support from, say, the phlogiston theory.

Any move away from atomism is in the direction of holism, and a theory of perception as far removed as logically possible from an atomistic theory is a holistic or, as it could be called, a "monolithic" theory. Human perception as portrayed by a monolithic theory might resemble the kind uncovered in the previous chapter: a vague, psychosomatic, total organic awareness of the environment (though the differentiation of organism from environment falls short of a thoroughgoing holism). A perceptual theory of this sort would, of course, be looked upon by most epistemologists with utter incredulity, though for my part I find it no more incredible than the atomistic theories of sense data examined. What is of interest about the "total organic awareness" theory of perception at the moment, however, is not its claim to serious consideration as the correct way of viewing human perception, but rather its heuristic value in providing methodological direction. As representative of the most distant alternatives to traditional sense-datum theories, and as standing to the latter about as holism stands to atomism, this amorphous, hard-to-conceptualize theory illustrates the other extreme of a scale of theoretic possibilities, possibilities which may be considered in terms of their positions on that scale. And the point I wish to make about modern psychologies of perception, once more, is that in general they have been moving away from atomism and in the direction of holism.

A theory located somewhere between atomism and holism is of course relatively atomistic and relatively holistic: atomistic relative to extreme holism and holistic relative to extreme atomism. And though a general characterization of such a theory would be next to impossible, since the theory could be located anywhere along the scale, nevertheless it is possible to give a functional or methodological characterization. Such a characterization would utilize the relative atomism of the theory by pointing out that the theory analyzes its subject matter into parts or elements which, because they are not logically simple, are further analyzable into simpler elements, but which, because they are as simple as the theory warrants, are not *significantly* further analyzable. To state the matter differently, the theoretic atoms are not logical atoms but logical molecules, grosser than logically necessary but as simple as theoretically significant. And a functional or methodological characterization would utilize the relative holism of the theory in question by pointing out that, while the theory does not conceive its subject matter as a unique monolith or totality compared to which every other whole is merely fragmentary, it does conceive its subject matter as a whole, whose parts may be considered in isolation only at the risk of distortion and loss of significance.

In other words, wherever a theory may be located along the scale whose extremes are atomism and holism, it is a contextual theory, analyzing its subject matter into molecular, more or less discrete, elements, but viewing these elements as significant because of their place within the whole. When the theory is about perception, the context in question is the perceptual situation. The point I am making about psychologies and epistemologies, finally, is that an epistemological theory of perception that could claim to have the empirical backing of recent perceptual psychology would in all probability be one which viewed perception contextually, in terms of the perceptual situation.[9]

[9] Such "recent" psychologies go back at least as far as William James. See John Dewey's "The Reflex Arc Concept in Psychology," *Psychological Review*, III (1896), 357–70; see also Arthur F. Bentley, "Situational vs. Psychological Theories of Behavior," *Journal of Philosophy*, XXXVI (1939), 169–81, 309–23, 405–13, reprinted in *Inquiry into Inquiries*, ed. Sidney Ratner (Boston: Beacon Press, 1954); Lewis E. Hahn, *A Contextualistic Theory of Perception* ("University of California Publications in Philosophy," Vol. XXII), 1942. Gestalt theories of perception have been instrumental in the trend away from atomism, though these have grounded their psychology in ontological assumptions unwarranted in the present context. Among present-day indications of the move toward contextual or situational approaches to perception are (1) such recent studies in the "personality" dimension of perception (that is, in the perceptual significance of the values, needs, etc., of the perceiver) as those of J. S. Bruner and Leo Postman (see Bruner and David Krech [eds.], *Perception and Personality: A Symposium* [Durham, N.C.: Duke University Press, 1949]); and (2) transactional psychology, stemming

The concept of the perceptual situation was encountered in the last chapter, not only in the extreme and unwieldy form of an undifferentiated psychosomatic perceptual state, but also in the conceptually more available form of Lewis' epistemological present. The epistemological present, in fact, is simply the perceptual situation from another point of view, that of an epistemologist taking time seriously. From this viewpoint, noticing and remembering, though they are elements of every perceptual situation, cannot be considered perceptually significant in isolation from one another, because when they are separated there is no longer a situation that could be significantly called perceptual.

The situational qualities of perception may be seen from other viewpoints than the temporal, however, for there are a great many things that make up perception besides the present-as-present which is noticed and the present-as-past which is remembered. There is, to mention one fairly important collection of elements in perception, the perceiver with his biological needs, his human values, and his assumptions (conscious or not) about the future, based on the past—all of them elements whose perceptual functions cannot be judged accurately outside the perceptual situation within which they occur. A growing body of empirical evidence is forcing recognition of the role played in perception by needs, values, and past experience,[10] and though the distinction between what we see and why we see it is undeniable, it is not an adequate reason for denying epistemological recognition to the role of needs and values in perception.

It is often maintained that regardless of the "veridicalness" of our sensations, or of how we select them out of the inventory of

---

philosophically from Dewey and Bentley, *Knowing and the Known* (Boston: Beacon Press, 1949), and represented by Adelbert Ames, Jr., *An Interpretative Manual for the Demonstrations in the Psychology Research Center, Princeton University: The Nature of Our Perceptions, Prehensions and Behavior* (Princeton: Princeton University Press, 1955); William H. Ittelson and Hadley Cantril, *Perception: A Transactional Approach* (Garden City, N.Y.: Doubleday & Co., 1954); and F. P. Kilpatrick (ed.), *Human Behavior from the Transactional Point of View* (Hanover, N.H.: Institute for Associated Research, 1952).

[10] See Bruner and Krech (eds.), *op. cit.*

sensory possibilities, or of how they came to be sensations, what alone has epistemological importance is what sensations consist in once we have them. The job of the epistemologist is to analyze them, not to speculate on their origins. This argument might carry conviction[11] were it not for the investigation of the previous chapter, which showed that no empirically acceptable method is available for laying bare the data of perception in order to examine them. The time-sanctioned method of hell-or-high-water analysis has grave defects stemming from its basic irresponsibility, and, disallowing declarations of epistemological priority based on intuition or on reconstructional convenience, only through empirical study of the process of perceiving can what is perceived be ferreted out for analysis. If the perception-sensation dualism is honored, the matter may be expressed by saying that, though the program of empiricism requires the analysis of sensation, the only legitimate approach to sensation is through perception, which is all we have to work with. There are no analytic shortcuts. At best, therefore, the empirical investigation of human perception is the normal and proper study of epistemologists; at worst it is an unfortunate but necessary detour. In any case, an empirical investigation brings into the open the role played by such perceptual elements as human needs and values, elements which do not exhibit that independence of the individual perceiving subject customarily thought to characterize whatever plays an essential role in perception. In fact, the subject-object dichotomy itself seems to lose its force so far as perception is concerned, and once more, an epistemological approach to perception that seems likely to result in as little distortion of the process as can be hoped for is one that begins with the context in which the process occurs: the perceptual situation.

As a context, the perceptual situation may be viewed from either of the two sides that every context has, the inside and the outside. Questions about perception, that is to say, may be either internal or external questions. And in terms of this distinction between internal and external questions, the problem of the

[11] Apart from the defects pointed out above, pp. 147–48.

formal and the nonformal in human cognition may be seen more clearly.

An internal question about perception is one referring to a particular perceptual situation, and it is answered by investigating that situation and stating the facts discovered. The matter is analogous to the internal questions about artificial languages that were considered in chapter ii. But there are subtleties about perceptual contexts that prevent the analogy with linguistic contexts from being complete, subtleties grounded in the privacy of the perceptual process. Investigation of a perceptual situation may teach us a great deal about it. We may inquire into the "objective" elements confronting the percipient and perhaps form a scientific opinion about what he ought to be perceiving, assuming normal and healthy sensory organs, neural activity, general bodily state, and environmental conditions. We may inquire into the physiological circumstances named and learn whether our assumptions about them are justified. We may study the percipient's history, his emotional structure and his tastes, and we may even, if so inclined and if acquainted with an introduction or two to the subject, psychoanalyze him. But, even armed with all these data, we cannot really form an accurate conception of what the percipient is perceiving. (Asking him is of little use, because the problem of calculating distortion due to conceptualization and articulation is at least as complicated as the problem of trying to learn what is perceived without asking the percipient.) Only the percipient himself is in a position to know what he is perceiving, and only the percipient himself is able, strictly speaking, to answer internal questions about perceptual situations.

Luckily, ability to pin down the significance of the formal-nonformal distinction in perception does not depend on ability to learn what someone else is perceiving; in fact, enough is known already for the purpose at hand. Any perceptual situation contains what may be called perceptual absolutes—elements which cannot be doubted by the percipient. These are the elements which structurally define the situation and in terms of which it is essentially characterized. They are the standards used by the percipient to interpret and evaluate all other elements in the situation; they are the elements about which he is certain enough to risk his actions. For a perceptual absolute to be doubted by a percipient would indicate not that the element might not be really an absolute but that a different perceptual situation is in question. In propositional terms, the denial of a proposition incorporating a perceptual absolute would be regarded either as occurring within another situation—in which case what is at issue is not a perceptual absolute after all—or else as self-contradictory. In these terms, that the characteristics of perceptual absolutes are formal is apparent, as is the existence of a difference between the formal and the nonformal.

But note that as soon as an internal viewpoint is exchanged for an external one, as soon as the discussion shifts from being about a particular perceptual situation to being about perceptual situations in general, retrenchment is necessary, for from an external point of view there are no absolutes of perception. There are no such absolutes because it is as impossible to generalize from one situation's "absolutes" to those of all situations as it is to generalize from one man's values, needs, and past experiences to those of other men. What were thought to be absolutes of perception turn out to be "functional absolutes" only. That every perceptual situation has its indubitables, its certainties, its defining or structural characteristics, is a proposition supported by the present inquiry, but what these indubitables, certainties, or characteristics are is a question to be investigated anew for every situation considered. Moreover, even as functional absolutes they are only as firm and as enduring as the perceptual situations within which they hold sway; and since most perceptual situations are short-lived and tentative, most perceptual absolutes are at any given moment "treated as if they were certain, but concurrently, at every moment they are held open for modification."[12]

The distinction between the formal and the nonformal as it functions in human perception can now be seen, for it is exactly the distinction between perceptual absolutes and other elements

[12] Ittelson and Cantril, op. cit., p. 30.

of perception. The formal or "absolute" perceptual elements are those which cannot be denied or rejected without also denying or rejecting the entire perceptual situation; so long as the situation is retained, those elements are indubitable. The nonformal factors in perception, on the other hand, are those about which doubts may be entertained without jeopardizing the status of the situation within which they occur; they are diagnosed in reference to the formal elements, which act as criteria for just such diagnostic perceptual activities.

The formal-nonformal distinction, therefore, is a functional one. It is to be found in every perceptual situation; in fact, a perceptual situation is best characterized in terms of where the distinction falls between its formal and its nonformal elements. But where the distinction falls within any particular context of perception is no indication of where it will fall within any other such context. What is formal, indubitable, and essential in one context may be nonformal, questionable, and accidental in another.

With these conclusions a turning point has been reached in the present inquiry, for one of the questions that seemed to impede progress concerned the sort of distinction the formal-nonformal one is as it manifests itself in human experience. The answer, at least so far as perceptual experience is concerned, is that the distinction always occurs within particular contexts or situations, that any such situation is characterized essentially by the distinction occurring within it, and that with respect to perceptual situations in general it may be said that all contain the distinction, but it may not be said where the distinction falls or whether any particular perceptual element is always formal or always nonformal.

It may be noted, moreover, that there is no discernible kind of experience so primitive that it does not contain the distinction. Every effort to pin down, in some empirically appropriate manner, an element in experience which could be said to be given, or epistemologically prior, or in any other sense basic or ultimate or indubitable, has failed. The distinction between the

formal and the nonformal does not seem to arise at some relatively sophisticated level of experience—or at least of human experience (the only kind that bothers me)—but must be said to
be present at the most primitive level that can be discovered.

Concomitant with and incidental to this discovery has come
another, one that will assume greater importance in Part III.
This is the discovery that no level of perceptual experience can
be discerned which is not pervaded by the needs and values of
whoever is having the experience. This proposition is directed
chiefly toward primitive levels of experience; there is little question of its truth at higher levels. There appears to be no raw or
neutral material given to us, out of which our needs and values
carve our personal worlds. The needs and values are always present and always operating.

3. THE EPISTEMOLOGICAL CONTINUUM

What I want to show now is that not only does our
most primitive experience contain the formal-nonformal distinction, but as the cognitive experience of men is "ascended" and
becomes more and more characterized by what is called "conceptualization," the same distinction is to be discovered present
in this experience and is to be discovered present in it in the
same way, which is to say contextually. In this all-important
matter of the distinction between what is formal and what is
nonformal about experience, there exists what may be called an
epistemological continuum.

When a philosophic empiricist concerns himself with conceptual thinking, he is especially concerned with how we get
from our immediate perceptual experience to our complex levels
of thinking, for if he can answer that question, then, by reversing
the process of conceptualization or abstraction, he has a way of
recovering the experiential content of abstract thoughts. When
sensation and perception have the air of crispness and clarity
given them by classic empiricist theories such as the sense-datum
theory, the evolution of abstract thinking out of concrete perceiving is one of those simple-to-complex processes, such as induction or construction or interpretation, which for the epis-

159

temologist may be tedious in practice but have no intrinsic difficulties. But the matter is entirely different when those clear classic ideas about immediate experience dissolve into a fuzzy collection of competitive hypotheses, each offering barriers of its own so far as getting to abstract thoughts is concerned. The contextual or situational approach that is being recommended recovers to a certain extent that earlier facility by shifting from a substantial or structural analysis to a functional or methodological one. What is of primary interest is not whether our primitive cognitive experiences consist in sense data or sensory blocks or intersensory clusters or psychosomatic monoliths, but that they occur within contexts. A proper field for empirical investigation would be the differences between the contexts within which our perceptual experiences occur and the contexts of abstract conceptual thinking, as well as the various ways in which the kinds of contexts could be ordered into a hierarchy. All that is of interest at the moment, however, is the proposition that abstract conceptual thinking does in fact occur contextually, and that so far as this matter of contexts is concerned there is an epistemological continuum including both the most primitive or immediate experiences discernible and the highest flights of abstract cognitive experience.

To speak of such a continuum is, of course, to deny in one important respect, at least, the sharp and radical distinction usually said to exist between cognitive experience which is perceptual and that which is conceptual. *All* cognitive experience occurs within contexts which are characterized, first, by the distinction between the formal and the nonformal elements belonging to them, and second, by the virtual impossibility of locating the same distinction between the same elements anywhere else but within the unique context in which it was first discovered, that is, of saying that any cognitive elements are always formal or always nonformal.

The idea of an epistemological continuum may perhaps be clarified by considering some of the more obvious objections to it that are bound to be made. One such objection could emerge from Price's distinction between cognitive elements which signify and cognitive elements which are signified. Of sign-cognition Price says: "it is at once thought and perception" because "ideas or concepts are somehow blended with immediate experience."[13] But he apparently finds these two features hard to reconcile, due basically, no doubt, to his belief that there has to be a level of cognition more primitive than sign-cognition—and this for reasons rooted in the can't-get-started argument that has already been mentioned.[14] This more primitive level of cognition would be, presumably, either all perception and no thought, or else mostly perception with just a smattering of thought. It would consist in the recognition of signs without using other signs; and because of the qualitative gap between this kind of recognition and the kind which does use other signs, the idea of an epistemological continuum would be a distortion of the nature of cognition.

The reply to the objection is that the sign-significate relation is a contextual one which can be isolated from the situation within which it rises only at the risk of profound distortion. Within any cognitive situation to which the term "signification" can be appropriately applied, a distinction can be said to exist between what is signified and the sign which signifies it; if no such distinction exists, application of the term "signification" is inappropriate. However, the sign of one situation is the significate of another. The sign-significate relation is a reciprocal one, and to ignore this reciprocal aspect can lead to such time-wasting puzzles as whether the egg signifies the chicken or the other way round.[15] Taken as an internal affair, there is a more primitive and a less primitive level of cognition in every cognitive situation. But the corresponding external assertion is false. There is no particular distinction of more primitive and less primitive

---

[13] Price, *Thinking and Experience* (London: Hutchinson's University Library, 1953), p. 90.

[14] Above, pp. 135–36.

[15] Price does remark that the sign relation is often reversible (*Thinking and Experience*, pp. 213–14). That he is aware of the contextual nature of signification is evidenced by his characterization of "being a sign of" as a three-term relation (*ibid.*, p. 92).

which characterizes every context of cognition, and there is no cognitive element which is most primitive in every situation within which it appears.

By taking a contextual viewpoint, incidentally, a generalized counterargument may be found for the can't-get-started argument. The germ of this counterargument is contained in remarks I have already made about the problem of circularity, which involves a special case of the can't-get-started argument, for the latter has both a linear and a circular form. Getting started may be a problem either because every alleged self-starter turns out to require an as-yet-undiscovered starting device of its own, in which case we are faced with an infinite regress, or because no member of an allegedly self-contained chain of two or more mechanisms is, when put to the test, a self-starter, in which case we are faced with a vicious circle. In either case the addict of the can't-get-started argument is driven to assume or declare a self-starter, with consequences which any self-respecting empiricist must find appalling. But just as circularity may be controlled by confining any instance of it within a relatively limited context, the more general problem of getting started may be handled by realizing that, while it is true that starting points are required in order to get processes under way, such starting points need not perform their function outside a relatively limited context. The self-starter of one context may be impotent within the next. Russell's argument about inferential and noninferential knowledge is adequate when considered as an internal matter only; within any cognitive context appropriately describable as inferential, something must be known without inference. But the noninferential character of this knowledge is entirely relative to context. Self-starters vary from one context to another, and what is inferred in one context must be assumed in another. No knowledge is significantly characterized as absolutely noninferential. Similarly with the necessity Russell sees for a lowest-type language: because a language is of lowest type in a linguistic analysis, there is no reason to suppose that it will possess that status in every other context of analysis. After all, what can't get started without a lowest-type language is not language but analysis, so that the question of which language is lowest is one relative to the purposes and specifications of the analysis.

But it may be wondered, despite all this dialectic, how in fact human cognitive experience does get started. It seems reasonable to assume that there is some rock-bottom experience that gets perception under way and could, to that extent, be called a general cognitive self-starter. Again, however, recognition of the need for starting points leads to the unwarranted demand for an absolute starting point. The fact seems to be that perception gets started in all sorts of ways, utilizing all sorts and combinations of sensory and extrasensory equipment; what equipment is utilized in any particular perceptual situation depends on the situation. Most likely, the kind and amount of equipment brought into play at these primitive levels of cognition is determined by what is needed by the perceiver in order to make sense of the situation, but "sense" is just vague enough and personal enough to keep this from being a very helpful way of putting things. More helpful, though still on the side of generalities, is the suggestion in a recent paper in psychology[16] of a hierarchy of perceptual thresholds which are stratified both quantitatively and qualitatively, which form sequences determined on each occasion of employment by the characteristics of the perceptual situation, and which trip off various response tendencies on the part of the perceiver. Such a concept could not happen along at a more propitious time, for it fits in admirably with the situational account of perception suggested above, indicating a strategy for pinning down some of the variables which underlie the starting points of perceptual situations, and tending to endow the whole approach with psychological respectability.

Another possible objection to the proposition that there is an epistemological continuum is the following. While some, and in fact most, cognitive situations may be said to be either erroneous

[16] Bruner and Postman, "Perception, Cognition, and Behavior," *Journal of Personality*, XVIII (1949–50), 26–27, reprinted in Bruner and Krech (eds.), *op. cit.*, p. 27.

or veridical, the disjunction cannot be significantly attributed to other cognitive situations; there may be a continuum of the former kind of situations, but the latter are in a class by themselves.

Part of the force of the sense-datum and similar theories of perception has always been that they enable one to talk about a sense of perception, usually called sensation, which cannot be erroneous. Whether the perceptual situation is described as veridical, illusory, or hallucinatory, whether the situation is a dream or an afterimage, we perceive, in this sense of "perceive," just what we seem to perceive. Now, if this indubitable sense of perception is considered, the perceptual situation is more "epistemologically" primitive than those considered previously, and it is exempt from the possibility of error simply because the true-false disjunction doesn't fit.

However, though there is a sense in which perception is immune from doubt, this argument misconstrues its significance. A kind of indubitable element in cognition has already been discussed and found to be present in every cognitive situation, the question of which elements are indubitable being a matter relative to the situation. And since there is a sense in which every cognitive situation is indubitable, the present objection does not impugn the idea of an epistemological continuum which includes every type and level of cognitive experience.

It might be said, though, that the point of the objection has not been grasped: it is not that every perceptual situation contains indubitable elements but that some perceptual situations contain nothing else. Within every situation, it might be said, there is a sub-situation, and this sub-situation contains just those elements of the larger situation that are indubitable. But this objection must face again all the difficulties, found in the last chapter to be insuperable, surrounding any attempt to delineate a kind of object—a sense datum, for instance—that is epistemologically prior to the object of perception in the larger sense. Failing this or any other attempt to show that the sub-situations mentioned really do play a role in human perception, the objection from indubitability must be overruled.

Another objection that may be brought against the idea of an epistemological continuum is more serious than those already looked at. This is the objection that as we travel "up" the epistemological scale we come to a sharp and radical gulf; because of this gulf, which is marked by the distinction between sign-thinking and symbol-thinking, the *scale* is not a *continuum*. This is by no means an *ad hoc* argument against the view that cognitive experience is continuous, for the distinction that a number of epistemologists, of whom Price will be taken to be representative, draw in terms of the expressions "sign-thinking" and "symbol-thinking" is the more or less common-sense one ordinarily drawn between perceptual and conceptual experience. The connection between the two distinctions may be seen in terms of a third—between thinking that is "tied" to, and thinking that is "free" of, sensation and the environment. The very nature of sign cognition ties it to sensations, because it consists at least partly in the perception of signs, which are sensory elements in the perceptual situation. But of course not all thinking is tied; a large part of our intellectual life is abstract and independent of our environment, and the difference between this and the other kind of thinking, according to the present objection, is enough to ruin the conception of a continuum that would include both.

There can be little doubt that a difference exists between the two kinds of thinking in question. And the difference is sharpened by such considerations as that symbols are easily producible and controllable by cognitive beings who employ them, whereas signs are not; that signification requires the presence both of sign and of significate, whereas only the symbol need be present in cases of symbolization; and that the sign relation may be reversible, whereas the symbol relation may not.[17] The only doubt that can be raised is about the significance to be attached to these considerations and to the difference they sharpen. In particular, it may be wondered which is more significant, and in what contexts: the differences between the two kinds of thinking or the similarities implied by the idea of an epistemological continuum.

According to Price, sign cognition is "the characteristic mode

[17] See Price, *Thinking and Experience*, pp. 212–14, 230–33.

of mental operation at a level of mental development where cognition and action are not yet sharply differentiated";[18] consideration of this remark will raise some interesting issues. What may be doubted is whether cognition and action are sharply differentiated in symbol cognition, as Price seems to think, or whether the apparent differentiation is due simply to failure to conceive action at this level with the same degree of subtlety that has gone into the conception of cognition at this level. The question, in other words, is whether there is not a "higher" level of action that is no more sharply differentiated from symbol cognition than Price's "lower" level of action is differentiated from sign cognition. If there is such a higher level of action, then of course the lower-level action that Price tells us is sharply differentiated from symbol cognition is not relevant to symbol cognition to begin with, and to maintain that the two are sharply differentiated is as significant as to maintain that there is a sharp difference between male squirrels and female zebras. I would not have raised the question if I did not think that there is, in fact, such a higher-level action, and I think it is quite obvious once it has been pointed out.

It can hardly be doubted that human beings expend a certain amount of energy in thinking, regardless of how quiescent their bodies may be—at any rate I will vouch that several hours of studying philosophy fatigues me, and moreover fatigues me at least partly in a way indistinguishable from what is customarily called physical fatigue. The obvious explanation is that I have been acting in some way, or doing something in a physical sense of "doing" that has been traditionally distinguished from "knowing." The relation of this doing or acting to the doing or acting that Price says is not differentiated sharply from sign cognition may perhaps be clarified by an analogy, though this particular analogy must be handled with care for fear that it may be overextended, or taken to be more than an analogy. The analogy is the relation between steam engines and calculating machines. Steam engines operate at a high level of energy, and their function is to deliver power; calculating machines operate at a low level of

18 *Ibid.*, p. 91.

energy, and their function is to deliver information.[19] But though the important consideration about a calculating machine is the information it yields and not the power it yields, nevertheless it consumes energy and becomes fatigued, and can thus be said to "act" just as much as a steam engine "acts," though in a more subtle and delicate—a higher-level—fashion.

What this adds up to is that thinking, like perceiving, is a kind of doing, and therefore it is not sufficient to try to distinguish between two kinds of cognition on the basis of whether one of them is or is not sharply differentiated from action. Nor can it be maintained that a sufficient basis for the distinction between two kinds of cognition has been provided here by the differentiation between two kinds of action, low-echelon and high-echelon action. The present differentiation is not between two kinds of action, because the present view of the action involved in cognition is the same as the present view of cognition—that there is a continuum, that "perception" and "conception," which are customarily taken to be kinds of cognition, are stages along this continuum, and that the most significant differences between them and between the levels of action they involve are differences of degree.

It could conceivably be argued that a crucial distinction has been ignored, namely, that while sign cognition is *for the sake of* the low-echelon action from which it is not differentiated, symbol cognition is not for the sake of the high-echelon action from which, according to the present account, it is not differentiated. The argument, however, would necessitate discussion of a third factor—motivation—which is even more speculative than the first two. Rather than worry about low-level and high-level motives, and about relations among low-level motives, high-level motives, action, and cognition, it seems more profitable to continue to ignore the alleged distinction.

There are, of course, differences of other kinds among stages of the epistemological continuum, particularly between situations that would ordinarily be called perceptual and those that

[19] See Norbert Wiener, *Cybernetics* (New York: John Wiley & Sons, 1948), pp. 50, 53–54.

would be called conceptual. Perhaps the most important of these differences is one mentioned by Price, that one kind of situation, the perceptual, seems to be tied much more closely to sensation than the other. It would be a great mistake to deny this difference, but there are one or two considerations about it that should be noticed. One is that, in the light of discussions in this and the previous chapters, the expression "tied to sensation" is not as free from vagueness as could be desired. Moreover, the reason the kind of cognition Price is talking about is "tied" to "sensation" is that it is sign cognition, and sign cognition involves the sign-significate relation that I suggested is a contextual matter which cannot be pinned down in general but only within some specific perceptual situation.

Finally, what Price has called symbol-thinking, though perhaps not "tied" in the same way sign-thinking is tied, nevertheless must be tied in some respect or there would be nothing to differentiate it from daydreaming or fantasy-thinking. Both sign-thinking and symbol-thinking are *responsible*, in a way that daydreaming and fantasy-thinking are not, and it may be supposed that there is some respect in which the former two are "tied" to their responsibilities. It is tempting to conceive this tie in terms of the cognitive situation within which both sign cognition and symbol cognition function. Responsible thinking, it could be said, must be carried on within well-delineated contexts which provide "limits of relevancy, fixed points of reference, something from which either thought or investigation can start and to which it can return."[20] When thinking is not firmly contextual, there is nothing to prevent it from shirking its responsibilities either by degenerating into the same state of intellectual turpitude that fantasy and daydreams enjoy or by rocketing into that "rarefied air where thought finds no obstacles to its flight, but, alas, no support."[21] If there is anything to be said for this suggestion about contexts and cognitive responsibilities, it would seem to indicate that, even apart from the present interest in

[20] W. D. Oliver, *Theory of Order* (Yellow Springs, Ohio: Antioch Press, 1951), p. 335.

[21] Morris R. Cohen, *Reason and Nature* (2d ed.; Glencoe, Ill.: Free Press, 1953), p. 146.

similarities between the two kinds of thinking, it is at least as important that sign-thinking and symbol-thinking both require well-defined cognitive situations within which to operate as it is that sign-thinking is tied more closely than symbol-thinking to those experiences involving common and ordinary, or low-echelon, biological actions.

4. THINKING AND ITS CONTEXTS

Because there is a continuity of cognitive activities, from the most primitive to the least primitive, whatever is said about any level of cognitive development has significance also for every other level. Since the remainder of the present work will deal largely with such highly developed forms of cognition as languages—natural and artificial—scientific theories, and logical and mathematical systems, it will be supposed that what is said about these media for thought will be not without significance for such other cognitive activities as image-thinking and perception, and that what has already been said about the latter is equally applicable to the former. For example, it will be maintained that precise thinking requires a precise context, and that the most precise kind of thinking requires the most precise kind of context, which is a logical or mathematical context—but behind this remark lie the beliefs that every kind of cognitive endeavor requires some kind of context, and that the features that make precise contexts precise are present also, though in varied degree, in all contexts.

A convenient device for dealing with cognitive contexts in this way is to give a behavioral twist to the considerations which seem to regulate our thinking. Such a consideration is the principle of identity, usually considered to be the central principle of logic. This is the principle, roughly, that every element in an argument should be held invariant and should have a fixed meaning throughout the course of the argument.[22] It is so central a principle that one might choose to ignore it on the ground that to call it a principle is to suggest that it could conceivably be

[22] This is a semantic statement of the principle, and it operates regardless of whether a particular formal system contains the theorem "x = x."

abandoned in favor of other principles, which is incredible. At any rate, whether identity operates according to a principle or not, it is so central to logic that it took a genius of the highest order to notice it. It is central not only to logic, however, but to all thinking; it has been taken to be not only a principle of logic but a principle of thought, the principle that meanings and symbols are or should be invariant within any context of thought. The question now is whether it is possible to formulate it not only as a principle of thought but as a principle of behavior. If a behavioral interpretation of the identity principle were allowed, thinking could be woven even more integrally into the fabric of human activity by means of a contextual account of both. Let me elaborate.

"Identifying" in a behavioral context need not mean "designating" or "naming" but only "distinguishing," "bringing into focus," or "attributing constancy to"—whatever the operation is that will enable us to rely absolutely on the invariance of an element throughout a situation. With this interpretation of the concept of identity the principle of identity may be extended still further in its application.

For one thing, the idea of contextual elements having absolute reliability suggests the indubitable elements in the perceptual situation that were described as formal in the sense of functionally absolute, and this in turn suggests that the principle of identity filters down at least to the perceptual levels of human experience. But since the minimal experience that even Price is able to discern is the experience of recognition, and since in order for recognition to occur its object must be (or must have been) identified, there is no discernible experience whatever which is so primitive that identification is not an element in it.

The behavioral nature of perceptual situations, as of the identificational activity that characterizes them, is the basis of a phenomenon that was mentioned earlier and that may be brought up now by way of illustration: that maximum visual differentiation occurs in foveal perception, and that as the retinal image becomes more peripheral it becomes more blurred. The corollary of this phenomenon is that at the periphery the retina is sensitive to motion, and a peripheral stimulation, if insistent enough to be noticed, is transformed into a foveal one so that the stimulus or some concomitant of it can be pinned down and brought into focus, which is to say, identified. This transformation of a peripheral stimulus into a foveal stimulus, it will be noticed, involves turning the eyes, the head, and occasionally the entire body; by anyone's criterion, therefore, it is behavior, behavior at a subconscious and hence relatively low cognitive level.

The principle of identity can thus be said, subject to further clarification, to govern human behavior at both extremes of the epistemological continuum, and it may be seen at work also in intermediate stages. In fact, it is with respect to contexts—which are present at all stages of the epistemological continuum—that the behavioral "principle" of identity operates. To ascribe identity is to inaugurate a context within which items of experience may be pinned down and preserved against change.

Strictly speaking, though, the "principle" of identity, at lower levels of behavior, is not a principle in the prescriptive sense at all, but rather a description of how behavior actually and naturally occurs; not until identification is a conscious process which can go wrong or be ignored—as when directed toward symbols—is a principle properly to be spoken of. At the symbol-thinking level, the principle of identity—still a behavioral principle, as well as a principle of thinking—governs the high-echelon kind of behavior that is engaged in whenever thinking is engaged in. At the symbol-thinking level, moreover, the identification process finds less resistance than at lower levels of cognition, and this is one of the considerations that makes it possible to talk about degrees of cognition along the epistemological continuum as being relatively low toward the "tied" or "sensory" end and relatively high toward the "free" or "conceptual" end.

The reason the identification process finds less resistance at the symbol-thinking level is that we create our symbols ourselves; because we create them we may control them, and because we may control them we may insure their exemption from the influence of time. Anything exempt from the influence of time offers no resistance to the activity of identifying, for exemption from the influence of time is exemption from change, and change is the biggest obstacle to identification.[23] It may be noted, though, that because we have created our symbols they are dependent on us for their stability, so that for the same reason that we may control them they are more apt to go out of control.

Exemption from change is not absolute, however; since there are degrees of exemption, it is possible to talk about different degrees of symbol-thinking. Besides words and complexes of words —the obvious symbols—the term, according to Price, covers pictorial symbols, gestures, mental images, and such nonverbal behavior as ritual actions,[24] and these different sorts of symbols may be kept invariant to different degrees. Perhaps the most important difference among kinds of symbols is the difference between those that are subjective or "in the mind," and others, such as verbal and pictorial symbols, that are outside the mind and that may be communicated and shared. Between these two kinds of symbols is a corresponding difference in the degrees of control we are able to exercise over them, in the degrees of their invariance, in the ease of ascribing identity to them, and in the difficulty of making the identity, once ascribed, stick. Mental or subjective symbols are subject to our own intellectual frailty. We have poor memories and vastly differing powers of conception, and to view symbol-thinking entirely in terms of symbols entertained in the mind would leave the most important features of our intellectual life a mystery. On any theory of thinking, therefore, symbols that are communicable and sharable—intersubjective symbols—must be invoked, even if only as guides to subjective or wholly mental symbols, in order to explain how we keep our cognitive objects as free from variance as we do. It is with recognition of intersubjective symbols that the importance of the *social* nature of symbol-thinking emerges. But even among intersubjective symbols there are differences, both with respect to invariance and with respect to another factor in symbol-thinking

[23] This I take to state a superficial characteristic of everyday experience. The depth of the reader's interpretation may be determined by his metaphysics.

[24] *Thinking and Experience*, pp. 145–46, 265 ff.

that has not yet been mentioned: ease of manipulation. Thus, while tribal rituals doubtless maintain an extraordinary degree of invariance over the centuries, thinking by means of them would be slow and expensive, and even hieroglyphics have yielded to less unwieldy symbols.

Invariance and ease of manipulation, as criteria for the extent to which the principle of identity may be implemented and conceptualization successfully carried on, seem to point to verbal or linguistic symbols as the means by which symbol-thinking is best engaged in. There is an important consideration in this connection that must not be overlooked, however: it is not enough merely to keep symbols invariant; the necessity for invariance applies also to what they symbolize. If what is symbolized changes, then the symbol, even though it remains invariant—in fact, because it remains invariant—is not performing its cognitive role as effectively as before. What is important is the symbolic relation, not the symbol itself. Even when symbol-thinking is narrowed down to verbal- or linguistic-thinking, therefore, there are degrees of exemption from change or—looking in the other direction—of recalcitrance to identification, and this question of degree is a function of how well we are able to control not simply symbols but symbolic relations. Words are notorious for the elusiveness of their meanings; ordinary spoken language is permeated through and through with slang and idiom, and the measure of our control over ordinary written language is reflected in the accuracy of the reports on usage to be found in the best dictionaries and grammars.

But again, we are best able to control what we ourselves have created, though we do not always make the most of the ability, and if we are able to create both symbol and what is symbolized, or if we are able to lay down rules to which the symbolic relations we use must conform, we can keep those relations invariant. Not only is symbol-thinking most successful, then, when carried on linguistically, but it is more successful when the languages employed are constructed by us, that is, are artificial, than when natural or ordinary languages are used. When symbol-thinking is done by means of artificial languages, we can get our cognitive situation well enough in hand so that our capacity for identification is at its height.

But there is yet one step to be taken, for all this becomes transparent within a formal logical system. It was in regard to logic that the principle of identity was originally discovered and formulated. The principle makes explicit the timelessness or cotemporaneity of the elements within a formal system, features heightened and elaborated by the laws of noncontradiction and of excluded middle. Logic demands its objects to be static, requiring, for example, the "tenselessness of quantification over temporal entities."[25]

By developing the concept of the epistemological continuum—along with its sub-concepts of identity, the cognitive situation, and the formal-nonformal distinction—to what is, in more than one way, its logical conclusion, I seem to have made it incredible, just as Hume, according to Russell, made the empirical philosophy of Locke and Berkeley incredible. For, from the point of view of cognitive contexts and identification, the acme of human thinking, the most fully developed stage along the epistemological continuum, is logic. And if asked what this pinnacle of cognitive invariance is about, one must answer: horseshoes, wedges, strokes, and dots, for the concern of logic is "to establish the precise meaning of such terms and to lay down the most general laws in which these terms are involved."[26] The truth is that, at the level of logic, cognition has become so self-conscious as to be ingrown.

Fortunately, however, there is no need to withdraw either the concepts or the analyses that made them seem desirable. Simply because the extremes of a continuum are inadequate to account

[25] Quine, "Mr. Strawson on Logical Theory," *Mind*, LXII (1953), 442.

[26] Alfred Tarski, *Introduction to Logic and to the Methodology of Deductive Sciences*, trans. Olaf Helmer (2d ed.; New York: Oxford University Press, 1951), p. 18. The quotation is not entirely accurate in this context, because the terms Tarski mentions are "not," "and," "or," "is," "every," and "some"; but as he points out in subsequent pages, these terms, as they emerge from the truth tables, differ in meaning from their ordinary usage, so that I am not distorting his meaning to speak of "wedges" instead of "or."

for what is everyday and ordinary, the explanatory value of the continuum need not be impugned. I am quite able, for example, to tolerate the concept of a moral continuum running from murderers and thieves at one end to saints at the other, without objecting that saintliness is possible only in a moral vacuum. Moreover, I am perfectly willing to agree that the saintly end is the higher end or the most fully developed stage of this kind of morality, even though I may have reservations about the value of saintliness as a norm and may even wonder whether morality, too, cannot become so self-conscious as to be ingrown. While aware, therefore, that the denotative significance of both extremes of the epistemological continuum is negligible if not null, and that human experience, including cognitive experience, is just as inexplicable in terms of formal logic as it is in terms of the other extreme—the animal mind which is, in Price's unsubstantiated view, "the Pragmatist's paradise"[27]—I see no reason for retracting anything said above about the epistemological continuum. There will be occasion in the next part to discuss the relations among various stages along the epistemological continuum, including the relation of linguistic experience to other kinds of experience. What is of concern here is that there is such a continuum.

All cognitive experience occurs within contexts or situations. These contexts are characterized by the "timelessness," or preservation from change, of the elements which may be abstracted from them. We create such contexts within which to carry on our cognitive activities by means of the process of identification, which has been called a principle of logic and a principle of thought, and now is being called a principle of behavior. This principle allows us to locate and familiarize ourselves with what become experiential constants. In some situations the operation of the identification process is at a subconscious level; these situations are "low-echelon" cognitive experiences. In other situations the process may operate at a subconscious level or it may be consciously implemented—more likely, it works both ways; these situations are usually thought to be experiences of sign-thinking.

[27] *Thinking and Experience*, p. 43.

Finally, the ascription of identity may be an entirely conscious operation according to an explicit principle of identity; such situations may be taken to be instances of symbol-thinking. Identity may be ascribed, in symbol-thinking, with varying degrees of completeness, which is to say that the principle may be more or less successful. It is most successful when the cognitive situation, or epistemological present, is a logical system; between sign-cognitive contexts and logical systems are different kinds of symbol-cognitive situations—image-thinking, gesture-thinking, picture-thinking and word- or language-thinking—which permit different degrees of success in ascribing identity.

There are, needless to say, vast differences among the cognitive experiences mentioned, and from certain points of view it is distorting the nature of human knowledge to place all these experiences within a single continuum and to call the differences differences of degree. From the present point of view, however, the experiences do belong within a continuum, the differences are differences of degree, and much bad epistemology has resulted from ignoring this facet of human knowledge. The biological, subconscious sort of action that is found at the lower end of the continuum is not missing from the upper end; it only appears to be missing when the concept of action is not refined in proportion to the refinement that went into the concept of thinking. "Of that which receives precise formulation in mathematical logic," moreover, "an important part is already vaguely present as a basic ingredient of daily discourse."[28] I pointed out in chapter i that logical words cannot be distinguished clearly from nonlogical words, and Price has shown that sign cognition has a logic not significantly different from formal logic. All cognitive experience is characterized by the presence of both formal and nonformal elements, though cognitive situations differ vastly with respect to which elements are formal or nonformal and where to draw the line between them.

One general statement that can be made is that the distinction is present in a behavioral sense at all levels of the epistemological

[28] Quine, *Mathematical Logic* (Cambridge, Mass.: Harvard University Press, 1951), p. v.

continuum. But, as we get into the realm of symbol-thinking, and, within this realm, to what might be called "propositional-thinking" (which certainly occurs on the linguistic level, whatever view be taken toward prelinguistic forms of cognition), the formal-nonformal distinction manifests itself also in a second way. This second way may be stated in terms of the relationship between symbols and what they symbolize. It emerges as soon as experience turns in upon itself, so to speak, as soon as one experience refers to another which is not an element in the first except symbolically. This second version of the formal-nonformal distinction is the analytic-synthetic distinction, for it is the distinction between propositional symbols whose truth depends on the experiences they symbolize and propositional symbols which are true independently of any experiences. If the question about formal and nonformal cognitive elements of either sort is an internal question about an individual situation, there is no trouble in answering it in specific detail, but as an external question a very general statement of the functional characteristics of the distinction is about all that can be asserted. How formal logic can be utilized philosophically without losing sight of its behavioral antecedents, and how behavioral characteristics of human knowledge can be recognized without losing the benefit of the most powerful intellectual instrument we possess, remain to be seen.

EMPIRICISM
AND
PRAGMATIC
RECONSTRUCTION

PART III

EMPIRICISM

AND

PRAGMATIC

RECONSTRUCTION

CHAPTER V

The Theory of Empirical
Significance

1. STATEMENTS, CONTEXTS, AND TOTALITIES

THE EARLY EMPIRICISTS, in wanting to clear away the deadwood of rationalist philosophies and so separate the significant from the nonsignificant, took human experience as their touchstone. They began by inquiring into the nature of experience, and they went on to promote a way of philosophizing which would be continuous with experience as their inquiries portrayed it. Good philosophy contains no ideas unless either analytic or empirically significant; an empirically significant idea is one that can be traced back to experience, and its empirical meaning is the experiences to which it can be traced back. No great effort is needed to recognize why a theory of meaning has always been a primary concern of empiricists.

Because it is concerned with significance, and because it takes human experience to be a touchstone for significance, the present account is an empiricist account. Where it differs from most other empiricist accounts is in its understanding of the nature of the experience to be taken as a touchstone and in the resulting changes in the way of philosophizing governed by that experience. In a way, philosophy in the present account becomes even more continuous with experience than the early empiricists thought it could be. This happens because it is not just in philosophic experience that significance is a problem and is something to be worked for but in all human experience, including the experience empiricism looks to as its touchstone; moreover, the quest for significance takes the same form both in relatively primitive or "low echelon" experiences, where it happens naturally, and in such "high echelon" experiences as philosophizing, where it must be self-consciously implemented and continually supervised. The form of this ubiquitous quest for significance is contextual, and contextualism, as it has emerged from the foregoing inquiry into perception and cognitive experience in general, provides a clue to the theory of empirical significance that it would be folly to pass up.

As an approach toward a possible contextualist theory of meaning, it is relevant to consider what linguistic elements are to be taken as the units of empirical significance. A certain parallelism has already been remarked between this matter of units of significance and the matter of context.[1] I referred to Quine's objections to the "term-by-term critique" imposed by the empiricist principle as first suggested by the British empiricists, a critique ameliorated by Russell's idea of definitions in use and by the verification theory of meaning, a theory about statements rather than terms. I said also that Quine finds even the "statement theory of meaning" too restrictive and wants to expand the unit of empirical significance to "the whole of science." That the unit of empirical significance should be greater than the statement is an idea that ought not be alarming. For in view of the contextual nature of human cognition, it is natural to suppose that the significance of any statement is a function not merely of its constituent elements and the way they are put together but also of the context within which the statement appears. And if this is the case, then a statement may be significant in some contexts and not in others, and its significance may change from context to context, so that it is more accurate to call the context the unit of significance than the statement.

Quine, however, espouses not simply a contextualist theory but, in view of his remark about "the whole of science," a much stronger theory which may be called the monolithic theory of significance. When this stronger theory is held, the parallel to the contextualist view of perceiving and thinking no longer holds. The cognitive situation in human experience obviously need come nowhere near comprising the whole of science, or even the whole of what the cognizing part of the situation knows

[1] See above, pp. 65–67.

about science. All that it need comprise is the bare minimum required by the cognizing subject in order to make sense of his world at a particular time and place for a particular purpose.

A closer look at the monolithic theory of significance as developed by Quine will be helpful. The theory leads him to what he takes to be the lack of immunity of any single statement in the entire body of knowledge to revision or rejection and, by the same token, to the possibility of holding fast to any single statement, come what may. "On the one hand we have language, as an infinite totality of said or appropriately sayable phrases and sentences. On the other hand we have our sense experience, which, by a process of psychological association or conditioned response, is keyed in with the linguistic material at numerous and varied places. The linguistic material is an interlocked system which is tied here and there to experience; it is not a society of separately established terms and statements, each with its separate empirical definition."[2] In an even more metaphoric vein Quine calls this interlocked linguistic system which is tied here and there to experience a "man-made fabric which impinges on experience only along the edges," or again, a "field of force whose boundary conditions are experience."[3] The point of the metaphors is the solidity of human knowledge as linguistically expressed; the differences among single statements so far as empirical significance or lack of it is concerned are differences of degree. Statements referring explicitly to sensory experience are at the periphery of the body of knowledge and tie it here and there to experience. Statements of ontology and statements expressing laws of logic are near the center. Scientific statements of varying degrees of generality range in between. And the confidence we have in any particular statement depends not only on how well it ties in with our experience, if indeed it can be said to tie in, taken by itself, at all, but also on its status within the

[2] W. V. Quine, "On Mental Entities," *Proceedings of the American Academy of Arts and Sciences*, LXXX (1951–54), 198. See Albert Hofstadter, "The Myth of the Whole: A Consideration of Quine's View of Knowledge," *Journal of Philosophy*, LI (1954), 397–417.

[3] Quine, "Two Dogmas of Empiricism," *From a Logical Point of View* (Cambridge, Mass.: Harvard University Press, 1953), p. 42.

total linguistic system. Our confidence may be controlled by something like what Reichenbach calls inductive consistency, or what Lewis calls congruence.[4] Duhem said in 1906, and Carnap reiterated thirty years later, that no scientific hypothesis can be tested alone; if experimental evidence is sufficient to require adjustments, the adjustments may occur anywhere within the system and may in turn have a reciprocal effect on the experimental evidence.[5] Now Quine would say the same of every statement whatever within the total system of knowledge.

In so far as Quine views empirical significance as attaching to linguistic units greater than statements, the analysis of analyticity in Part I of the present book and of cognitive experience in Part II tends to corroborate his view. And in so far as he believes no statement to be immune to revision, the present findings about the analytic-synthetic distinction are entirely consistent with his belief. But in so far as he goes beyond a contextualist theory to a monolithic theory of significance, Quine receives no support from the foregoing analysis. Nor do considerations of scientific methodology sanction the monolithic theory. While it is correct to say that a scientific hypothesis cannot be experimentally verified in isolation, it does not follow that the entirety of scientific knowledge must be conjoined with it. In relation to any given hypothesis the statements of science have varying degrees of relevance. Science is comprised of different fields, each field contains branches, and the branches in turn consist in what may be called theoretic systems. Some theoretic systems, for example the laws of optics, are relevant to a large number of hypotheses in all fields; others, such as the laws of thermodynamics, are less frequently relevant; and such others as the laws of phylogenetics

4 Hans Reichenbach, "Are Phenomenal Reports Absolutely Certain?" *Philosophical Review*, LXI (1952), 155; C. I. Lewis, *An Analysis of Knowledge and Valuation* (2d printing; La Salle, Ill.: Open Court Publishing Co., 1950), pp. 338 ff.

5 Pierre Duhem, *La théorie physique: son objet et sa structure* (Paris: Chevalier & Rivière, 1906), pp. 347 ff.; Rudolf Carnap, *The Logical Syntax of Language*, trans. A. Smeaton (London: Routledge & Kegan Paul, 1937), p. 318.

have so little relevance outside their immediate area that any effort to include them in most formulations is a wasted one.

Or at least the belief that every statement of science is relevant to every other statement is as much a metaphysical article of faith as the belief that every statement has its own experiential counterpart. The grain of truth in the monolithic theory is its denial of what may be called "absolute irrelevance": any statement whatever may be held relevant to a given statement. But any statement may also be held irrelevant to a given statement, and scientific practice consists, in part, in the determination of which statements are and which are not to be held relevant to the matters under inquiry. In other words, while it is true that statements about the external world do not "face the tribunal of sense experience" individually, it is not true that they do so "as a corporate body." Rather, selected groups of statements stand trial; whether a statement belongs with a certain group as co-defendant depends on whether it is relevant and, if so, how relevant; the determination of relevance is a matter to be decided on the basis of the individual circumstances. The groups of statements are what I am calling contexts, and the consideration I have just mentioned is one reason why I am arguing for a contextualist theory of significance as opposed both to a statement theory and to a monolithic theory.

A context, as a unit of significance, is more *limited* than the totality of statements, though not so limited as a single statement. By the same token, if the entire body of knowledge is to be accounted for contextually, there must be a *plurality* of significant units, since no limited context can account for all our knowledge.

The kind of context I am talking about now—scientific contexts as units submitted to experience for confirmation—is fairly advanced in the epistemological continuum. It is a linguistic kind of context, and its member contexts contain analytic and synthetic elements. When any individual context is submitted to experience for confirmation, it is vital to know which statements within the context are analytic and which synthetic, because any discrepancies between the context and the experiences to which it is submitted must be charged up to the synthetic statements rather than to the analytic. Such discrepancies cannot be attributed to the analytic statements because it is the analytic statements that enable us to understand the meanings involved in the context, and any attempt to compromise a context's analytic statements will result in chaos so far as our own understanding of the context is concerned.

However, reasons were advanced in Part I why the analytic-synthetic distinction is not the sort that can be pinned down once and for all. One cannot say where the distinction falls within a particular context unless one is familiar with the context or has actually examined it to see which statements are analytic and which synthetic. Nor can one generalize; because the analytic-synthetic distinction falls at a certain place in some specified context, there is no warrant for asserting that it will fall at the same place in other contexts.

The analytic-synthetic distinction, I suggested, is a special case of the formal-nonformal distinction, a special case which is confined to one part of the epistemological continuum. But a generalized formal-nonformal distinction occurs in all parts of that continuum; in fact it was the ubiquity of the formal-nonformal distinction that led me to speak of continuity in the first place. The more general distinction, moreover, has many of the same characteristics as the analytic-synthetic distinction, the interesting common characteristic at the moment being the impossibility of ascribing a particular separation between formal and nonformal to more than one experiential context. Nevertheless—and this is my reason for mentioning here the distinction between formal and nonformal—the difficulties we have in pinning down this distinction in experience do not seem to inhibit experience from happening. Experience happens; it happens contextually; every context within which it happens contains formal and nonformal elements; and the division between these two kinds of elements is indigenous to a particular context. We may or may not be able to make sense of experience after it happens; but if we do, it is because we have been able to delineate, within an experiential context, the distinction between formal and non-formal. And because the particular context of experience we are able to make sense of by means of any such distinction is limited, too limited to be able to account for more than a small fraction of our total experience, there must be a plurality of such distinctions.

The special case of the analytic-synthetic distinction differs from the more general formal-nonformal distinction in that contexts in which the special case occurs are at one remove from experience and do not exist unless we consciously create them. But linguistic contexts, like experiential ones, are essentially characterized by the formal-nonformal distinction's precise location within them. And the common impossibility of generalizing on any instance of the distinction affords a clue to the understanding of linguistic contexts, a clue that has already been seen in connection with experiential contexts and that points to a necessary condition for testing scientific contexts. The clue and the condition are twofold, for any individual scientific context must be relatively limited, and this relative limitation requires that there be a number of such contexts.

Thus, though there must be a sharp distinction between analytic and synthetic statements within any context that is to be confronted with its experiential consequences, and though such a sharp distinction is indigenous to the context, nevertheless empirical science is not inhibited thereby, any more than human experience is inhibited by the analogous circumstances in which it must occur. Human experience occurs in a vast number of ways, and what we can learn about any single experiential context will not take us far toward piercing to the heart of any other. What we can learn is that every such context contains functional absolutes, and any particular context is uniquely characterized by the precise nature of the functional absolutes it contains. Similarly, every scientific and linguistic context contains functional absolutes in the form of analytic truths, and the precise nature of its functional absolutes or of the distribution of analytic and synthetic truths within it essentially characterizes a linguistic context.

I said that when, in the testing of a scientific context, there is a discrepancy between the context and the experiences with which it is supposed to agree, it is the synthetic rather than the analytic members of the context which must be held accountable. This is true but misleading.

For one thing, it is not customary to think of testing a context; the scientist (whether in the field, the laboratory, or the study) has a hypothesis, which he may or may not attempt to formulate rigorously. If he does formulate it, chances are that it will be a single empirical statement which experiential test will be expected to confirm or disconfirm. However, this simple procedure, which dictates ordinary ways of thinking about science, occurs only in the earliest stages of a science or in the simplest facets of everyday experience. Hypotheses undergo all sorts of ramifications: they become complex, and their parts are chiseled ever more sharply; and the experiences which might confirm or disconfirm them in the straightforward manner of the naïve examples are more subtle than human sensitivities can record and more tangled than human intelligence can unravel. In the theoretic systems thus developed, some elements are on the experiential surface, so to speak, and more or less straightforwardly testable, and other elements are basic, are not so testable, and can be altered only at the cost of great disturbances throughout the system. Such theoretic systems, linguistically clothed, approach in essence if not in scope the monolithic system Quine describes so well, except that these systems can be exchanged for new ones, whereas all Quine can do is patch his up by redistributing its parts and their truth values. These systems are what I am calling contexts, and they are what I am describing as the units of empirical significance.

But I have said both that such contexts are the least units able to undergo empirical test and that negative test results, if any, are attributable to the synthetic rather than the analytic elements in the contexts. If this latter assertion is correct, it is not the context as a totality that is tested but only its synthetic constituents. This means either that the unit of empirical significance is something smaller than a context or else that the contexts involved differ from those already discussed in containing no analytic statements but only synthetic ones. I will try to clarify.

It may be remembered that, in the course of the examination of rational reconstruction, Quine's objections to the statement theory of significance were said to be obviated when statement and meaning are seen within an artificial language, and that under that condition the statement theory and the contextualist theory coincide. One of the reasons why an artificial language is so advantageous, in fact, is that its member statements may be considered in isolation without losing any of the significance they possess by belonging to a context. The reason for this, of course, is that the context is built right into each of its statements. The statements contain only logical terms, undefined predicates belonging to the context, and predicates defined in terms of the undefined predicates; these are put together to form statements according to methods prescribed in the context. The synthetic component of a linguistic framework may therefore be separated from the analytic component, and an individual member of the former put to experiential test in isolation from its contextual colleagues. In order to preserve consistency with previous remarks, though, it must be added that when such a synthetic statement is tested alone and explicitly, the whole context is undergoing an implicit test; the isolated statement carries the indorsement if not the banner of its context. But it is time to speak once more of internal and external affairs.

The contextualist theory of significance I am advocating has two sides, the two sides that every context has. Looked at externally, a linguistic context of the sort mentioned above is an indivisible chunk of significance. Either it is swallowed whole or else it is entirely rejected, regardless of how it makes its initial sensory appeal. From an internal viewpoint, though, the constituent elements may be isolated and discussed on their own merits. The seasoning may be tasted and judged or, if the palate is subtle enough, discounted and the genuine flavor sampled. My metaphor is interfering with my accuracy, however: when viewed externally, an empirical context may be likened to an organic whole, but the appropriate figure for the internal aspect of it is a machine. The point of the internal approach is to be able not only to disassemble the linguistic framework but also to get it back together.

As an internal matter, at any rate, individual empirical statements belonging to an artificial language are testable in that isolated and clearcut manner that empiricists used to talk about before the disenchantment. To every such statement "there is associated a unique range of possible sensory events such that the occurrence of any of them would add to the likelihood of truth of the statement, and . . . there is associated also another unique range of possible sensory events whose occurrence would detract from that likelihood."[6] But as an external matter it isn't so. Any statement's significance is attributable partly to experience and partly to meanings analytically determined. How this twofold significance is to be divided is impossible to say unless the statement is seen within a linguistic context over which we are able to exert enough control to keep its elements constant and to trace the line between its analytic and its synthetic statements. And the significance so determined does not belong to the statement as such; it belongs to the statement by virtue of its status within the context and only in so far as it belongs to the context.

2. A CONTEXTUALIST THEORY OF SIGNIFICANCE

The discovery that empirical significance resides within contexts and is not properly attributed to entities apart from contexts tells us where to look for empirical significance but not how to recognize it once we are there. The question now to be faced is, What characteristics are common and peculiar to empirically significant contexts?

In order to give an initial direction to the inquiry, we may recall that a possible answer to the question is in terms of the ideal language L_B and of the rendering of empiricism as the principle that "no statement in L_B contains any descriptive constant other than primitive descriptive constants in L_B and con-

6 Quine, "Two Dogmas of Empiricism," pp. 40–41.

stants definable in terms of these."[7] As an answer to the question about empirical significance, what this amounts to is the explication of *significant* as "well formed in L_B," of *analytic* as "analytic in L_B," of *experience* as "(designated by) primitive descriptive constants in L_B," and so on. But since the monolithic theory of significance has already been rejected, L_B can be at most one among many contextual repositories of empirical significance, and a description of significance relative to L_B is only the answer to an internal question. As the answer to an internal question, it is as unimpeachable as it is philosophically unimportant. The philosophically important questions about a contextualist theory of meaning are, of course, external questions.

External questions about empiricism, in so far as they require decisions rather than investigations, may be answered by proposals rather than assertions. From an external viewpoint, for example, Bergmann's ideal language rests on nothing more solid than a convention, or a series of conventions, so that when L_B is considered as the habitat of empirical significance, empirical significance must be considered a matter of convention. There is the convention of the distinction between analytic and synthetic statements in L_B, with its subsidiary conventions about the distinction between logical and nonlogical words (which, for Bergmann, is tantamount to a convention about truth tables) and about what pairs of expressions are synonymous. There is the convention about the designata of the primitive descriptive vocabulary of L_B—sense data, qualities of sense data, and external relations of contiguity among sense data—but it is enough to point out on the basis of chapters iii and iv that, as a proposed explication of *experience*, "(designated by) primitive descriptive constants in L_B" leaves something to be desired even apart from what the particular primitive descriptive vocabulary and designation rules of L_B are. Moreover, whatever other context might be chosen to exhibit empirical significance, if it is precise enough to serve the purpose, it will rest on conventions.

But this conventionalist position into which empiricism is transformed when empirical significance is confined within some

[7] Above, p. 64.

specific artificial context and when empiricism is done as rational reconstruction is certainly not the position that people who have traditionally called themselves empiricists have thought they were embracing; in fact it seems to be quite alien in spirit to that position. There is an arbitrariness, if not a capriciousness, about this conventionalism which is akin to the kind of philosophizing the early empiricists thought they were getting away from. I could, of course, forget that the conventions are conventions and stay within L_B; by wearing a not altogether unknown sort of philosophic blinders, I could come to believe that there is nothing external to the context. My philosophic demands would then be met by empiricism-in-L_B, and I could devote myself to propagation of the faith. But if I am impressed with the similarities between this position and certain types of avowedly rationalist philosophies, and if I have not lost my sympathy for the original intent of empiricism, then the vast difference between internal and external vantage points will weigh against such easy acceptance of rational reconstruction through the method of the ideal language.

However, if rational reconstruction did not require reconstructionists to put all their empirical significance in one language—if rational reconstruction could involve a *plurality* of languages—it would be more likely to have importance for empiricism, if only because its ability to accommodate the plurality of scientific contexts could no longer be ruled out. Discussion of a pluralistic approach to rational reconstruction will be postponed for a while in favor of some other contextualist considerations about meaning.

An assertion has "cognitive significance," according to Hempel, if it can be said to be either true or false, and a cognitively significant assertion has empirical significance if it is neither analytic nor contradictory.[8] Like "analytic" and "synthetic," the

[8] Carl G. Hempel, "Problems and Changes in the Empiricist Criterion of Meaning," *Revue internationale de philosophie*, XI (1950), 41–63; reprinted in *Semantics and the Philosophy of Language*, ed. Leonard Linsky (Urbana:

terms "true" and "false" can be sharply defined, or explicated,
only within a sharply delineated context. In fact, Tarski's semantic conception of truth has been noted as an example of the sort
of explication wanted for analyticity (though it may also be
noted that Tarski has been able to come closer to a *general*
semantic conception of truth than anyone has been able to do
for analyticity). But if "true" and "false" are sharply definable
only within a sharply delineated context, the same must be said,
on Hempel's view, for cognitive significance. This contextual
quality of cognitive significance might have been predicted even
without consideration of the true-false disjunction, however, for
if a statement is to have significance by itself at all, it must appear
within the kind of context demanded by the true-false disjunction—which is to say, the kind of context that will underwrite
the statement theory of significance.

So far there is clear sailing. But when the tack is altered from
cognitive to empirical significance, the argument seems to falter.
It would have been expected that once having characterized cognitive significance it would be enough merely to define the
species by adding "nonanalytic," following the example of Hempel. However, though this might suffice to characterize empirical
significance in an internal sense, it would suffice to characterize
it in an external sense only if the context within which the statement theory and the true-false dichotomy hold is also a context
whose synthetic statements happen to possess empirical significance; this can be determined only if empirical significance can
be characterized independently of cognitive significance and non-
analyticity. That a statement should be synthetic and either true
or false is no guarantee of its empirical significance, unless only
empirically significant statements are supposed capable of being
synthetically true or false. But this supposition, at this stage of
the inquiry, would serve only to shift the major difficulties of

University of Illinois Press, 1952), pp. 163–85. Present reference is to the
latter, p. 163. Also Hempel, "The Concept of Cognitive Significance: A Reconsideration," *Proceedings of the American Academy of Arts and Sciences*,
LXXX (1951–54), 61.

empiricism from questions of meaning to questions of truth. Therefore, while empirical significance is to be located only within contexts containing cognitive significance, not every such context can be said to contain empirical significance.

The problem of arbitrating among cognitively significant contexts in order to ferret out those that are also empirically significant might perhaps be postponed by settling for a concept of degree of empirical significance. Such a concept should make it possible to talk about significance independently of any particular context, and it ought to make it possible to talk this way whether the unit of significance is the term, the statement, or the context. A concept has already been mentioned—degree of independence of meaning—which might conceivably be interpreted as a concept of degree of empirical significance applicable to terms.[9] Carnap, it may be remembered, suggested that logical signs contribute less to the meanings of the statements within which they occur than do descriptive signs and therefore have a lower degree of independence of meaning. He was able to distinguish among logical signs with respect to independence of meaning, but he was unable to draw a hard and fast line between logical signs and descriptive signs. If "independence of meaning" is replaced by "empirical significance," Carnap's idea may be accepted in the present context and may be extended to the point of distinguishing among nonlogical words on the basis of degree of empirical significance. Thus, "feverish" has more empirical significance than "neurotic," and "neurotic" than "demonic," because "feverish" contributes more than "demonic" to the empirical significance of statements within which the respective words occur. Statements containing "demonic" necessitate more initial suspension or hesitation on the part of the reader or hearer than do statements containing "feverish": more must be understood about the former statements before the intended meaning of "demonic" can be known than need be understood about the latter statements before the meaning of "feverish" is known. We can, so to speak, meet "feverish" statements halfway, but not "demonic" statements.

[9] See above, p. 46.

Immediately, however, qualifications are necessary. For one thing, the whole matter is relative, as Carnap points out.[10] I myself am surer of "feverish" than of "demonic," and I am able to attribute more significance to a statement containing the former than to one containing the latter. But for a practitioner of witchcraft, "demonic" would doubtless have at least as much empirical significance as "feverish"; the difference would be measurable roughly by the number and variety of experiential tests he would require or be willing to accept as evidence for proper application of the former in proportion to the number and variety of tests in the latter instance. A second qualification is that one must guard against the mistaken ideas that the significance of a statement is the sum of the significances of its constituent words (an idea which ignores the importance of syntax) and that the significance of a word is *entirely* independent of the statements in which it occurs. Third, to talk about the significance of statements even as something that can be known by means of interpreted constituent terms and rules of syntax is to assume that statements, terms, and rules all belong to artificial linguistic contexts, because only within such contexts does the statement theory of significance prevail. But then it was wrong to think that "degree of significance" could be discussed in terms of any unit of significance, and I am driven right back to a contextualist position. There is still a fourth qualification: the expression "degree of significance" is not unequivocal. It can mean "relative frequency of occurrence within empirical contexts," in which case its use is confined to descriptions of existing artificial empirical language frameworks. Or it can mean "aptitude for use in constructing new empirical contexts," in which case its meaning transcends existing contexts. But in either case—and in fact in all of the qualifications just mentioned—the effect is to shift the emphasis back to the contexts with respect to which degree of significance is relevant. Thus the prospects of illuminating the concept of empirical significance by means of a noncontextualist concept of degree of significance seem to have faded away, and

[10] Carnap, *Meaning and Necessity* (Chicago: University of Chicago Press, 1947), p. 7.

with them the possibility of avoiding the problem of arbitration among contexts.

It was remarked at the end of the first chapter that external questions about contextual matters may be answered either by statements of degree or by proposals for conventions to establish new contexts or evaluate old ones, and that to the extent that either kind of answer is relied on the other is ruled out. Conventions about empirical contexts, however, must either presuppose the understanding of empirical significance which is the object of the present search, or else be marked by the kind of capriciousness that has been found not to accord with the intentions of empiricists. But statements of degree of significance, in the absence of independent knowledge about what makes contexts empirically significant, seem able to yield only statistical information about linguistic contexts people have constructed. This information has a certain value for talking philosophically about empirical significance, and there will be occasion to mention it again, but its applicability for present purposes is much too limited. The concept of degree of empirical significance is as inimical to the desire to draw a sharp boundary between meaningful and meaningless statements as the concept of empiricism-in-L_B is inimical to the desire to develop a philosophic position which is genuinely about the world we experience at the same time that it points the way to solutions of philosophic problems. Arbitration among contextual candidates for empirical significance seems, once more, to provide the only solution to the vexing problem of philosophic empiricism that is holding up the present inquiry.

The kind of arbitration in question does not involve a selection of the context within which empirical significance is for all time to be revealed. Selection of such a privileged context would be a hopeless task, and no single context could escape the indictment already imposed on the idea of rational reconstruction within a single artificial language. The kind of arbitration that is meant involves investigating empirical significance as built into a plurality of contexts.

The concept of a plurality, or of a pluralistic approach to the problem of empirical significance, has been cropping up more and more frequently during the course of the discussion. That cognitive experience consists in a plurality of cognitive situations was seen in the last chapter. A cursory glance at scientific methodology has shown that scientists, in seeking confirmation or infirmation of hypotheses, submit groups of statements—theoretic contexts—to experiential test. Such a context, in comparison with the total body of human knowledge (Quine's monolith), is limited. But then, in order to account for the total body of knowledge, a plurality of contexts is required. Again, no ideal linguistic context can be by itself a touchstone for empirical significance, for all the reasons pointed out in chapters ii and iii. Finally, the concept of a plurality of empirical contexts avoids both confinement to the concept of degree of significance and the necessity for proposing a convention amounting to a once-and-for-all criterion for empirical significance.

The idea of a plurality in connection with criteria of significance, moreover, is not unknown in recent literature on the subject. Hempel, in the article referred to on the concept of cognitive significance, shows not only that the concept needs to be "relativized" to systems but that systems themselves cannot be "dichotomized" into significant and nonsignificant. What is called for, according to Hempel, is an appraisal and comparison of different systems in certain respects, respects for which standards and theories need to be developed.[11] The appraisal and comparison of systems, and of the criteria which govern them, thus emerge as crucial to empiricism, and it seems plausible to suggest —and I do suggest—that in most respects the *concept of empirical criteria for appraising, comparing, and constructing contexts* is and should be supplanting the *concept of empirical significance* as paramount in the work of philosophic empiricists. A large part of the remainder of the present work will be devoted to these considerations; what is of interest at the moment is the pluralistic aspect of the empiricism which emerges.

11 "The Concept of Cognitive Significance," pp. 72, 74.

A resistance to the concept of a plurality may be anticipated. This concept is not the sort that lends itself to the strongly intrenched philosophic desire for enduring conclusions, particularly those, in recent philosophy, about meaning and significance. The theory of meaning and of meaningfulness has assumed such a central role in present-day empiricist philosophy that a decisive and final split between what is significant and what is not is too precious, in the beliefs of many philosophers, for a rigid and unique criterion of empirical significance to be allowed to dissolve into a plurality of criteria.

Nevertheless, one may realize that the meaningful-meaningless distinction is a functional or methodological one, like others that have emerged in the present inquiry; that nature, whether human or nonhuman, exhibits no such distinction as that between meaningful and meaningless; that the infirmities necessitating such stopgap measures as a criterion with which we can separate what is significant from what isn't are our own infirmities; and that the criterion and the separation have only the purpose of pulling us out of a trap we have sprung on ourselves. When one realizes all this, he may also realize that if the concept of empirical significance is to perform the duty it was originally intended for without causing more damage than it was designed to repair, it must be a functional concept, flexible enough to meet any exigency, though powerful enough to meet it squarely.

The concept of empirical significance is one that we must be ready to apply at any time, for it is a concept by means of which we are able to make sense of our world and to act intelligently. It is not a concept that can be painstakingly delineated in advance of any application of it, however, for we can never be sure that we have anticipated every kind of occasion for its use. To attempt to legislate its application once and for all would be the part of folly, not wisdom. It would be to institutionalize that rigidity of behavior which, as we learn from the history of the race, inhibits us from adapting to a constantly changing world with the degree of success required before we can forget about adapting and concentrate on the good life.

What can be legislated once and for all is the *function* of

empirical significance: in any cognitive situation we must be
prepared to distinguish between what is empirically significant
and what is not. This means that we must be able to distinguish,
within whatever situation or context is at issue, between symbols
which belong to the context as members either of its primitive
or of its defined vocabulary and symbols which do not. It means
that we must be able to distinguish between sequences of member symbols which are well formed and sequences which are not.
And if it is desirable to separate out of the class of cognitively
significant statements those statements which have empirical
significance—or, at least, as much empirical significance as is permitted by the context—we must be able to distinguish between
statements which are analytic or contradictory (those which, in
Carnap's terminology, are L-determinate) and statements which
are true or false synthetically.

The concept of empirical significance is not limited to symbol-
thinking contexts, however, but is important at every level of the
epistemological continuum. That it should be thought of primarily in connection with symbolic contexts is due partly to
those contexts' being the places where significance is most apt to
go astray, and partly to an equivocacy in the word "significance."
Throughout this book "significance" has been used with the
exact sense of "meaningfulness"; in this sense it denotes what
empiricists have always required ideas or words or statements or
contexts to have, and to have in definite and rigorous ways, in
order to be empirically acceptable. But the more common and
less technical sense of "significance" is more closely allied with
"meaning" than with "meaningfulness," though it is "meaning"
in a vaguer sense than empiricists have given it, a sense conveyed
to a greater or lesser degree by such other words as "relevance,"
"value," "consequence," and "importance." Significance in this
more usual sense is, in the present inquiry, significant enough to
warrant closer examination.

It may be recalled from the previous chapter that the so-called
principle of identity can be construed not only as a principle of
logic and of thinking but also as a general principle of behavior;
the activity of identifying was thought to be an essential part of

cognition occurring at every stage along the epistemological continuum. Cognition was held to be partly determined by human values, and this too was said to be true at every inspectable level of cognition, no matter how "primitive" or how abstract. The point of citing these suggestions from chapter iv is that they may be thought of, without doing violence to the facts of cognition, as adding up to the idea that a large part of our cognitive activity at every level consists in picking out from the environment what is significant or, as a metaphysical alternative, in attributing significances within the cognitive situation.[12] The significance thus encountered in cognitive situations provides a link between the two senses of "significance" mentioned and indicates that coupling them amounts to more than an epistemological pun, because the significance that plays this cognitive role has both the customary sense of relevance, expediency, value, and so on, and the technical philosophic sense of possessing cognitive or empirical meaning.

It may be said, moreover, and without breaking faith with the intent of traditional empiricism, that the ordinary sense of the term is the paradigm for the technical sense. In setting up the concept of empirical significance, after all, what empiricists have wanted to do is to recapture the experiential import or value or relevance of abstract conceptual discourse, and this experiential import or value or relevance is exactly what is meant by "significance" in its most basic sense. Where empiricists have gone wrong is in striving to perfect their concept of significance to such a rigid and foolproof stage that they could get on with philosophy and rely on significance to fend for itself. The reason this course was the wrong one is that their experiential paradigm is itself never rigid and foolproof. Experiential significance is always contextual, and the contexts within which it is located vary to a degree that requires it to be flexible and tentative. In low-echelon contexts, it is true, significance can be relied on to fend for itself, but in high-echelon contexts, which are the ones empiricists concern themselves over, this is not the case.

[12] See William H. Ittelson and Hadley Cantril, *Perception: A Transactional Approach* (Garden City, N.Y.: Doubleday & Co., 1954), pp. 19 ff.

The phrase "cognitive or empirical meaning," used above, camouflages a difficulty, because, as suggested earlier, cognitively significant contexts are not always empirically significant; in fact, the problem of picking out those that are remains to be solved. A context is cognitively significant if it is sharply enough delineated so that the true-false dichotomy obtains within it, and it is empirically significant if, in addition, its synthetic components are empirically significant. That the empirical significance of its synthetic components may in turn depend on the empirical significance of the context points only to the complexity of the problem. The problem is interesting in connection with the epistemological continuum because at lower levels of the continuum it does not exist. If a cognitive situation is present at lower levels of the epistemological continuum, it is not only cognitively significant but empirically significant. It is when the conscious attempt is made to construct high-echelon contexts that the phenomenon of cognitive-significance-without-empirical-significance first occurs. Identity may be faultily ascribed, significances faultily attributed, and distinctions—particularly the formal-nonformal distinction, which in the upper reaches of the epistemological continuum becomes the analytic-synthetic distinction—faultily drawn. We become so concerned with the subtleties and ramifications of our conceptual frameworks that we do not notice or do not care when cognitive significance is no longer accompanied by empirical significance. To be sure, we can go astray at lower levels, but if we do, the pressure of events is an effective and more or less immediate remedial agent; poor judgment in attributing significances at higher levels too often gets compounded and, by reason of its influence in developing formal structures, perpetuated. Perpetuation brings with it inflexibility, and when the quest for significance at these levels is guided by an inflexible conception of what is meaningful and what is not, poor judgment is in many cases scarcely avoidable. Experience, even high-echelon cognitive experience, does not conform to rigid specifications. If the conception of meaningfulness is as rigid as some philosophers want it to be, the difficulty is not so much that poor judgment is used in attributing significances as that no judgment is used.

As the gap between the ordinary and the technical kinds of significance becomes wider and empirical significance becomes more of a problem, philosophic attempts to meet the problem become more sophisticated, tend to ignore the ordinary kind of significance, and result in a further widening of the gap. The present account may be understood as seeking to restore the experientially prior kind of significance to philosophic empiricism without losing whatever benefits have been won through concern for a rigid criterion of meaning. The vehicle for the restoration is the contextualist theory of significance, which not only prevents the extreme rigidity that leads to suspension of judgment in dealing with empirical contexts but also gives rise to a philosophic concept of significance that does justice to and is continuous with experienced significance. The concept of significance emerging from a contextualist approach is continuous with experienced significance because the latter is contextual, and rigidity is prevented because a contextualist theory is pluralistic, adapting its criteria to whatever context is to be evaluated. From the viewpoint of a contextualist theory, finally, the empiricist criteria to be used for evaluating contexts outweigh in interest and importance the concept of empirical significance itself. Appropriately, then, an examination of these criteria—pre-eminently the criterion of precision—follows. It may be hoped that the examination will help clarify what has until now been an abstract discussion of significance.

3. PRECISION AND SIGNIFICANT PRECISION

Among the characteristics of theoretical systems by which the systems may be compared and evaluated with respect to empirical significance, Hempel lists four:[13]

a. the clarity and precision with which the theories are formulated, and with which the logical relationships of their elements to each other and to expressions couched in observational terms have been made explicit;

[13] "The Concept of Cognitive Significance," p. 74.

    b. the systematic, i.e., explanatory and predictive, power of the systems in regard to observable phenomena;

    c. the formal simplicity of the theoretical system with which a certain systematic power is attained;

    d. the extent to which the theories have been confirmed by experiential evidence.

The last three of these criteria—systematic power, formal simplicity, and degree of confirmation—have, as Hempel points out, received a certain amount of attention in recent years, though they require a considerable amount more. As it happens, however, it is the first and least discussed of the criteria, clarity and precision of formulation, that has a special importance in the present inquiry. The importance derives from a profound philosophic significance that attaches to clarity and precision.

    In his reply to Quine's attacks on the principles of empiricism, Bergmann differentiates between two kinds of philosophic reconstructionists or theorists whom he calls sketch theorists and blueprint theorists.[14] The difference between the two is a difference in the accuracy and detail of the ideal language, and corresponds to the difference between the sketch the architect submits to his client and the blueprints he submits to his contractor. Carnap's *aufbau* and Bergmann's ideal language are both sketches, and in fact it is the sketchiness of the former that Quine is pointing to when he cites its chief shortcoming as focusing on the primitive connective "is at."[15] On the other hand, sketch theorists accuse blueprint theorists of indulging in an excessive fondness for both ordinary English and science; science rightly tries to deliver blueprints, but philosophers "in this respect as in all others, are not scientists."

    A good example of the different ways in which sketch theorists and blueprint theorists handle certain problems is their treatment of the counterfactual conditional, an issue Bergmann

---

    14 Gustav Bergmann, "Two Cornerstones of Empiricism," *The Metaphysics of Logical Positivism* (New York: Longmans, Green & Co., 1954), pp. 87 ff.

    15 "Two Dogmas of Empiricism," p. 40.

singles out and one discussed earlier in the present work.[16] Disposition terms may be sketched by means of the apparatus of logical atomism (which Bergmann associates with sketch theory) so long as what is called "idiomatic accuracy" is not demanded— and idiomatic accuracy, whether scientific or "ordinary," would be demanded only by a blueprint theorist. Thus, while the term "soluble" cannot be introduced into a sketch language, the conjunction of "a is immersed in water" and "a doesn't dissolve" may be outlawed, and this is sufficient to translate "a is soluble" with what may be called the "syntactic accuracy" of logical atomism. If, on the other hand, idiomatic accuracy is demanded and one wants to blueprint the term rather than sketch it, the only recourse is to give up syntactic accuracy within a relatively atomistic context and try something else, for instance a modal logic or a framework allowing potentialities. With a qualification to be noted later, increase in either idiomatic accuracy or syntactic accuracy is achieved only at the price of decrease in the other.

The conflict of these two kinds of accuracy is a familiar one, and it takes many forms. Often the term "accuracy" is associated with the atomistic kind but not the idiomatic, which is thought of as anything but accurate. The defect of the former from the viewpoint of the latter is its unavailability for practical application and its inability to follow through on programs; rational reconstructions are sketched, said to be possible "in principle," and left in a programmatic and idiomatically inaccurate condition.[17] Reversing the situation, the demand for idiomatic accuracy is felt by reconstructionists and other sketch theorists to lead to a conceptual unwieldiness inimical to the justification and explication toward which philosophers should aim. Because the opposition of the two kinds of accuracy is at the heart of the present thesis, I will discuss it in greater detail.

[16] Bergmann, op. cit., pp. 88–89. See his "Comments on Professor Hempel's 'The Concept of Cognitive Significance,' " The Metaphysics of Logical Positivism, pp. 260–63; and see above, pp. 68–71.

[17] See Morton G. White, "A Finitistic Approach to Philosophical Theses," Philosophical Review, LX (1951), 299–316.

Borrowing a couple of old rationalist expressions, I will say
that the atomistic accuracy of sketch theory has more *distinctness*
but less *clearness* than the idiomatic accuracy of blueprint theory,[18] and I will try to explain what I mean by clearness and
distinctness in this context by employing the concept of explication. When a term is explicated, it will be remembered, part
of its constituent meaning is isolated from the rest and given a
precise formulation, usually by exhibiting it within a precise
framework. We explicate a concept by doing to it what Kant said
analytic statements do, by "breaking it up into those constituent
concepts that have all along been thought in it, although confusedly." Thus, the concept of solubility may be explicated in
terms of the denial, within some language L_1, of the predicate
"is immersed in water and doesn't dissolve"; in fact, by replacing
denial with unlawfulness and following out the same line of
thought, the concept of empirical lawfulness can be explicated
as nomologicality-in-L_1. The example suggests that the process
of explication results in an increase in distinctness; vagueness is
diminished, and a decision procedure exists for disposing of borderline cases. Nor is it difficult to see that it is in the sense of
distinctness that rational reconstruction aims at precision; the
greatest precision, and the highest degree of distinctness, is afforded by logical atomism, for within a context governed by
logical atomism every complex term breaks down almost of its
own accord into constituent terms which themselves have no
constituents.

So much for distinctness. It is distinctness that will be meant,
hereafter, when the word "precision" is used. To the extent that

[18] See Descartes, *The Principles of Philosophy,* in *The Philosophical
Works of Descartes,* trans. Elizabeth S. Haldane and G. R. T. Ross (New
York: Dover Publications, 1955), I, 237; W. Windelband, *A History of Philosophy,* trans. James H. Tufts (2d ed.; New York: Macmillan Co., 1901),
pp. 392, 398; Alan Gewirth, "Clearness and Distinctness in Descartes," *Philosophy,* XVIII (1943), 17–36; Norman Kemp Smith, *New Studies in the
Philosophy of Descartes* (London: Macmillan & Co., 1952), pp. 55–60,
263 ff.; Norman Dalkey, "The Limits of Meaning," *Philosophy and Phenomenological Research,* IV (1943–44), 406 ff.; Raphael Demos, "Doubts
about Empiricism," *Philosophy of Science,* XIV (1947), 218. The distinction is found in these authors in various ways and with various names, but it
marks essentially the same difference. Demos, for example, uses "immediate"
and "clear," respectively, for the present account's "clear" and "distinct."

a term is thought not to be precise it will be said to be vague, without distinguishing among vagueness, ambiguity, and confusion. A term is vague if its borderline cases are undecidable or if it has a number of different meanings; to establish a decision procedure for borderline cases or to isolate and sharpen one of these meanings is to gain precision in the sense of distinctness.[19] "A is soluble," therefore, is a vague statement-function; not only may it mean "not 'a is immersed in water and doesn't dissolve,'" but it may also have the senses, among others, of "a, if it is immersed in water, is soluble if and only if it dissolves," "if a were immersed in water it would dissolve," "a has the property of dissolving in water," and "a contains a potentiality for dissolving."

Syntactic accuracy within a context of logical atomism, it was said, is achieved only at the expense of what Bergmann calls idiomatic accuracy. Though the unreconstructed or unexplicated expression "a is soluble" is vague in that it has more than one sense (not every one of which is precise), it has idiomatic accuracy. In ordinary contexts its meaning is clear enough. Its meaning would be stated, if statement were required, simply as "a dissolves in water," and a demand for elaboration might elicit the counterfactual conditional. To rule these meanings out through philosophic explication, moreover, would be to invite the charge of "idiomatic inaccuracy." It is in terms of idiomatic accuracy that a first approach may be made toward narrowing down the meaning of "clearness," though unfortunately a rigid specification of the concept is no more attainable than a rigid specification of the concept of empirical significance, and for exactly the same reasons. Clearness and distinctness are inverse functions of one another. If a term is explicated in a series of steps, each explicatum serving as explicandum for the following step, the result is a progressive increase of distinctness and decrease of clearness. Moreover, neither is dispensable. To paraphrase an eminently empiricist maxim, precision without idiomatic accuracy is empty, clearness without distinctness is blind.

[19] See Bertrand Russell, "Vagueness," *Australasian Journal of Philosophy*, I (1923), 84–92; Max Black, "Vagueness," *Philosophy of Science*, IV (1937), 427–55; Hempel, "Vagueness and Logic," *ibid.*, VI (1939), 163–80; I. M. Copilowish, "Border-Line Cases, Vagueness, and Ambiguity," *ibid.*, 181–95; A. C. Benjamin, "Science and Vagueness," *ibid.*, 422–31.

However, I am oversimplifying. For one thing, clearness and
distinctness are relative, and matters of degree; it is a distortion
of the case to say flatly that "a is soluble" is clear and not distinct. It is more clear and less distinct than, say, "not 'a is immersed in water and doesn't dissolve,' " but to use the terms in
some absolute sense is improper. Second, there is a relativity
about distinctness even apart from clearness. Increase in distinctness is not, considered in general, a simple and linear matter.
There are kinds of distinctness, for what is vague and leads to
borderline cases in one context may be precise in another. Only
within a particular context—that is, for a specified kind of distinctness—may degrees of distinctness be said to range themselves in a linear progression. Third, the remark that clearness
varies inversely as distinctness must be qualified, for there seems
to be a point at which loss of distinctness is accompanied by loss
of clearness. So long as it is a question of sketches versus blueprints, the inverse function can be said to hold without qualification, but when the depths of vagueness are plumbed, from
artificial languages to natural language, from linguistic meanings
to sense meanings, from definite meanings to dim feelings and
undifferentiated sensations, then clearness itself begins to give
way to obscurity.

If I may speak, subject to the first two qualifications, of a distinctness scale running from "utterly vague" to "perfectly distinct," I can make my point by saying that both ends of this
scale are veiled in obscurity. However, I must then make another point: the obscurity which conceals the vague end of the
scale is not the same obscurity as that which hovers about the
distinct end. The former is the obscurity of the dumb and in-
choate, of the cognitively meaningless, while the latter is the
obscurity of the overintellectual, of the empirically meaningless,
and it may be ventured that both empirical significance and a
certain measure of distinctness are necessary conditions for
clearness.

The experiential analogue of all this is begging to be mentioned. The analogy, of course, is between the distinctness scale

207

and the epistemological continuum, and it helps make clear that the question of clearness and distinctness is significant at lower levels of cognitive behavior as well as at those higher levels where it becomes conscious and reflective.

The analogy between the distinctness scale and the epistemological continuum can be seen when the clearness criterion is applied to the continuum. If we start with low-echelon cognitive situations and work toward the upper end of the continuum, clearness makes its first appearance when a cognitive situation first emerges, which is to say at the lowest discernible cognition level of the continuum; it increases along with cognition levels up to the point at which empirical significance begins to diminish, and then itself diminishes as cognition-levels continue to increase. Thus, clearness bears much the same relationship to cognition levels as it does to degrees of distinctness.

Incidentally, the characteristics of experience below the lower threshold of clearness, and even the existence of such experience, are problematic. Some degree of clearness is a necessary condition for cognitive experience, and therefore any experience below the threshold of clearness is noncognitive. If anything is to be known about a noncognitive kind of experience, it must be known by reconstruction. Of course, mystics, metaphysicians, and poets make all sorts of claims about the nature of what is experienced when vagueness and obscurity are both maximized; however, the importance of the claims lies not in their alleged revelation of a subcognitive experience but in the index they offer to the characteristics of experience at the thresholds of clearness and cognition. Different persons have different sensitivities, and there is no reason to think that the same is not true about thresholds of cognition, that some persons who make claims about privileged experiences do not actually have lower thresholds of cognition than most of us.

Wherever the threshold may be, however, and whatever, if anything, may lie beneath, in general the characteristics of experience are these: Clearness increases as the epistemological continuum and the distinctness scale are ascended, through the point at which experiences get articulated, to the point at which ordinary languages are replaced by technical languages, and natural languages by artificial ones. So far as clearness is concerned, this is the point of diminishing returns. Beyond this point the conflict between clearness and distinctness begins to be more and more noticeable; "nonformalists" come into conflict with "formalists," blueprint theories with sketch theories, and idiomatic accuracy with atomistic accuracy.[20]

Much the same may be said about clearness and distinctness that has been said about empirical and cognitive significance; in fact, within the present context the concepts of clearness and of empirical significance are so nearly indistinguishable that no harm will be done by considering them to be identical. If a context in the lower stages of the epistemological continuum has cognitive significance, it has empirical significance too, whereas contexts at higher stages are likely to have the former without the latter. Similarly, in low-echelon cognitive activities clearness and distinctness usually increase and decrease as a pair, for the fight against confusion is a fight also against obscurity. We work, at these levels, to maximize precision, and the quest for clearness, or for empirical significance, may be depended on to take care of itself.[21] It is when cognition becomes a conscious process of creating frameworks and of ascribing identities and significances within these frameworks that precision begins to outstrip clearness.

Precision, like cognitive significance, tends to be pursued for its own sake. This absence of ulterior motive is harmless when precision carries clearness in its wake and when whatever has

[20] Note that for Descartes there can be no distinctness where there is no clearness (op. cit., p. 237). The phenomenon of distinctness-without-clearness has always been a threat to philosophy, and it was at least as grave a threat in Descartes' time as in the present. But when rooting out the scholastic version of the phenomenon, Descartes sowed the seeds for the emergence of the contemporary version.

[21] Adelbert Ames, Jr., shows that in order to gain the behavioral advantages that come with simultaneous awareness of a multiplicity of significances, the latter must be low-order rather than high-order, and to this end we have "developed the capacity to be aware" of lower order significances ("Reconsideration of the Origin and Nature of Perception in Situations Involving Only Inorganic Phenomena," Vision and Action: Essays in Honor of Horace M. Kallen, ed. Sidney Ratner (New Brunswick, N.J.: Rutgers University Press, 1953), pp. 260–62.

cognitive significance has empirical significance also. But the fact is that it is not *maximum precision* which governs our cognitive behavior but *significant precision*. The limit to the degree of precision we attain in low-level cognition is determined by significance in the sense in which it is experienced, which is to say, by empirical significance. We strive, in any cognitive situation, for the maximum degree of precision that is relevant or important or valuable in that situation. What is misleading is that in low-echelon situations this degree of precision is the maximum degree attainable, so that the kind of difference which could support a distinction between two kinds of precision is missing. It is when we have established control over our cognitive situations —particularly at the sophisticated level involving symbols—that attainable precision can exceed what is empirically significant and that we fail to draw the proper distinction between maximum and significant precision.

In other words, precision within any particular cognitive situation is stratified, forming a scale between maximum confusion and maximum precision. At some point along this scale may be found the highest degree of precision compatible with empirical significance, the latter being determined by the context. This point may be called the point of significant precision. The cognitive behavior of human beings, which includes such activities as identifying, attributing significances, and drawing distinctions, is governed by a *principle of significant precision*, the principle that in any context precision is to be maximized so far as is empirically significant.

In cognitive situations where precision and significance of any sort are gratefully acknowledged because hard won, the idea of significant precision and the principle which utilizes it are gratuitous. As much precision as we are able to achieve in low-level cognition is bound to be significant; as a result, a *principle of maximum precision* would be more useful here and certainly less apt to divert our attention from the main problem, the problem of attaining not excessive precision but sufficient precision. At higher stages of the epistemological continuum, however, where significant precision and maximum precision diverge, the principle of significant precision, far from being gratuitous, is essential to intelligent behavior. Nevertheless, our cognitive activity, notably in philosophy, very often seems to be governed by the principle of maximum precision—even, oddly enough, when we are most concerned about the empirical significance to which that principle is least likely to lead us. The opposition of the two principles which involve intellectual precision sets the stage for the methodological discussion to follow, for pragmatic reconstruction is a methodological approach to philosophy which governs itself rigorously by the principle of significant precision.

Before that methodological discussion, however, it may be worth pointing out that in areas of endeavor where the plea for applicability is likely to find a readier hearing than it is in philosophy, the idea of significant precision is not unknown. An engineer, in carrying out the decimal expansion of pi, does not carry on the process indefinitely; there is a point, determined by the nature of the computation and the accuracy of other factors involved, beyond which further precision would be insignificant. A twenty-place representation is more precise than one with four places, but the extra precision is insignificant when the figure is to be used for setting a control which is itself accurate only to two places, and a three- or four-place representation is accurate enough to bring two sections of a bridge span together. A lecturer, in covering himself against anticipated criticism, will determine criteria for the maximum permissible loophole in relation to his audience. The precision required to insure against criticism from his professional society is greater than the precision necessary for the local parent-teacher association, and the obscurity and insignificance of the former degree of precision for the latter audience is measurable in terms of yawn frequency. Again, the flashcard method of teaching recognition to plane-spotters was designed with significant rather than maximum precision in mind, a fact not unrelated to some basic characteristics of vision.[22] The triviality of these examples should not be permitted to obscure the principle they exemplify—the principle of significant precision.

[22] See Hoyt L. Sherman, *Drawing by Seeing* (New York: Hinds, Hayden & Eldredge, 1947).

CHAPTER VI

Pragmatic Reconstruction

1. EXPLICATION VERSUS APPLICATION

THE EMPHASIS in philosophic empiricism has recently shifted, as mentioned, from the concept of significance to that of criteria for evaluating the contexts within which significance emerges. If the present view is correct, the criteria which have become of central importance to empiricism are pragmatic criteria. The expression that will be used to designate the philosophic method which focuses on these criteria and on the contexts they are to be applied to is "pragmatic reconstruction."

Pragmatic reconstruction as a philosophic method is contextual. Until a context has been constructed, even the grossest raw materials are lacking for high-echelon thinking. Of course, a context of some sort is always present, since we are experiencing creatures, but a context within which we can engage in subtle yet rigorous thought must be one within which we have control, and we can have most control (though we also run the highest risk of losing it) within contexts we have constructed ourselves. If we are in complete control of a context, we are able to answer in terms of it the fundamental questions empiricists have traditionally raised. The statement theory of significance is applicable, and we are able to give a criterion by means of which we can know at a glance whether a statement is or is not cognitively significant. Moreover, because the distinction between analytic and synthetic statements is transparently clear, we are able to say without hesitation whether any statement is empirically significant. And because there is no doubt in our minds about which part of the significance of a synthetic statement is formal and which factual, we are also able to say what the statement's empirical meaning is.

The tragic flaw lies in the limitations of the context. The reason we are able to give such definite answers to the questions is that we have already agreed on certain conventions by which we were able to construct a context in the first place. In fact, the questions just cited point to exactly those central issues which are most convenient for delineating contexts, so that the assertions we can make so confidently might well be the conventions we originally decided on. Our confidence in the correctness of our answers is thus rooted in our determination not to renege on our conventions; at least this is the case provided we have not already conveniently forgotten that there were conventions. In either case, our viewpoint is limited to the particular context, and every question is considered only as an internal question.

But there are external questions too; otherwise the context could never have been constructed to begin with. From an external point of view it becomes clear that the context within which our empiricist confidence seems to blossom so is a limited one. It is limited to a domain of experience or of language which is narrow enough and selective enough that, when filtered through the categories of the context, it presents that simple, unified, manageable appearance that invites both theoretic investigation and practical manipulation, activities for whose sake the context was delineated in the first place. The external viewpoint that recognizes the limitations of the context recognizes also that it is but one of many. Every context isolates a different experiential or linguistic domain or superimposes a different categorial structure on the same domain, so that a number of contexts are needed. And what dictates the selection of a domain or of a categorial structure is, to the extent that the selection is conscious and controlled, the purpose to be served by the context. Since a context of the sort I am talking about depends for its existence entirely on conventions, the ultimate criterion for evaluating a context is whether or not it serves the purpose for which it was constructed.

Purpose is, of course, an eminently pragmatic term; the criteria for determining whether any context does or would adequately serve a specified purpose are pragmatic criteria, and the philosophic method most concerned with these criteria is pragmatic reconstruction. The philosopher who approaches a problem by the method of pragmatic reconstruction recognizes both the necessity for working within well-defined intellectual contexts and the inadequacy of any single context to do more than reconstruct a narrow segment of language or of experience for a limited purpose. Any context he adopts he considers as if it were closed, solitary, and absolute, as if every question that could be asked either has a definite and final answer in the context or else is meaningless. But at the same time, he must carry with him continually the awareness that his adoption of the context is a provisional one, subject to cancellation at any moment. The position of the pragmatic reconstructionist is fragile and frustrating; he can say nothing about the world, he can offer no solutions to philosophic problems, without full consciousness that what he is saying is no more reliable than the context—ultimately a convention—within which it originated and that it may have to be withdrawn momentarily. There is a tension between absolute and provisional acceptance of a context, between accepting it as a closed system and holding it open, ready for expansion or replacement. The pragmatic reconstructionist, to rephrase the predicament slightly, is plagued by the circularity of everything he says; whatever his assumptions, they must eventually be questioned. As noted earlier, however, the alternative to circularity is philosophy by fiat, or by the method of unquestioned assumptions, an alternative whose exponents avoid the misgivings of the pragmatic reconstructionist as well as his insistence on leaving no problem unexamined.

The name "pragmatic reconstruction" naturally suggests opposition to rational reconstruction, and though there is little in pragmatic reconstruction that does not find a place somewhere in rational reconstruction, the intent and emphasis of the two are different enough to justify talking about different philosophic methods. In any case, an enumeration of a few of the more prominent differences in intent and emphasis will be convenient for throwing into relief some of the details of pragmatic reconstruction.

Both philosophic methods utilize frameworks, for one reason or another, and with a few exceptions (such as Bergmann's method of the ideal language) both utilize a plurality of frameworks. Yet there is a difference in intent between the way in which the two methods view this contextual pluralism. From the viewpoint of pragmatic reconstruction the older approach, even when contextualist and pluralist in practice, exceeds the bounds of empirical propriety. The reason for its transgression is its tacit and unempirical assumption that for any experiential domain there is a framework best suited for its reconstruction, a framework which, if not possessed to begin with, may be approximated more and more closely by trying out a plurality of frameworks. For pragmatic reconstruction, on the other hand, there is a plurality not simply of candidates for best-suitedness but of "best-suited" frameworks themselves; no framework is *best* suited, even as a limit, for any domain that is to be reconstructed. Which framework should be imposed on any particular subject matter is a question to be answered carefully (for the question is complex) and tentatively (for the answer may be wrong). What is primarily involved is, again, purpose.

Pragmatic reconstruction may be further differentiated by means of the principles of maximum precision and of significant precision, which govern rational and pragmatic reconstruction, respectively. The difference between some kinds of rational reconstruction and others is that some reconstructionists allow exceptions to the rule and others do not. Bergmann allows no exceptions: all philosophic problems are dissolved by discoursing about the ideal language, the ideal language is a framework of logical atomism, and logical atomism incorporates the maximum degree of precision.[1] But others, wanting to investigate some of the issues that slip through the net of logical atomism, allow within their frameworks a studied element of vagueness that

---

[1] The maximum degree of precision, strictly speaking, exists only in uninterpreted artificial languages. See Carl G. Hempel, "Vagueness and Logic," *Philosophy of Science*, VI (1939), 163–80, in which he says that, because vagueness is a semiotic (in the sense, here, of extrasyntactic) relation, the question of vagueness does not arise within uninterpreted artificial languages.

represents an infringement of the principle. Thus, an intensional language may be desirable for investigating certain philosophic problems connected with disposition terms, empirical law, and causal necessity; when seen within an extensional language, the problems, though seen distinctly, are seen obscurely or in idiomatically inaccurate terms.[2]

For pragmatic reconstructionists both methods may be useful. If it serves the purpose of the reconstruction—as it well may —a problem may be exhibited within a framework rigged according to the most rigid specifications rational reconstructionists can devise. Or, like the more flexible among rational reconstructionists, the pragmatic reconstructionist may tolerate a degree of vagueness in the construction of a framework in order to increase the empirical significance, or the clearness, of the problem at the expense of its distinctness. However, relaxation in standards of precision need not be thought of in terms of "exceptions to the rule." In fact the method of pragmatic reconstruction is better represented if, instead of tacking exceptions onto the principle of maximum precision, the latter is replaced by the principle of significant precision, the principle that the degree of precision to be sought within any context is the greatest degree that is empirically significant.

The function of the principle of significant precision is to satisfy the philosopher devoted both to precision and to the preservation of his subject matter. By now, presumably, the point is clear that gain in precision is likely to be accompanied, at upper cognitive levels, by loss in idiomatic accuracy or empirical significance. Every reconstruction is for a purpose, which determines what is and what is not significant; the cardinal principle is the seemingly obvious one that the reconstruction should suit the purpose which brought it about, or should be significant. All this is only to say that a reconstruction should reconstruct what it is intended to reconstruct, without losing it. And the reason for mentioning what ought not to require mention is that when reconstruction in philosophy is ruled by the principle of maximum precision, just such disappearance of what was to have

[2] See, for instance, Rudolf Carnap, *Meaning and Necessity* (Chicago: University of Chicago Press, 1947).

216

been reconstructed is likely, because few purposes are served by contexts which possess maximum precision.

It may be noted, however, that when a purpose *is* served by a context having maximum precision, the task may be handled by pragmatic reconstruction; even all-out rational reconstruction may be countenanced occasionally under the principle of significant precision. In such cases maximum precision and significant precision coincide. The purpose of a pragmatic reconstruction may even be to erect an ideal language which will allow the exhibition of the whole body of science in sketch form; then pragmatic reconstruction would coincide with the super-all-out rational reconstruction investigated in Part I.

Rational reconstruction occurs within the context of justification, or as Bergmann interprets it, the context of *explication*. The context of justification, it will be remembered, is Reichenbach's name for a device by which distinct meanings and deductive chains are substituted for confused meanings and "psychological" processes; the context of the latter is the context of *discovery*. Bergmann shifts slightly, from justifying thought processes to explicating meanings. A meaning is explicated when an empirical context has been constructed which contains a representative of the meaning. Whereas Bergmann's rational reconstruction involves one ideal context which is supposed to be complete in the sense that it contains a representative of every meaning worth holding on to, other forms of rational reconstruction adapt the context (which need not be complete in Bergmann's sense) to the meanings or experiential domains. In either case, whether the context is complete or incomplete, its construction is dictated ultimately by those empiricist ideals which are to be found in the classic empiricist writings.

From the vantage point of pragmatic reconstruction, however, an explication of a meaning in the manner just described is only one of a plurality of "explications." Such an explication involves any number of philosophic theories—theories about what there is, theories about the nature of "direct experience," and so on. What is most important is not the fact of explication but the purpose of explication, for what context is chosen for reconstructing any area of language or of experience depends entirely on how the context is to be used, which is to say, on its application. Pragmatic reconstruction may now be further delineated if said to occur not within a context of justification or of explication but within a context of *application*.

There are many variable factors entering into pragmatic reconstruction that may be accommodated by contexts of application but not by contexts of explication. A few of these factors should be noticed. Pragmatic, like rational, reconstruction is concerned with the results of processes of thinking and of scientific investigation as distinguished from the processes themselves. Unlike rational reconstruction, though, pragmatic reconstruction, when it suits its purpose, concerns itself also with the processes of thought as distinguished from the results of the processes, so that it finds use for the context of discovery as well as for that of explication. In fact, from the vantage point of the context of application, the distinction between the contexts of explication and of discovery loses its initial crispness. Thus, for the pragmatic reconstructionist the inductive origin of scientific knowledge is a fact to be reckoned with in the justification of knowledge, and the reckoning can take place neither entirely within the context of justification cut off from that of discovery, nor entirely within the context of discovery cut off from that of justification.

Carnap's recent investigations of probability and induction are an example of pragmatic reconstruction in this sense. He has attempted to explicate the beliefs scientists hold when they reason inductively, that is, discover, and he has done so with reference to the beliefs actually held by competent scientists.[3] But

[3] See Carnap, "On Inductive Logic," *Philosophy of Science*, XII (1945), 72–97; "The Two Concepts of Probability," *Philosophy and Phenomenological Research*, V (1944–45), 513–32; reprinted in *Readings in Philosophical Analysis*, ed. Herbert Feigl and Wilfred Sellars (New York: Appleton-Century-Crofts, 1949), pp. 330–48; reprinted in *Readings in the Philosophy of Science*, ed. Herbert Feigl and May Brodbeck (New York: Appleton-Century-Crofts, 1953), pp. 438–56; *Logical Foundations of Probability* (Chicago: University of Chicago Press, 1950); "Inductive Logic and Science," *Proceedings of the American Academy of Arts and Sciences*, LXXX (1951–54), 189–97.

when justification is cut off from discovery, as Reichenbach claims it should be, Carnap's is seen as a "psychological brand of justification"; what is wanted according to Reichenbach is not to copy the mistakes of scientists (who "often have strange beliefs") but to lay down rules in the light of which any particular inductive inference either is justified or is unjustified.[4] What Reichenbach overlooks is the significance of the "non-rational factors" in scientific discovery. These factors not only are "important and fruitful," as Carnap recognizes,[5] but represent an element of human knowledge that epistemologists concerned with valid thinking and fruitful theorizing cannot afford to ignore or to abandon to psychologists, from whom they have cut themselves off.

There can, according to Reichenbach, be no rational reconstruction for a fallacious argument as a whole, because a fallacious argument contains two steps separated by an irrational "jump" which cannot be reconstructed. All that can be provided is one reconstruction for the part of the argument between the premises and the irrational jump, and another reconstruction for the part of the argument between the irrational jump and the conclusion.[6] This pinpoints a difference between rational and pragmatic reconstruction, for in the context of application the irrational jump may be fully as significant as the rational slides, and for some purposes much more interesting. The reconstruction of the fallacious argument, as it emerges from the context of explication, is—aside from being no longer fallacious—very different from the argument to be reconstructed. For what emerges is two arguments, each with its premises and its conclusions, and how to get from the premises of the first argument to the conclusion of the second is as much a mystery after the reconstruction as it was before. But what is frequently of interest to the pragmatic reconstructionist is that scientists do get from those

---

[4] Hans Reichenbach, "The Verifiability Theory of Meaning," *Proceedings of the American Academy of Arts and Sciences,* LXXX (1951–54), 41–60; reprinted with omissions in *Readings in the Philosophy of Science,* ed. Feigl and Brodbeck, pp. 93–102. Present reference is to p. 96 in the latter.

[5] "Inductive Logic and Science," p. 195.

[6] *Op. cit.,* pp. 96–97, n. 5.

premises to that conclusion, and the existence of an irrational jump doesn't seem to diminish the utility of the argument even if it does compromise its logical validity. If a reconstruction could be given which would include the irrational part of a successful argument as well as the rational part, much would have been learned. However, I started out merely to suggest that some of the factors in pragmatic reconstruction which necessitate the use of application contexts rather than explication contexts are factors involving contexts of discovery. It was only by way of strengthening this suggestion that I mentioned the artificiality, from the viewpoint of applicability, of distinguishing sharply between the contexts of justification and discovery.

A consideration which greatly inhibits the number of permissible frameworks for rational reconstruction is that such frameworks, when intended to be reconstructions of human knowledge along the lines of traditional empiricism, must have a primitive vocabulary consisting of terms which, when interpreted, become experiential terms. No such categorical rule governs pragmatic reconstruction, however, and its absence allows a great number of contexts which are otherwise ruled out. The reasons for eliminating the rule from pragmatic reconstruction should also be fairly apparent. The empirical significance a framework has simply because its primitive vocabulary contains terms purporting to designate elements in our immediate experience is negligible unless accompanied by arguments to show that the designated elements are in fact "immediately experienced." No such arguments are currently to be found, however. Any assignment of experiential terms to an artificial language represents a guess about the sensory end of the epistemological continuum; from the vantage point of reconstruction both ends of this continuum shade off into ontology, and the lack of experiential terms should cause no more alarm than the lack of classes of classes of classes.

There are, however, applications which do require a context to have an experiential basis of some sort; these are the test or experimental applications that both pragmatic and rational reconstruction are concerned with to a great extent. A scientific context incorporating a theoretic system may have to contain experiential terms: it may have to be tested, and to be tested is to be "tied down" to experience. Furthermore, the experiential terms chosen must be such as to facilitate testing, or there might as well be no experiential terms at all. But these terms are better called *test* or *observation terms*, in order to make clear that their function is to facilitate scientific experimentation and not to stand as the linguistic counterpart of our most intimate and direct experience. Advocates of so-called "thing-languages" as opposed to sense-datum languages frequently confuse scientific expediency with epistemological priority. That the two are distinct does not mean that a perfectly respectable case cannot be made for the explicit view that epistemological priority or some degree of it attaches to observation terms *because of* their scientific expediency. At any rate, when any sort of hypothesis is to be submitted to experience for confirmation or infirmation, the pragmatic reconstructionist will reject any context not containing observation terms. He will do so not because such a context lacks empirical significance but simply because it isn't applicable in these circumstances.

But there are other circumstances, equally important to science, which do not require the framework of reconstruction to contain observation terms. It may be, for example, that the reason for constructing a language is to learn more about the relations among terms in a theoretic system which are nowhere near the sensory periphery. In such a context observation terms might be unnecessary, and they could be a definite hindrance. And if observation terms could be not only unnecessary but undesirable, then obviously a context applicable to these circumstances is guided not by empirical criteria of the sort empiricists have always tried to pin down, but by criteria more customarily applied to theoretic contexts.

These criteria, once more, are pragmatic in character, along with the kind of reconstruction in which they are of primary importance. If the criterion of precision, for instance, is to be a workable one in philosophic reconstruction, it must be continually adapted to the context in which it is to be applied. Continual adaptation is made possible by a principle of significant precision, which regulates the degree of precision allowable within any context and regulates it ultimately with reference to what is significant in human experience—a point of reference to which empiricists can scarcely take exception. Other criteria, too, are entirely relative to the purpose served by the context within which they are invoked. Moreover, from one viewpoint—a not insignificant one, considering that the method of pragmatic reconstruction is an extension of basic modes of cognitive behavior —all contextual criteria operate as one. Only at a comparatively self-conscious stage of inquiry, where the inquirer attempts to unravel the intricate cognitive maneuvers which have led him to a tentative termination of inquiry, are these criteria picked out one by one and designated as "simplicity," "clarity," and the rest. This broader criterion takes various shapes within various contexts, and how it is defined depends on how it is to be applied. The purposes of one pragmatic reconstruction may be served best by considerations of simplicity; in another reconstruction, the issue of degree of confirmation may assume a crucial importance. And the relative weight attached to such issues will determine the criteria by which contexts are to be judged. No criterion can be laid down in advance of specification of the purpose which the criterion is to serve. Purpose once specified, criteria emerge; in accordance with them a choice of context is made; and the method of pragmatic reconstruction is then a process of alternately improving the criteria in view of their performance, and of constructing new contexts in view of the criteria improved. What happens to philosophy when done this way must now be considered.

2. INTERNAL QUESTIONS, EXTERNAL QUESTIONS,
   AND ANTECEDENT FRAMEWORKS

When approaching philosophic problems—or any other kind—by means of a plurality of contexts, it is essential not to confuse internal and external questions. This is especially true for pragmatic reconstructionists, whose program is designed to meet responsibly the problem of circularity, recognizing that there is a condition to be cured but not curing it with a treatment more calamitous in its philosophic consequences than the condition itself.

Consider, as an illustration of the necessity for keeping internal and external questions distinct, the relation of evidence to hypothesis in theoretic systems. This relation may take widely different forms depending on the particular framework within which it is exhibited. Considered in general, the relation of evidence to hypothesis, whatever else it may be, cannot be considered a deductive relation. If deduction is to occur, there must be a set of rules that will give directions for transforming certain statements into certain other statements—in this case, statements explaining experiences into statements describing experiences. Moreover, the statements themselves must be formulated in certain definite ways in order that the transformation rules can be effective. Statements in natural languages, however, are seldom so formulated. Any sense of "deduction" in which the deductive process is carried on without going beyond the linguistic apparatus provided by ordinary language is an unacceptable sense in so far as the deductive process alone, given the validity of the statements that go into it, is expected to vouch for the validity of the statements resulting from it.

Within a rigid and sharply delineated artificial language framework, however, the requirements for deduction are present, and the deductive relation can be exhibited. But even here, no single set of transformation rules governs the relation within every such framework, if only because different frameworks have different formation rules. To specify a single set of rules would be to preclude possible frameworks within which the relation of evidence to hypothesis may fruitfully be viewed. To consider the relation as deductive, therefore, it must be seen within a particular artificial language framework. One must not take for granted that when that particular framework has outlived its usefulness, and the relation is transplanted to another framework, the relation will continue to be deductive. It must be investigated anew whenever a different framework is considered. In fact, one of the most important reasons for investigating the language of science and for constructing languages to suit certain scientific purposes is that the relation of evidence to hypothesis may be deductive, for over a deductive relation we may exercise control to a degree otherwise unobtainable.

Now, given a particular hypothesis and the evidence for it, different sorts of questions may be asked. One question is whether a given theoretic system, say classical mechanics, is such that the hypothesis may be expressed within it, and that from the hypothesis so expressed, together with relevant auxiliary hypotheses also within the system, the evidential statements may be deduced. This sort of question is what Carnap calls an internal question. It is a question asked about a particular system or language or context, and it is answered by a definite assertion, to be found and verified by investigating the framework in question. Another question is which theoretic system will accommodate the hypothesis and evidence as a deductive team in a manner requiring fewest primitive terms, or least alteration of existing hypotheses. This sort of question is an external question. It calls not for an assertion but for a decision. It is, as Carnap makes clear, a practical question, not a theoretic one.

The results of ignoring the rule against confusing internal and external questions are now apparent. To mistake the internal question for an external one would be to suppose that the particular context by virtue of which the question is really internal is the only context possible, and that when an answer has been given there remains nothing further to be said on the subject. And to mistake the external questions for internal ones would be to suppose that there is some single context by virtue of which the questions may be answered definitely by inspection—or, if inspection is impossible because the context has not yet been discovered or is universal, then answered definitely on the basis of calculation or of speculation. In either case circularity has got out of control. If an internal question is taken to be external, the circularity is no longer provisional; and if an external question is taken to be internal, it is no longer limited.

The consequences of confusing internal and external questions may be seen again in connection with the difference—mentioned earlier—between ontology and language commitments. There are questions, in Quine's happy phrase, about what there is, and there are questions about what one's language form commits one to in the way of entities. Questions of the second kind are internal questions. They are of a factual nature, to be answered by examining the language form in question. They are questions about language forms, not about ontology.

One may also ask, however, whether the entities which a given language form commits one to agree with what there actually is. Or one might ask which language form would best agree in this respect with what there actually is. If these external questions are to make sense, one must already have an idea of what there is; this, as will be seen, requires an antecedent framework of some sort, a context within which the question "what is there?" is significant. Given an antecedent framework and an antecedent conception of what there is, the external questions call for a decision about language forms within which what there is may be exhibited. And to confuse external with internal questions on this issue is to confuse ontology with semantics.[7]

A new note has apparently been struck by the concept of *antecedent framework*, and I want to develop the concept now, both for its own sake and because at the same time I can deepen the discussion of pragmatic reconstruction. Antecedent frameworks are the source of cognitive significance for external questions. There can be no cognitive significance where conditions for cognitive activity are not present; in other words, there can be no cognitive significance outside a cognitive situation. The nature of cognitive situations is such that if cognition is to remain active, open, and flexible, a number and variety of such situations are required; in philosophy, where consciously created frameworks are high-level extensions of low-level situations, cognitive significance emerges in relation to a series of frameworks.

Consider a framework L_n. Internal questions about L_n—questions, say, of the ontological sort—are answered on the basis of what is revealed by an examination of L_n, and the answers are

[7] See above, pp. 67–68, 78–79.

cognitively significant because they refer to a cognitive context. But external questions about L_n do not refer, at least not in the same way, to L_n. If these questions and their answers are to have meaning, there must be another language, L_{n-1}, in reference to which their meaning can be known. L_{n-1} is an antecedent framework. It is within L_{n-1} that one determines which internal questions to ask about L_n, and L_n was selected or constructed to begin with because it seemed an appropriate convention on the basis of considerations developing within L_{n-1}.

But now the same questions may be posed about L_{n-1}. Where did its characteristics come from? If the cognitive circumstances are still under control, there must be an antecedent framework of L_{n-1}, in reference to which external questions about L_{n-1} have cognitive significance. Within such an antecedent framework, L_{n-2}, the kind of information can be learned about L_{n-1} that can be learned in L_{n-1} about L_n. Thus, there is a series of artificial languages—. . . , L_{n-2}, L_{n-1}, L_n, . . .—any one of which is an antecedent framework for the subsequent language and has an antecedent framework in the previous language. Frameworks are antecedent relatively, and for the same reason the distinction between internal and external questions is entirely relative. An external question with respect to a language form L_n is an internal question with respect to an antecedent framework L_{n-1}.

The apparatus just sketched makes possible a somewhat more detailed account of pragmatic reconstruction in philosophy. As a reference point, the group of problems may be used clustering about the counterfactual conditional, causal law and necessity, "connections" and disposition terms.

Take the term "soluble" once more, and in particular take both the statement "sugar is soluble" and an extensional artificial language which for the sake of definiteness will be called L_4. Within L_4 appears the statement "if sugar is immersed in water, then it dissolves," which is the L_4 representative of the statement "sugar is soluble." The latter, however, itself appears in a language if the proper controls are not lacking, so that there is another language, L_3, containing the statement "sugar is soluble."

L_3 is an antecedent framework of L_4, and it is by means of L_3 that the appropriate external questions may be asked—questions involving conventions on the basis of which "sugar is soluble" is to be seen more precisely. Mention of precision, moreover, suggests that L_3 and L_4 have relative positions on the "distinctness scale," that "if sugar is immersed in water, then it dissolves" is more distinct than "sugar is soluble." But now look at some facts about L_4. When "sugar is immersed in water" is false in L_4, then not only is "if sugar is immersed in water, then it dissolves" true; by the truth table for material implication, "if sugar is immersed in water, then it doesn't dissolve" is also true. These facts about L_4 are interesting, and perhaps even disconcerting, but they have no special significance until the discovery is made within L_3 that the adequacy of L_4 so far as explicating "sugar is soluble" is concerned is now somewhat tarnished. The answers to the pertinent external questions need revision, because the decision to exhibit "sugar is soluble" within L_4 no longer seems wise.

Suppose now that a new language, L_5, is constructed and that it contains the so-called reduction sentence "if sugar is immersed in water, then it is soluble if and only if it dissolves."[8] For this language both L_3 and L_4 are antecedent frameworks, because external questions involving L_5 may refer to either or both of the others. And once more, answers to certain internal questions about L_5 may, when viewed externally, impugn its utility so far as "sugar is soluble" is concerned. Thus, both the indeterminateness of reductions as against definitions and the existence of synthetic consequences of analytic statements make it desirable, from one point of view at least, to push on to still another language, L_6.[9] This new language, say, does not contain a representative of "sugar is soluble" because "soluble" is missing from its vocabulary, but the statement is built into it by means of a semantic rule which prohibits the conjunction of "x is sugar," "x

[8] See Carnap, "Testability and Meaning," *Philosophy of Science*, III (1936), 440 ff.

[9] See above, p. 69.

is immersed in water," and "x doesn't dissolve" from appearing in the language.

It will be noticed that the linguistic progression from L_3 to L_6 is approximately a progression along the distinctness scale, for L_6 may, consistently with what was said about it, be the kind of framework talked about earlier in which concepts and propositions may be exhibited with the syntactic accuracy afforded by logical atomism, an accuracy in comparison with which the "sugar is soluble" of L_3 is vague indeed. However, a progression from less distinct to more distinct is—at this level—also a regression from less obscure to more obscure, and in order to avoid losing sight of this aspect of the process it is well not to forget the various antecedent frameworks through which the process has passed. If, in progressing from L_5 to L_6, one still has L_3 firmly in mind, then it is difficult to see how the obscurity of the rule "not 'is immersed in water and doesn't dissolve' " as a metaportrait of solubility can be overlooked. And since to overlook that obscurity would be to go counter to the principle of significant precision, it may be taken as a helpful maxim of pragmatic reconstruction that no antecedent framework ought to be wholly forgotten.

It is not true that because the succession of languages L_3 to L_6 is a sequence with respect to distinctness from the viewpoint just discussed, the languages will distribute themselves the same way for every pragmatic reconstruction. If, for example, the purpose of the reconstruction were not simply to explicate the statement "sugar is soluble" but to account for its empirical lawfulness, a different approach and a different attitude toward various contexts would be taken. L_3 could be of little use, from the point of view of distinctness, if all that could be done with its help were to state what it is whose lawfulness is of present interest, though if L_3 permitted the statement " 'sugar is soluble' states an empirical law," it would be a good language to use for a jumping-off place, or for a preliminary framework. L_4, with its "if sugar is immersed in water, then it dissolves," does not convey the idea of lawfulness, but the same statement in an intensional language might facilitate a second approximation. Thus, suppose L_{4a} is such a language and contains the adverb "necessarily." This would yield "if sugar is immersed in water, then it necessarily dissolves," and the adequacy of the language now depends on the acceptability of "necessarily." The necessity involved cannot, of course, be a matter of definition, because it is empirical, not logical, necessity. A step in the direction of distinctness might be represented by the adoption of a language within which Reichenbach's concept of nomological statement—a concept which enables him to define physical necessity—can be utilized; a third approximation would then be possible in a language L_{4b} which contained the statement " 'if sugar is immersed in water, then it dissolves' is a nomological statement in the sense of Reichenbach."[10] But the acme of distinctness is still L_6, because the unconstitutionality in L_6 of state-descriptions containing "x is sugar," "x is immersed in water," and "x doesn't dissolve" builds into L_6 not only "sugar is soluble" but also " 'sugar is soluble' states an empirical law." The obscurity of the language for purposes of the present reconstruction is reflected by the identity of this explication with the one that would be offered for " 'sugar is soluble' states a logical law"; there is no difference in L_6 between the nomologicality of "sugar is soluble" and that of "no bachelor is married," and logical and empirical necessity are indistinguishable. At any rate, the sequence of languages from clear-but-vague to distinct-but-obscure, found to be applicable to the problem of causal lawfulness, differs from the sequence useful in reconstructing the very similar problem of disposition terms. And, in general, the sequence in which frameworks are stratified varies from one reconstruction to the next.

The examples so far show that there is in pragmatic reconstruction a kind of tension between maximizing precision by means of more and more precise language frameworks and preserving empirical significance by clinging as long as possible to antecedent frameworks. Naturally, the tension could not be alleviated simply by sticking to the original framework. To stick to

[10] Reichenbach, *Elements of Symbolic Logic* (New York: Macmillan Co., 1947), chap. viii.

the original framework would be to give up the method of pragmatic reconstruction; in fact, it would be to give up philosophizing, for some movement among conceptual frameworks is essential in order to avoid a complacent acquiescence in a categorial structure, an acquiescence inimical to the sort of activity traditionally called philosophy.

But there are more forces than mere contextual inertia pulling the pragmatic reconstructionist away from the direction of maximum precision. There is the desire and the need to investigate antecedent frameworks, for full harvest of any statement's empirical meaning demands an investigation not only of the context within which the statement appears but also of the context within which the circumstances exist that made the statement worth uttering in the first place. If the statement is the answer to a question, the considerations prompting the question and the context in which the considerations emerge are factors which from the viewpoint of pragmatic reconstruction are as important as those which lead to ever more precise frameworks.

Given any artificial language framework, pragmatic reconstruction calls for two operations besides the investigation of the framework itself. One is explicating the concepts in the framework, and this involves constructing frameworks which allow the concepts to be exhibited with greater degrees of distinctness. The other operation consists in what might be called, after Kant, the "ampliation" of the concepts in the framework; this operation involves the exploration of antecedent frameworks, which reveals the empirical significance of the concepts. Given a language framework L_n, the first operation requires the "ascent" through more precise frameworks, and the second operation requires the "descent" through antecedent frameworks. In practice, of course, both "ascent" and "descent" are limited, the first by uninterpreted formal systems and the second by natural or ordinary or everyday language. The extent of the precision afforded by the uninterpreted formal system is matched only by its empirical obscurity, and its utility derives primarily from its value as a prototype for other systems, whether the latter are interpreted formal systems or formalized empirical systems. The utility of uninterpreted formal systems is considerable from an empiricist viewpoint; whatever the purpose of the pragmatic reconstructionist, he cannot afford to ignore frameworks within which a high degree of precision can be achieved, and a concern for such frameworks will direct his interests toward logical calculi. Precision is at an ebb, on the other hand, in natural languages, so that their utility and interest for pragmatic reconstruction is of an entirely different sort. I now turn to an examination of them.

3. NATURAL LANGUAGES AND ANTECEDENT FRAMEWORKS

The descent from L_n through its antecedent frameworks brings the reconstructionist eventually to what may be named L_0, a natural language. Of course the schema is idealized, for the n in question would seldom have a value greater than 1 or 2; that is, more than one or two steps would seldom be required to get back to L_0, and in practice it is more customary to travel from L_0 to L_n than the other way round.

Between L_0 and any L_1 there appear to be great differences, abbreviated by the terms "natural" and "artificial" or "ideal"—though I will shortly argue that these apparent differences are exaggerated and most accurately to be conceived as differences of degree. Control over natural languages is negligible compared with control over artificial ones, for expressions are used for various purposes within natural languages and so have different meanings in different occurrences; new expressions are continually infiltrating into the languages; and because meanings are seldom precisely and adequately specified, unambiguity is rare (though, it should be added, it is rarely needed). Moreover, the generality of natural languages, measured in terms of type, number, and range of values of its variables, is enormous in comparison with artificial languages. Again, the distinction between formal and factual, or between analytic and synthetic, is not rigidly perpetuated within natural languages, as it is within artificial ones, and even if it were, it could not be known what part of a synthetic statement's meaning is linguistically determined and what part is oriented toward the world of extralinguistic facts.

Despite their defects, natural languages are the "L_0" to which the descent through antecedent frameworks leads. The pragmatic reconstructionist, whenever his concern for empirical significance dominates his concern for precision, eventually finds himself investigating ordinary language and answering questions about it in order to determine what questions to ask about artificial languages and what basis to lay down for conventions about new linguistic contexts. Ordinary language is the context by which questions that are external with respect to any ideal language can be guaranteed cognitive significance even if no artificial language is available to provide it.[11] But of course questions internal to natural languages cannot be answered with the degree of certainty and of precision possible in artificial languages, and this fact forces reconsideration of the nature of internal and external questions.

Internal questions, as introduced by Carnap in connection with artificial language forms, are questions referring to particular frameworks; thus they are answered by definite assertions based on the outcome of investigations of those frameworks. External questions, on the other hand, are questions involving practical decisions about frameworks; answers to them are in the form of proposals about establishing frameworks or of statements of degree about standards for comparing frameworks. But when the framework at issue is the natural language L_0, internal questions cannot be answered definitely, because an investigation of the structure of natural language is not at all like an investigation of artificial languages. This was amply demonstrated in the first chapter of the present work, where, on the basis of an investigation within natural language of such concepts as logicality, synonymy, and analyticity, it was found that no definite assertions could be made, but only statements of degree. "Or" has a high degree of logicality, the pair "bachelor" and "unmarried

---

[11] Ordinary language, according to Warner A. Wick, is "the linguistic philosopher's substitute for common sense" ("Minds, Artificial Languages, and Philosophy," *Philosophy and Phenomenological Research*, XIV [1953–54], 234). In this essay, and in his "The 'Political' Philosophy of Logical Empiricism" (*Philosophical Studies*, II [1951], 49–57), Wick presents a point of view which includes a number of general features of the present one.

man" has a high degree of synonymy, and "no bachelor is married" has a high degree of analyticity. More definite assertions than these would lay claim to a degree of certainty unwarranted by natural language.

Thus, when the reconstructionist pushes the external questions back through antecedent frameworks in an effort to cut down the conventionalist aspect of reconstruction and linguistic analysis, he comes to rest eventually in the framework of natural language. And this is a framework in which internal questions no longer can get the definite answers obtainable in artificial languages. What is called for at this stage of pragmatic reconstruction is a careful investigation of natural language, with a wary ear out for all the subtleties and contextual nuances of colloquial speech to which the so-called ordinary-language philosophers have developed such an extraordinary sensitivity. Just as it is to the general advantage of the pragmatic reconstructionist to follow a concept up the distinctness scale of artificial language frameworks as far as possible, so it is also to his general advantage to learn as much as possible about the various guises under which the concept shows up in everyday language. The first is the advantage of precision and the second of clearness, applicability, and a sense of direction.

So much for the internal questions of ordinary language. When external questions of ordinary language are considered, a new dimension altogether is added to the discussion. If external questions referring to ordinary language are to have cognitive significance—if there are to be considerations in view of which certain questions are thought relevant to ordinary language and certain others not—then there must be an antecedent framework within which this significance is to be found. And the new dimension emerges when the concept of a framework antecedent to L_0 is considered, for such a framework, whatever it may be, is not linguistic.

Some idea of the nature of the antecedent framework of L_0 can be got by thinking of it in terms of both the epistemological continuum and the distinctness scale. In those terms it should be a cognitive context of the sort wherein the activity called "nonverbal symbol-thinking" occurs, and it should be less precise than L_0. How it compares with L_0 in clearness, or empirical significance, depends on the context of application within which the comparison is made. If one wishes to argue that nonverbal thoughts are refractory when it comes to articulating them, it may appear that any gain in distinctness accompanying verbalization is more than offset by a loss in clearness; thinking is never entirely verbalizable. But if one's concern is for conceptual intersubjectivity, or empirical availability—if, for example, problems of social intercourse are primary—the shift to L_0 from its antecedent framework will be viewed as a gain in clearness as well as distinctness. Because of this relativity of the clearness-obscurity relation, the utility of L_0's antecedent framework for the pragmatic reconstructionist must depend entirely on the purpose of his reconstruction. In general it must depend on whether the context of application corresponds more closely to what has been called the context of discovery or to what has been called the context of justification or explication. Opposite errors are often made in this respect: on the one hand, to burrow so deep into the context of explication that nonverbal thinking goes wholly unrecognized and epistemology becomes entirely a matter of language and, on the other hand, to become so fascinated with the context of discovery that verbalization is seen as distortion, the genetic fallacy is elevated to the stature of a methodological precept, and the question of valid thinking as opposed to invalid thinking is completely ignored.

It may be noted, incidentally, that the antecedent framework of natural language could conceivably be a preconceptual form of cognitive experience rather than a context of nonverbal symbol-thinking. It might be thought—in fact, many empiricists have thought—that there is a direct route from immediate experience to language, and that by means of this we are able to anchor our verbal knowledge securely to our least mistakable experiences. The device for getting from the meanings resident in immediate experience to linguistic expression of those meanings is a kind of cognitive element which is quasi-linguistic and quasi-experiential. It has been variously called a protocol sentence, an expressive statement, and a report or basic proposition, and it is the pineal gland of contemporary empiricism. I have suggested, in connection with Lewis' expressive language, that the belief in a language which is available to us, and is also a direct and hence indubitable transcription of experience, is a belief not consonant with empirical propriety. Any language which could share the indubitability of "immediate experience" would share also its elusiveness and obscurity, and any language which was available to us could have no more indubitability than provided for by the canons of the scientific method accounting for its availability.[12]

If there were a realm of sense meanings which had the characteristics and served the purpose Lewis speaks of, it would quite clearly be an antecedent framework of L_0. But there may be such a realm, excepting only that it lacks the characteristic of being transcribable by an expressive language which is indubitable in some empirically significant sense of indubitability. If such a realm existed, it could still be thought of as an antecedent framework but, because of the problem involved in getting to it, not as an *effective* antecedent framework. Lewis suggests a way of getting to sense meanings, involving induction based on linguistic and nonlinguistic behavior; this could provide the inductive certainty obtainable through scientific methods but not the desired indubitability. Nevertheless, inductive certainty is enough for empiricists, and it is the goal of the science of pragmatics. Pragmatics is a broad study that deals, according to Morris, "with all the psychological, biological, and sociological phenomena which occur in the functioning of signs."[13] Presumably by now the circularity bugaboo has been eliminated, and with it the need for pausing to counter the objection that such a study presupposes

[12] See Reichenbach, "Are Phenomenal Reports Absolutely Certain?" *Philosophical Review*, LXI (1952), 147–59; Nelson Goodman, "Sense and Certainty," *ibid.*, 160–67; C. I. Lewis, "The Given Element in Empirical Knowledge," *ibid.*, 168–75. The papers comprise a symposium entitled "The Experiential Element in Knowledge."

[13] Charles W. Morris, *Foundations of the Theory of Signs*, Vol. I, No. 2, of *International Encyclopedia of Unified Science* (Chicago: University of Chicago Press, 1938), p. 30.

EXPERIENCE AND THE ANALYTIC

the validity of the very knowledge for which it is intended to provide a foundation. The pragmatic branch of semiotic is an enterprise in which the pragmatic reconstructionist ought to place full confidence. The "descent" through antecedent frameworks must, when it reaches the level of natural language and seeks an effective antecedent framework for it, take account of any theories which may have developed out of evidence uncovered through pragmaticist inquiry.

To speak, as I have been, about *the* antecedent framework of L_0 is misleading, because it suggests that some single prelinguistic cognitive context is a unique point of departure from nonlinguistic to linguistic contexts. There are any number of such points of departure and, therefore, any number of such antecedent frameworks. What makes it seem natural to speak of *the* antecedent framework of L_0 is that L_0 itself appears to be one vast, sprawling framework, a framework that is antecedent to every L_n and that ought itself to have a single framework antecedent to it.

The truth is that our everyday language is properly characterized not as a single language but as a plurality of languages. Even this is an oversimplification, because what is called natural language is actually a complex network of intertwining languages. Nor should this be so surprising, because natural languages serve an essentially social function and might be expected to mirror a complex network of intertwining social relationships. There are political languages, scientific languages, and esthetic languages, and there are everyday languages reflecting social roles determined by vocation, avocation, income, sex, education, and all the other factors that can be abstracted from the social scene.

The point is not to smuggle in sociological observations but to support the claim that any attempt to get beyond ordinary language to its antecedent framework is entirely dependent on *which* ordinary language one is concerned about. Furthermore, the same considerations are relevant to the appeal to natural language as an antecedent framework of some L_1; it no longer suffices to speak of L_0 as the antecedent framework of every L_1, because only a portion of natural language is required as a framework within which questions external to some artificial language form become significant. Thus, a pragmatic reconstruction whose purpose is to inclose some hypothesis of physics within a context that will exhibit its testable consequences may, faced with some L_n, travel backward through antecedent frameworks until L_0 is reached—but the L_0 is not the whole of natural language, it is only a part of that part of natural language which physicists find efficacious for testing hypotheses. And if the reconstructionist is further concerned to reach a nonlinguistic sensory framework antecedent to this L_0, he will isolate from the set of nonlinguistic cognitive contexts only those applicable to his particular reconstruction. With this comment about the plurality of natural languages, the concept of pragmatic reconstruction may be deepened yet further.

Mention of the pluralistic nature of ordinary language should dispel certain doubts about the scope of pragmatic reconstruction. It may be thought that the method's usefulness is limited to those disciplines or to those portions of disciplines that lend themselves easily to formalization, that if applied to other disciplines pragmatic reconstruction would lead to premature formalization—an occupational malfunction which sins against the very principle of significant precision that is at the heart of the method. Thus, any attempt to superimpose formal frameworks on such disciplines as art criticism or political theory or vocational guidance might be said to surround these activities with an aura of precision far transcending the degree permitted them under the principle of significant precision. And though pragmatic reconstruction pays lip service to natural languages and their antecedent frameworks, it might be objected that the emphasis is all on artificial languages. It might be objected that the reconstruction of a nonformalizable discipline could simply oscillate back and forth monotonously and indefinitely between L_0 and its antecedent framework, for all the guidance pragmatic reconstruction has to offer.

However, the discussion of the plurality of natural languages enlarges the scope of pragmatic reconstruction by showing that the method has ample resources to draw on before, or even without, making the transition from natural to artificial languages. Instead of imposing artificial language forms on his material, the reconstructionist may hand-pick, from among the teeming community of ordinary languages, the linguistic subsets which satisfy the relevant criteria of selection and within which his material may be expediently exhibited. For every subset thus selected, there rise additional problems concerning an antecedent framework, so that any fears about the inhibition of nonformalizable activity due to intimidation at the hands of pragmatic reconstruction are groundless. The principle of significant precision, applied to such disciplines, itself demands that they remain within hailing distance of natural languages. And the conception of natural language developing out of the foregoing discussion insures against the inactivity that might result from confinement to a monolinguistic medium and its antecedent framework.

A modified picture of an "ideal" language is revealed in this light, because ideal languages are no longer opposed to natural languages in the sharply defined way indicated when they are called "artificial" instead of "ideal." To pick out from everyday language a subset adequate for some definite conceptual purpose is to separate desirable meanings from undesirable ones, to free meanings from ambiguity, and to supply meanings and truth values otherwise lacking. But these are the characteristics used earlier for describing languages at once ideal and artificial. There seems to be one main difference between artificial languages and the sort of subsets of natural languages that must be employed for conceptual purposes: the former are entirely creative and have empirical significance only to the degree that their primitive descriptive terms are interpreted, whereas the latter are not so much created as "assembled." This difference is mitigated, however, in consideration of the twofold manner in which the creation of artificial languages can occur. In addition to interpreting a purely formal language framework, the reconstructionist can obtain an artificial language by formalizing an existing empirical language, and formalizing an empirical language does not differ essentially from isolating subsets of natural languages. In fact, the whole distinction of natural from artificial or formal languages seems less clear and distinct than it was, and it is perhaps best conceived as a matter of degree. So far as formalized languages are concerned, a remark of Church's is enlightening: "the difference of a formalized language from a natural language lies not in any matter of principle, but in the degree of completeness that has been attained in the laying down of explicit syntactical and semantical rules and the extent to which vaguenesses and uncertainties have been removed from them."[14]

To isolate subsets of natural languages, then—which is the least that any discipline must do if it is to be allowed even a pretense of having control over its subject matter—differs only in degree from the activities described earlier under the name of artificial language construction. The concept of a hierarchy from L_0 to L_n must be modified in order not to suggest any permanence about the order followed in any particular reconstruction. Within a reconstruction the order may be dictated by any one of a number of factors, most prominent of which are the principle of significant precision and the purpose that determines how it is to be applied.

With this de-emphasis of linguistic differentiation, and the resultant collapse of programs of philosophic analysis centering on some particular kind of linguistic analysis to the exclusion of others, it becomes apparent that for pragmatic reconstruction any language whatever is permissible except within particular contexts of application where it is excluded by considerations of purpose and significant precision. The value of the heavy concentration on artificial languages in the preceding discussion has been mainly heuristic. Linguistic pluralism, linguistic conventionalism, and linguistic pragmatism are most easily introduced and defended in terms of artificial languages, though, once introduced and defended, these aspects of pragmatic reconstruction

[14] Alonzo Church, "The Need for Abstract Entities in Semantic Analysis," *Proceedings of the American Academy of Arts and Sciences*, LXXX (1951–54), 106–7.

become extended to natural languages as a matter of course when similarities between natural and artificial languages are pointed out. Languages are never ready-made for the pragmatic reconstructionist; they can never be taken on faith. While a language he develops may seem ordinary or extraordinary depending on the circumstances, the fact remains that if he is in command of his linguistic medium, he has in one way or another himself contributed to its development.

CHAPTER VII

Empiricism as Pragmatic Reconstruction

1. FACTS, FORMS, AND NORMS

I CONSIDERED in chapter iv some arguments that have been used to deny that factual data and scientific explanations have epistemological relevance, arguments including the proposition that epistemology is a radically different kind of activity from science, and I adduced counterarguments with which to meet these. Since, except in particular instances where there are particularized arguments to the contrary, it is the expansion of sources of knowledge and not their curtailment that philosophy requires, the effect of these counterarguments is to reintroduce, where necessary, scientific data and theories into philosophic inquiry. This poses for the philosophic methodologist the question of what exactly the relationship is between science and philosophy.

In chapter i of the present work, moreover, the distinguishability of logical and nonlogical words and statements was found to be seriously impaired by the necessity that words or statements so distinguished be contained within rigid and precisely delineated linguistic frameworks. The distinguishability is impaired because philosophic inquiry, like all other inquiry, tends continually to transcend any rigid and precisely delineated framework within which it is inclosed. But when distinguishing between the logical and the nonlogical becomes a problem, the methodologist in philosophy must face up to the larger problem of the relationship between logic and other branches of philosophy, and in general the relationship between formal and nonformal disciplines.

Again, in the investigation of human cognition in the fourth chapter, particularly the investigation of low-echelon cognition, consideration of human values loomed large on the epistemological horizon. It was discovered, for instance, that when the needs and the values of the perceiver are ignored, a distorted and vastly oversimplified account of perception results. However, when human values are considered to play an essential role in human cognition, a concern for philosophic methodology must lead to a reconsideration of the customary differentiation between value theory and other branches of philosophy.

Philosophers have long enjoyed the advantages, dialectical and otherwise, to be had by distinguishing sharply between the cognitive and the noncognitive and between the formal and the nonformal, whatever form the distinctions have taken and however they have been called. The advantages have been as great for empiricists as for any other philosophers, for apart from their well-documented stake in the formal-nonformal distinction, empiricists have been anxious to exclude all value or "emotional" elements from the territories of science and of analysis; they have been anxious to fence in a purely ethical domain which would share no embarrassing common ground either with the factual or with the analytic, and the cognitive-noncognitive distinction has enabled them to accomplish both these aims. Moreover, a sharp boundary between science and philosophy has permitted philosophic empiricists to enjoy a reputation for anchoring their ideas firmly in scientific fact and human experience, while managing to avoid existential commitment to theories designed to explain the facts or to assist in the understanding of experience. The factors I have cited, however, force a reconsideration of these distinctions, of the division of philosophic labor based on them, and of the general relationships of the several branches of philosophy to factual inquiries, to logical investigations, and to each other.

To deny that scientific facts and theories have no direct relevance for epistemology is not necessarily to adopt the exaggerated view that the subject matter, methodology, and conceptual tools of science and philosophy are identical, but only to adopt the view that the scientist and the philosopher each has a stake in the activities of the other. There exists what might be called—to take a familiar tack—a methodological continuum ranging approximately from the laboratory at one extreme to the proverbial armchair at the other; to designate what occurs on one side of a certain point on this continuum as "science" and what occurs on the other side as "philosophy" is either entirely arbitrary or else a provisional designation intended to serve a definite but limited purpose. Science and philosophy both operate to advantage, on the present view, when employing the method of pragmatic reconstruction. For both, circularity—the abhorrence of which has made the distinction in question seem desirable—is best controlled when confined within limited and provisional contexts, and such control is best insured by pragmatic reconstruction.

Of course, the reconstruction of scientific issues within sharp and definite language frameworks is an activity in which the scientist seldom engages. There is no reason why he should not engage in the activity, and occasionally he does, but it is much too self-conscious for anyone but modern philosophers to engage in very often. In general the reconstruction is imposed on scientific problems by persons more commonly known as philosophers. What is important is that scientific theories are formalizable; whenever a problem rises which warrants the trouble, the problematic context may be formalized to whatever degree is desirable and the problem seen more precisely. The philosopher, on the other hand, may if so inclined mark off the province of the scientist and declare himself officially uninterested—but the delineation of that province varies from domain to domain, so that elsewhere the same philosopher must handle issues ostracized before as scientific. None of this, however, reflects against the continuity between science and philosophy.

What has been taken to reflect against that continuity is that even though the reconstructionist activity mentioned may, if insisted on, be conceded to be both a scientific and a philosophic activity, as a philosophic activity it belongs to a single and rather limited part of philosophy, the part called philosophy of science. Thus, Bergmann thinks that the only logical interactions between science and philosophy are those which can be seen when newly discovered facts make philosophic analyses useless (rather than wrong) and when scientific problems rise which require philosophic analysis for their solutions. But the latter task, according to him, is "the limited task of the so-called philosophy of science," and it must not be appealed to by arguments for the general philosophic usefulness of artificial or ideal languages. That usefulness may be seen in reference to the fundamental questions of philosophy, but "the appeal of science merely confuses the issue."[1]

It is true that philosophic problems which arise in connection with scientific activity fall within the province called philosophy of science, just as it is true that philosophic problems which arise in connection with political activity fall within the province called political philosophy. However, the significance of these truths is mainly that philosophy is concerned with all sorts of things, and a convenient way of dividing up the field is with respect to the sorts of things it is concerned with. But differentiation by content does not entail differentiation by method, and there is no reason to think that while reference to the "fundamental questions" will indicate that some methods are more useful than others, reference to less fundamental questions will indicate that other methods have more use. Moreover, the appeal to science, far from confusing the issue, illuminates it. Before it disappears in the smoke screen which seems suddenly to have enveloped the discussion, the issue is whether the aims and methods of science and philosophy are different enough to justify the radical distinction that both philosophers and scientists have drawn between the two. And what I am still maintaining is that there is a continuity between science and philosophy. Not only is the traditional ground for distinguishing sharply between them undermined, but both involve the method of pragmatic reconstruction. The main differences between the ways science and philosophy involve the method of pragmatic reconstruction are, first, that scientists actually construct linguistic frameworks or formalize their theories only when obstacles rise, or when they

[1] Gustav Bergmann, "Professor Quine on Analyticity," *Mind*, LXIV (1955), 254–58.

become self-conscious, and, second, that philosophers are a little freer to disregard the rule about observable consequences. This last difference lays a special obligation on the philosopher not to let the method get out of control, for freedom to disregard the rule about observable consequences can easily lead to obscurity, of either the underdistinct or the overdistinct variety. But the point is that these are inessential differences and that—once more preserving the spirit if not the letter of traditional empiricism— the methodology most appropriate for exhibiting the most salient features of science is also the methodology that emerges from a careful consideration of philosophic method.

Enough has been said about the formal-nonformal distinction that no corroboration is needed at this late stage of the discussion for the belief that the distinction, a crucial one for the processes of intellect, can never be made except functionally. With respect to philosophic methodology an important question that emerges is the question of how logic fits into the scheme of things.

Formal systems in general, whether they are constructed as such or result from the formalization of comparatively nonformal systems, are useful as structural prototypes for more substantial contexts. The demarcation of a class of systems that are not only formal but logical, however, is no less subject to ambiguity than the tracing of a border between systems that are formal and those that are not. That demarcation, if it could be made un-ambiguously, would rely heavily if not exclusively on the distinction between logical and descriptive words that was found, in the first chapter, to contain a strong element of convention. Any word, it was suggested, may function as a logical word in so far as its descriptive component is ignored. Certain words, it is true, occur more frequently in logical systems than others, and though the choice of these words is ultimately a convention, un-derlying the choice is the utility the words have for facilitating logical transformations. The words that occur pervasively in a logical way are those which seem to lose relatively little of their significance when their descriptive component is ignored. Never-theless, there hangs over the whole matter a veil of indecisiveness

245

which obscures the kind of vision that could reveal a sharp and permanent distinction between logical words and nonlogical words or, more generally, between logic and other branches of philosophy. Logic is a legitimate and vital branch of philosophy, but it is identifiable as logic solely by its peculiar way of trying both to ignore those qualities of words and statements we usually find most significant and to recognize as significant certain other qualities we usually ignore. These latter qualities are variously called formal and logical and syntactic. The view I am taking and the proposition I am arguing is that the differences between form and nonform, between logic and nonlogic, and between syntax and semantics show up and are significant only within limited and provisional contexts, the sort that provide the media within which pragmatic reconstruction may be carried on.

That it is a gross distortion of the nature of human knowledge to portray it as devoid of any value element by now needs no documentation. The epistemological distinction between cognitive and noncognitive, the key to which is the absence or presence of value, simply has no basis in any empirical difference. Nevertheless, the distinction is so crucial that it is difficult to see how epistemologists could get along without it. There is a way, moreover, of utilizing the distinction without hypostatizing it—by taking it in a functional sense, with the aid of contexts. Recognition of the cognitive and the noncognitive need not lead to the false alternatives, or share the discredit, of intellect and emotion as psychological faculties, reason and faith as epistemological criteria, or fact and value as ontological domains.

Within a domain of the sort used for pragmatic reconstruction, considerations of value may be ignored in favor of "purely cognitive" considerations just as considerations of fact may be ignored in favor of "purely formal" considerations. The resulting distortion of the nature of knowledge may be overlooked because the domain is both limited and provisional. It has been set up for a purpose; the purpose requires that value elements in knowledge situations be ignored; and there is no excuse for supposing that the domain "corresponds to" or is otherwise indicative of the real characteristics of cognitive experience. All that is needed is continual recognition that a particular context is only a context, and that the elimination of values is only within a relatively narrow scope.

So far as empirical meaning is concerned, what we have to start with is significance as it emerges at the most "primitive" levels of cognition empirically available, and at this level significance is at least as much a matter of human value as of anything else. A greater falsification of the state of things cannot be imagined than to prune low-echelon cognition of its value component by distinguishing between cognitive and noncognitive elements. By the same token, no true empiricist can assent to dividing significance into cognitive and noncognitive significance, except tentatively, in the spirit of pragmatic reconstruction.

2. SOME METHODOLOGICAL PROBLEMS IN THE
THEORY OF KNOWLEDGE

Aside from settling or dissolving boundary disputes among logic, epistemology, value theory, and science, the issues just discussed are important for methodological reasons. One of the variables among pragmatic reconstructions, and one of the questions that must be decided in advance of any reconstruction that is to serve the purpose for which it is designed, is the drawing of the several boundary lines. We deal with the cognitive by ignoring, to a certain extent, the noncognitive; but the noncognitive can be ignored entirely only for a very limited number of reconstructions, certainly far fewer than empiricists have seemed to think. What we must decide for any reconstruction of knowledge is how much of the value component present in our experience is to be excluded from the reconstruction. We deal with the formal by ignoring, to a certain extent, the nonformal; but there are degrees of formality, corresponding to the degrees to which the nonformal may be overlooked, and the degree chosen for any reconstruction must take into account the purpose the reconstruction is to serve.

Furthermore, just as the "purely cognitive" and the "purely formal" are ideal limits toward which many philosophers have thought it profitable to aim, the "purely factual" (or as it has been called in another connection, the purely descriptive) has provided a foundation for much bad methodology. Should an entirely factual or nonformal context seem desirable for a reconstruction, the context must be accorded no more philosophic privilege than an entirely formal or an entirely cognitive context. And exactly the same is true of the noncognitive that is true of the nonformal; any attempt to mark off an entirely noncognitive realm (or, as it has been called in some contexts, entirely emotive) must reckon with the considerations that have been brought to bear against the cognitive, the formal, and the nonformal, in their unsullied states. My purpose at present, however, is not to malign contexts in which important elements of experience are refused acknowledgment but to point out the necessity for deciding, with respect to every context of pragmatic reconstruction, what proportion of the various experiential elements would best suit the needs of the reconstruction.

Other variables of pragmatic reconstruction involve the drawing of other boundary lines. There are, for example, the many distinctions blurred in Parts I and II because objection was taken to the philosophic significance customarily attached to them. Nevertheless, these distinctions must be made in a functional or methodological sense whenever certain areas of knowledge are reconstructed. The analytic-synthetic distinction, of course, needs to be traced whenever a framework of any sort is to be constructed, for without it we have not yet brought order out of chaos. Tracing the analytic-synthetic distinction in turn requires a firm grip on some or all of the elusive matters discussed in connection with the distinction: matters including definition, synonymy, and the distinction between the logical and the nonlogical. Besides the analytic-synthetic distinction, there are the less pervasive boundary lines to be drawn in the reconstruction of certain areas of human knowledge. These are the boundary lines between the given and the nongiven, the noninferred and the inferred, the noticed and the remembered, the present-as-present and the present-as-past, and the extradermal and the intradermal. There are numerous possibilities for dividing any single pair, and the presence of several pairs within a single reconstruction insures that pragmatic reconstruction is not likely to be inhibited for lack of alternative contexts.

Another decision to be taken in the preliminary stages of any reconstruction is the selection of primitive terms. The elements taken as primitive in a linguistic framework within which or from which human knowledge is to be reconstructed have presumably been determined within an antecedent framework. Within the framework to be constructed the elements have epistemological priority, but within the antecedent framework their priority is methodological only, and the philosophic difference between methodological and epistemological priority is vast.

An antecedent framework within which epistemological priority might reasonably be expected to be meted out, if it were expected to be meted out at all, is the one I have mentioned as being antecedent to natural language, a framework that may be designated as "experiential." But the point that the nature and constituency of this framework is anybody's guess, or at least the outgrowth of anybody's analysis, has been labored too long. Starting with total perception, irrespective of questions about immediacy, and analyzing this into perceptual elements which are "given," or have epistemological priority, the question of which elements have epistemological priority is a question of where the analysis ends; and where the analysis ends is, for pragmatic reconstructionists, determined for each analysis in the light of the purpose of the reconstruction. Not simply maximum precision but maximum significant precision is the goal of analysis performed in the name of pragmatic reconstruction. Maximum significant precision may, depending on the context of application, award epistemological priority to psychosomatic totalities of sensation, to their somatic portions, to sensations combining the customary five sense modalities, to sensations of any single sense modality, to "qualitatively homogeneous blocks" of these, or to the old familiar sense data, which may be either kept intact or split up into such "atoms" as (in the case of visual data) hue, saturation, and brilliance. Analysis need not stop even here, for if the context of application requires it, these perceptual atoms may be taken as correlates to physiological and physical complexes which are further analyzable. And the most that can be said of any primitive elements among these is that they have methodological priority, that within a particular context for pragmatic reconstruction these elements fulfil the requirements better than any others.

Should it be objected that a primitive basis must, for the reconstruction to meet the conditions imposed by empiricism, be governed by something like Bergmann's principle of acquaintance,[2] then there is the opportunity to make clear that the so-called principle of acquaintance or anything like it, as far as pragmatic reconstruction is concerned, gives the widest possible latitude in the selection of primitive bases. In advance of a particular occasion of its employment, nothing whatever can be ruled out, from sense data to material objects to classes of classes to ghosts. It is true that material objects will fill the need more often than ghosts, but this has to do not so much with a principle of acquaintance as with a principle of applicability—the principle which governs the context of application.

The most popular primitive bases for the reconstruction of knowledge have been sense data and appearances of material objects. The resulting frameworks have been called "sense-datum" or "phenomenalist" languages and "thing" or "physicalist" languages, respectively. It is worth noting, incidentally, that Quine —though he presents cases for both the phenomenalist and the physicalist conceptual schemes, compares the acceptance of an ontology with that of a scientific theory, and counsels "tolerance and an experimental spirit"—speaks of "the epistemological point of view" and, taking it, awards epistemological priority to the

---

[2] "To be an empiricist means to adopt an 'empiricist meaning criterion' or 'principle of acquaintance,' i.e., to assert the sufficiency of a class of undefined terms that refer to the sort of thing philosophers call the phenomenally given in contradistinction to, say, physical objects" ("Logical Positivism," *The Metaphysics of Logical Positivism* [New York: Longmans, Green & Co., 1954], pp. 6–7).

phenomenalist scheme.[3] Quite apart from the unwarranted supposition that the phenomenalist vocabulary comes closer to an
accurate description of our immediate experience, Quine's loose
dealing with epistemological priority affords the epistemologist
scant opportunity to display the experimental spirit. Once having located the epistemologically prior framework, the epistemologist's duty seems clear, and it leaves no room for tolerating
physicalism or any other nonphenomenalist scheme. The plea
for tolerance is a fitting one, but Quine scarcely facilitates the
granting of it, at least in epistemology. More in accordance with
the experimental spirit is freedom on the part of the epistemologist to adopt any basis whatever. Phenomenalism, physicalism,
or any other linguistic framework may be called for when the
purpose of a reconstruction is best served by it,[4] and the only
kind of priority a framework may be said to have on this account
is methodological priority for the reconstruction in question.

Along with selecting a primitive basis for the pragmatic reconstruction of human knowledge, and drawing the relevant distinctions, other decisions need to be made. It has to be decided,
for instance, how much of human knowledge is to be reconstructed and, concomitantly, what kind of accuracy is to be
aimed for in the reconstruction. The decisions are concomitant
because the amount of epistemic coverage possible is limited by
the accuracy of the coverage. Conversely, given a particular area
of knowledge to be reconstructed, a certain kind and degree of
accuracy may be possible but not another. If a reconstruction of
scientific knowledge in its entirety is wanted, then, as has been
seen, "blueprint" accuracy must be foregone, and we must make
do with sketching our subject in *aufbau* style. But if a reconstruc-

[3] W. V. Quine, "On What There Is," *From a Logical Point of View*
(Cambridge, Mass.: Harvard University Press, 1953), pp. 16 ff. See also
Quine's "Two Dogmas of Empiricism," *ibid.*, pp. 44 ff., and Albert Hof-
stadter, "The Myth of the Whole: A Consideration of Quine's View of
Knowledge," *Journal of Philosophy*, LI (1954), 403 ff.

[4] See Rudolf Carnap, "Testability and Meaning," *Philosophy of Science*,
IV (1937), 9 ff., and Hans Reichenbach, "The Verifiability Theory of
Meaning," *Proceedings of the American Academy of Arts and Sciences*,
LXXX (1951–54), 50–51.

tion of a small subarea of knowledge is wanted—say, a small set of theoretic constructs and relations among them—then blueprints may be drawn up. The difference here, it might be said, is the difference between theoretic and practical accuracy. Practical accuracy, if built into a framework, allows a reconstruction to be carried out as thoroughly as the reconstructionist is inclined; theoretic accuracy allows it to be carried out only "in principle." And whereas blueprinting a small subarea of scientific knowledge can be accomplished with practical accuracy, only theoretic accuracy is attainable in a reconstruction of more comprehensive domains of human knowledge.

The degree of precision built into a framework determines the extent to which the knowledge reconstructed with the aid of the framework may be refined. Given the precision of logical atomism, an extreme degree of refinement is possible, whereas the comparatively lumbering apparatus provided by intensional frameworks allows only grosser elements of knowledge to be reconstructed. The other side of the coin is, of course, that the more precise apparatus is so light and agile that it skips nimbly over many kinds of knowledge we want also to reconstruct. When this happens, the reconstruction is obscure; to regain and preserve clearness, or empirical significance, the principle of significant precision becomes operative and prevents precision from outstripping significance.

Note, however, the relation of the combined primitive questions of precision, clearness, and scope of reconstruction to the question of primitive bases. If a certain primitive vocabulary has already been chosen, the number of alternatives in the matters of accuracy and scope have been cut down. If "necessarily" appears anywhere in the list of connectives or if statements must be able to refer to potentialities in order to be true, those kinds and degrees of accuracy and scope possible only with the help of logical atomism are ruled out. Therefore, it would be an oversimplification to speak of deciding first on a primitive vocabulary and then on the scope and accuracy of a reconstruction; all these decisions must be made jointly, unless some one consideration so far outweighs the others for the purposes of a recon-

struction that its determining influence on the other decisions is
of small or agreeable consequence.

The rational reconstruction of human knowledge within one
all-encompassing linguistic framework substitutes deductive or
"linear" relationships among linguistic elements for the haphazard relationships to be discovered among the bits of knowledge that actually function in human thinking. The substitution
has its purposes, of course, and in so far as this is the case such a
reconstruction may be pragmatic as well as rational, but in so far
as rational reconstruction has no other purposes some pragmatic
reconstructions are nonrational. A difference between the two
kinds of reconstruction has been suggested in the case of Reichenbach's irrational jump.[5] From the pragmatic reconstructionist's
position, though the jump is irrational from one viewpoint it
may be rational, or at least less irrational, from another. Thus,
given just such a piece of unreconstructed belief as Reichenbach's
example, pragmatic reconstruction enables us to attack the problem in innumerable different ways. For example, if the jump appears less abrupt when exhibited within a sociological or psy-
chiatric framework, we have learned something about human
knowledge, something that may serve a philosophic purpose,
even if we have not given the sort of justification or explication
of the jump which from another viewpoint it is the sole task of
philosophy to give.

The linear approach taken by rational reconstructionists to the
problems of knowledge is but one of a number of approaches
open to pragmatic reconstructionists. Though any particular
framework utilized in pragmatic reconstruction is linear in de-
sign—which is to say that relations among elements are strung
out in such a way that it is easy, by means of operations permissible within the context, to get from any one element to any
other—this is not true of the frameworks themselves. Depending
on the initial clearness and distinctness with which the subject of
a reconstruction is conceived, there may or may not be some
obvious principle according to which the sequence of frameworks

[5] See above, pp. 219–20.

taken up and discarded in the course of a reconstruction is serially ordered.

The order may be of degrees of precision, aiming toward maximum precision, or it may be from obscurity to significance, where significance is a direct function of precision up to a point and an inverse function beyond that point. The reconstruction may move from natural languages to uninterpreted formal languages, or it may move from natural languages into nonlinguistic domains of experience by way of pragmatics. It may travel toward empirical observability, or it may travel away from empirical observability. It may lead into the domain of natural science, or it may lead into the domain of metaphysics. It may even be that the order of sequence is a mystery to all but the reconstructionist, who is at liberty to "home" on his subject in any way that seems appropriate to him or that offers a possibility of opening up fruitful explorations. In exploring the byways of pragmatic reconstruction the bonds of relevance—not to mention more intimate kinds of connection—may get stretched to tenuous lengths, but so long as the reconstructionist does not lose sight of the external questions in his enthusiasm for certain internal ones, he is not transgressing the limits of pragmatic reconstruction.

However, failure to distinguish between the two kinds of questions leads to all sorts of philosophic disasters. In the case of a scientific theory it leads to the curtailment of activity whose focal point is outside the theory, and thus effectively insures against any scientific development of the order of magnitude of the theory in question. In the case of a metaphysical system it leads to the sort of disdain for experience, intolerance of ideas, and ingrown scholasticism with whose repudiation empiricism has traditionally been associated. And in the case of an ideal language, or any other conceptual framework with its own legislation about admissible kinds of experience, the blurring has consequences similar to those mentioned in connection with metaphysical systems, except that so far as empiricism is concerned the consequences are calamitous—repudiation of the framework is apt to be construed as repudiation of empiricism itself, the sort of repudiation currently (and periodically) associated with the phrase "return to reason."

3. THE SCOPE AND LIMITS OF EMPIRICISM

Should it be wondered what sort of metaphysical activity may be engaged in under the aegis of empiricism, various answers are possible. A theory about metaphysics which fits in well with the requirements of pragmatic reconstruction is Pepper's "root metaphor" theory: a metaphysical system is a "world hypothesis," "framed in the first instance on the basis of a rather small set of facts and then expanded in reference so as to cover all facts."[6] Similar to Pepper's approach to metaphysics as metaphor is Emmet's conception of metaphysics as analogic thinking.[7] Of course these metaphoric and analogic conceptions of metaphysics, though themselves compatible with pragmatic reconstruction, are not metaphysical theories; the metaphysical theories the conceptions are about are empirically acceptable only when viewed hypothetically, which is not the way metaphysicians have traditionally viewed them. So long as there exists an antecedent framework within which external questions referring to a system are significant (as provided, for instance, by the metaphoric and analogic theories about metaphysics), the internal-external distinction, and along with it the control demanded by pragmatic reconstruction, may be maintained. But so long as a system has an antecedent framework, it is not a metaphysical system in the traditional sense.

Mention of the idea of antecedent frameworks suggests a way of looking at metaphysics that is even more closely tied to the idea of pragmatic reconstruction. Any pragmatic reconstruction can, if necessary, be carried backward through its antecedent frameworks until one is reached which has no framework antecedent to it. This is the *ultimate antecedent framework* for the reconstruction. To the degree that a context figures within prag-

[6] Stephen C. Pepper, "The Root Metaphor Theory of Metaphysics," *Journal of Philosophy*, XXXII (1935), 369; see also his *World Hypotheses* (Berkeley: University of California Press, 1942).

[7] Dorothy M. Emmet, *The Nature of Metaphysical Thinking* (London: Macmillan & Co., 1945).

matic reconstructions as an ultimate antecedent framework it may be called metaphysical.

From the point of view of the reconstructionist, such ultimate antecedent frameworks constitute what may be called *working hypotheses*, and every reconstructionist must have such hypotheses, however vague and incompletely worked out they may be, in order to carry on his reconstructional activities. In the normal course of those activities it does not occur to him to doubt his working hypotheses; he has no reason to doubt them, and it would hamstring him intolerably to be forced to doubt them. However, if the reconstruction should for any reason focus on these working hypotheses, his willingness to jeopardize them by placing them in a position such that other frameworks are antecedent to them is the test of whether or not he is a pragmatic reconstructionist. What is essential to pragmatic reconstruction is that every framework, however high its priority in certain reconstructions, may figure in other reconstructions where there are other frameworks antecedent to it. Again, however, the objection is proper that so long as a context has an antecedent framework at all it is not really metaphysical, and that therefore I have not yet explained how metaphysics can be part of pragmatic reconstruction. The only reply is that so long as a context is held to be absolutely immune to external questioning—the kind of questioning that demands an antecedent framework—it cannot be part of pragmatic reconstruction.

There is, nevertheless, a real function to be performed by a kind of metaphysical activity that falls under the rubric and shares the spirit of pragmatic reconstruction. In speaking just now of working back through antecedent frameworks, I did not make clear how very different this activity is from that which travels in the direction of precision, which is the direction of explication and analysis. The difference is much more than one of direction, for while any framework contains within itself the information required for an intelligent choice of a more precise framework, it does not contain the information needed to choose an antecedent framework. Choosing an antecedent framework involves considerations quite different from those controlling explication and analysis, considerations which suggest that something close to metaphysics is being done. Among these is the desire that various piecemeal reconstructions be compatible by having compatible conceptual and methodological bases, or even that they be parts of one not-so-piecemeal reconstruction. This desire can lead to a system-building activity which, at least in degree of comprehension aimed at, is certainly metaphysical, though of course no system can be held as irrevocable by empiricists as metaphysicians have customarily held theirs to be. There is, moreover, the desire to justify piecemeal reconstructions by means of antecedent frameworks within which judgments of value—ignored but nevertheless functioning within the piecemeal reconstructions—may be made explicit. And there is the desire to work out a set of fundamental propositions, about the world or about human values, which could serve as a hyperultimate antecedent framework, a framework antecedent to every reconstruction except, of course, one whose purpose is to investigate that antecedent framework. All these desires are legitimate ones for the pragmatic reconstructionist, and all require for their gratification a kind of philosophizing that in almost all respects must be called metaphysical.

It may be pointed out, incidentally, that such a hyper-ultimate antecedent framework is just the sort of thing that philosophy is traditionally supposed to provide for the spiritual comfort of mankind. Recent neglect by empiricists, if not of mankind's spiritual comfort, then of rock-bottom propositions about things and values, may be said to have left a hiatus in contemporary intellectual life, though without—it appears in retrospect—any compensatory gain for philosophy. In the absence of such a compensatory gain, and as long as no belief is granted immunity against investigation, there is no reason why philosophers, even empiricist philosophers, should be denied the right to traffic in fundamental beliefs. By trying out frameworks incorporating them, pragmatic reconstruction reopens the possibility of a careful investigation of the most fundamental beliefs men hold.

But I am talking too much about metaphysics, as empiricists usually do. The initial preoccupation of empiricists with metaphysics has long ago served its purpose of making philosophers self-conscious about their theories and what their theories are about; the oversimplification that had an initial utility in bringing about the rapid elimination of nonsense has brought in its wake a kind of nonsignificance of its own. My suggestion is that through pragmatic reconstruction we can eliminate this new kind of nonsignificance without suffering a full backward swing of the pendulum.

It may be wondered whether the philosophic position I have tried to rescue from a rationalist cul-de-sac is really the empiricism I claimed needed rescue to begin with. When philosophic method is governed by the loose sort of canons to which I have given the name of pragmatic reconstruction, it can no longer be guaranteed that any significant element of human knowledge is tied down to human experience in the way the early empiricists wanted it tied down. For one thing, the only epistemic element that can be tied down at all is a whole context or system, so that any lesser element is significant only as it figures in a system. But empirical significance cannot be guaranteed even for a system. All that can be guaranteed by pragmatic reconstruction as it has been developed in these pages is the empirical significance of a definite and particular system for a limited and particular purpose, and, it may be said, this is no more than a travesty of what empiricists have from the beginning wanted to accomplish. Moreover, some of the criteria appealed to—clearness, applicability, significant precision—are themselves not without a whisper of the appeal to self-evidence and intuitive certainty in terms of which I have characterized rationalist philosophies and even satirized some empiricist philosophies. In effect, the pluralist kind of reconstruction here outlined, discussed, and promoted gives the go-ahead to any kind of system-building whatever, for no hint has been given about how to pick out from among this plethora of contexts, situations, systems, and frameworks those which empiricists can be fully confident are pervaded with significance because anchored firmly to experience. The warning against confounding internal and external questions, it may be said, is of some utility in preventing the acceptance of any one system as the eternal and immutable repository of empirical significance, but only at the cost of depriving empiricists of any criterion for accepting one system even as *more likely* to be empirically significant than another. The whole matter has been made relative to purpose, and, purpose being the subjective sort of thing it is, anyone can have any purpose, and therefore any system at all can have empirical significance.

The puzzlement is understandable, but the charge is unjust. It hinges on mistaking the proposition that any system can be empirically significant for the proposition that no system is more empirically significant than any other. The first proposition I assert and the second I deny. Let me try to explain the ground for my denial of the second.

The original empiricist principle that, in order to be empirically significant, every idea should be derived from experience may be translated as the principle that the ultimate antecedent framework of every cognitive context should be experiential. Taking "ultimate antecedent framework" in a previously suggested sense, the principle may be expressed by the statement that the empiricist should take as his working hypotheses that experience is the touchstone for the significance of his assertions and that he must be prepared at any time to justify the latter by showing their relationship to the former.

But the mark of the empiricist, as also suggested, is his willingness to jeopardize his working hypotheses, or ultimate antecedent framework, by placing them in a position of subservience to another framework or set of hypotheses. Much of the present work has been devoted to just this, the test framework being experiential in one or another sense of the word, and the framework by means of which the test was carried out being methodological. By focusing on the methodological factors involved in the principle of justification by reduction to experience, it was found that there are a number of concepts of experience, most of them vague, and that therefore any appeal to experience as the sole arbiter of significance is doomed to frustration. Any such appeal is completely dependent on which concept of experience is being appealed to, and because there is a plurality of such concepts, there is—entirely apart from the vagueness of many of them—a plurality also of criteria for significance. It is true that the results of the inquiry into experience in chapter iv point to a pluralist conception of experience, and along with it to a pluralist conception of empirical significance, but the issue is whether the kind of empiricism that emerges is close enough to the intentions of the classic empiricists to warrant continued use of the name.

It is possible that the empiricist viewpoint may be conveniently expressed through bypassing experience and dealing instead with some closely related concept. A closely related concept that has both historic and conceptual connections with empiricism is that of science; and it may be that however difficult it is to capture experiential elements and convert them into linguistic elements, these are only dialectical difficulties and do not obstruct scientific avenues to experience. Though operationism and the verification theory have surrendered much of their utility as ways of expressing the epistemological significance of science, there is still the contextual theory of significance. Some contexts are and some are not ratified by science, and scientific ratification may be said to be tantamount to the possession of empirical significance.

It may be noted, for one thing, that scientific ratification or, to slip into a more familiar vocabulary, scientific confirmation, is not a straightforward matter of being confirmed or being unconfirmed. Rather, it is a matter of being confirmed to some degree, so that the most that can be got out of scientific confirmation is degree of empirical significance. Nevertheless, a concept of degree of significance is better than no concept at all, and it is all I need at the moment, because what I am concerned with at the moment is denying the proposition that no system of knowledge has more empirical significance than any other.

But there is something wrong with this independent appeal to scientific confirmation. Given the concept of experience, it is easy enough to get to the proposition that degree of confirmation is a clue to degree of empirical significance, because by "empirical" here is meant "experiential" and the confirmation in question is confirmation by experience. But without the concept of experience to mediate between science and empiricism, it is not apparent that the appeal to science as the backbone of empiricism has anything stronger behind it than an unreasoned belief in scientific infallibility.

A possible reply is that no independent concept of experience is necessary, because an understanding of the way science works brings with it its own conception of experience. Science works through its explanatory concepts and propositions; the latter have predictable consequences; and the nature of the consequences is a sure index to the nature of the experience to which empiricists want significant contexts to be tied. The trouble with this reply is that there is, as I have mentioned, a continuity of the kinds of activity that may qualify as scientific. Science may be said to range continuously from the armchair to the laboratory, and predictability is relative to the methodological level under consideration. Lack of predictable consequences at a particular "prediction level" does not mean there are no consequences at another level, and presence of consequences at a particular level does not guarantee their applicability. The conclusion seems to be that any conception of experience we are to get out of considerations of scientific method we must have brought to those considerations ourselves.

Another possibility for penetrating to the heart of empiricism without making direct use of the idea of experience is through the idea of *intersubjectivity*. A significant part of the empiricist revolt against rationalism was and is directed against the philosophic method of arriving at allegedly objective truths on the basis of such subjective criteria as self-evidence and intuitive certainty. The motivation of Locke's attack on innate ideas was to rid philosophy of the subjective controls that seemed to be governing it. That the controls which the early empiricists substituted for those of the rationalists are no less subjective to us is merely an irony of intellectual history. It is no less ironic, however, than the subjective character of logical clarity or syntactic precision as criteria by means of which so many latter-day empiricists have thought they were preserving the intent of empiricism. Every attempt to subject philosophy to controls or standards said to guarantee its objectivity has seemed to result in loss of control somewhere along the line, and eventually in a return to subjectivity. And I have little doubt that much of the narcissism of modern epistemology can be traced to the oscillation between objectivity and subjectivity that has characterized so much of the history of philosophy in modern times. My suggestion is that the best remedy for this philosophic ataxia is the concept of intersubjectivity.

To seek out intersubjective agreement in philosophy is to recognize the impossibility of attaining objective truth—if not to recognize the dubious nature of the concept—without abandoning the attempt to reach criteria of adequacy grounded in considerations less subjective than intuitive certainty. And the avoidance of subjectivity is more crucial for empiricism than the attainment of objectivity. Moreover, when intersubjectivity is recognized as a more appropriate philosophic goal than objectivity, some of the thorniest problems of recent philosophy are seen to be, if not pseudo-problems, then at least problems deserving of much less attention than they have been getting. Problems about ontological commitments by natural language, for example, lose their air of urgency if not of intrigue when natural language is viewed as a vehicle for intersubjective communication. Natural-language commitments may then be viewed not as clues, accurate or misleading, to objective reality, but as indexes to the kind of ontology that facilitates communication among human beings and therefore facilitates social behavior. Quine states the connection between ontology and natural language nicely when he says, "men have believed in something very like our common-sense world of external objects as long, surely, as anything properly describable as language has existed; for the teaching of language and the use of it for communication depend on investing linguistic forms with intersubjectively fixed references."[8]

With consideration of intersubjectivity, science comes back into the picture. Science faded out of the picture, it will be remembered, because without a definite concept of experience to mediate between science and empiricism the appeal to science would have no reasonable justification. Intersubjectivity, however, provides just the sort of mediating concept that is needed. As an empiricist criterion, I have suggested, its use leads to consequences close to the underlying motives of empiricists. Furthermore, intersubjectivity is the ground of scientific method, for however devious the methodological routes that science takes between the experiences that call for and those that justify its employment, sooner or later the test of intersubjectivity must be passed. And it must be passed at whatever "confirmation level" is most appropriate, that is, wherever along the methodological continuum experiential consequences have been predicted.

But experiential consequences will usually be predicted at whatever level is thought suitable for testing purposes, and test suitability in turn is dictated by considerations of intersubjectivity. Given a hypothesis to be tested, it must be inclosed within a suitable theoretic context, and one must decide how the context is to be "tied down" to experience. One must decide which statements are to be put into such an intimate relation with experience that a single negative experiment will lead to their denial; which statements are to be given such an exalted status that no experiential evidence could compromise them; and which statements are to be placed in intermediate positions and where. The kind of experience to which the system is to be submitted is a matter of intersubjective availability.

Intersubjectivity emerges as a central concept of philosophic empiricism, and scientific method may be considered in several ways the institutionalization of intersubjectivity, or at least the place to look for a conscious and cautious exploitation of it. Because of this, it may be expected that the test procedures ap-

[8] Quine, "On Mental Entities," *Proceedings of the American Academy of Arts and Sciences*, LXXX (1951–54), 200.

proved by scientists are a clue to the nature of experience in that evidential factors appealed to by scientists have, on that account, a measure of empirical significance. But I do not want to lay too much stress on this significance which accrues by virtue of scientific test procedures, because there are other factors which may outweigh it; I have gone to these lengths to discover it merely in order to show that while it is true that on my view any system whatever may have empirical significance, it is not true that no system has more empirical significance than any other system.

I want to point out now that, though intersubjectivity turns out to be of central importance to empiricism, and is determinant of empirical significance more often than not, empiricists, once they have grasped this importance, must always be allowed to ignore it. Intersubjectivity, in other words, is a reference point and not an ironbound criterion. There are times—and they are frequent—when philosophy demands fresh vantage points, and at such times rigorous insistence on intersubjectivity and on the scientific method which implements it is inimical to philosophic advance. Moreover, not only intersubjectivity but any kind of methodological legislation is a barrier at such times to the forward movement of philosophy. It is the same in every field of intellectual endeavor: consolidation and systematization of knowledge may be and ought to be governed by legislation, but speculation and discovery, whose fruits are to be consolidated and systematized, cannot and ought not be legislated.

Absence of legislation, however, does not absolve intellectual workers of responsibility, even in areas of speculation and discovery. While speculation requires relaxation of legislative controls, responsible speculation requires that, though any control may be relaxed within any context, no control may be relaxed within every context and within no context may every control ever be relaxed. What this requirement presupposes, moreover, is a strict accounting for individual contexts and therefore a firm grip on the distinction between internal and external questions. Given such a grip, we cannot lose ourselves within an individual context, whether it is an artificial language, a system of meta-physics, or a scientific theory.

Responsibility, except in the most superficial of senses, is not the sort of thing that can be legislated; it goes naturally along with competence in any field. Philosophy, when competent, is responsible. But, though adequate methodological legislation can help prevent incompetence in philosophy and can occasionally, in certain narrowly conceived domains, by itself insure competence, for the most part philosophic competence and incompetence result not from being governed by adequate and inadequate methodologies but from being done by competent and incompetent philosophers. A philosopher who is competent tries among other things to take experience seriously by being constantly on his guard, even (and especially) when he departs deliberately from what is intersubjectively sanctioned as experientially significant.

Very likely this is true whether the philosopher calls himself a rationalist or an empiricist. But rationalist or empiricist, responsible or irresponsible, it is all too easy to be misled. The history of philosophy shows that once experiential significance is misplaced, an incredible amount of time and labor may be required before it is located again. The consequences to philosophy in the meantime are calamitous. So appalling does this seem to the philosophic empiricist that he finds it worthwhile, in the name of significance, to try to build into his philosophy methodological safeguards which will prevent the occurrence of such intellectual setbacks. That these safeguards import into philosophy difficulties of their own has been documented, along with the nature of the added difficulties, but though the difficulties demand attention, they do not necessitate abandonment of the safeguards. All they necessitate is a reconsideration of the safeguards and of the empiricism that revolves about them. Such a reconsideration I have tried to give, and pragmatic reconstruction is a way of doing philosophy that gives promise, in the light of that reconsideration, of helping empiricists to overcome their major difficulties while developing a greater sensitivity to what is significant in human experience.

INDEX

Index

Accuracy, 251 f.; idiomatic, 204 ff., 216; practical and theoretic, 252; syntactic, 204 ff., 228; *see also* Distinctness; Precision
Acquaintance: knowledge by, 134; principle of, 68 n., 250
Action: and cognition, 166 f.; high-level and low-level, 166 f., 176; and motivation, 167
Ames, Adelbert, Jr., 141, 154 n., 209 n.
Analysis, 94 ff., 99, 152 f., 155; being the end result of, 94 ff., 100, 113 ff.; and epistemological priority, 99, 249 f.; functional, 160; philosophic, 63, 115, 239; and purpose, 115
Analytic meaning; *see* Meaning
Analytic statements: as auxiliary statements, 19 n.; as distinguished from synthetic statements (*see* Analyticity [2]); explicit and implicit, 25 f., 83; as following from semantic rules, 54, 58, 61, 71; in L_{I}, 52 ff., 61, 85 f.; in L_{B}, 64, 79, 191; in L_{I}, 60, 85; as limiting kind of statement, 13 f.; as transformable into logical truths, 33 ff.; as true by definition, 33 ff.; as true in every state-description, 53, 58, 61; verification of, 13 f., 55 f.
Analyticity ([1] as property belonging to analytic statements), 26 ff., 39, 45, 50 ff., 71; general and specific questions of, 56, 60 f., 84 f.
Analyticity ([2] as distinction between analytic and synthetic), vii f., 17 f., 47, 59, 61, 83 f., 185 ff., 191, 212; and admissibility of factual evidence, 148 f.; and conceptual analysis, 148 f.; and empiricism, 11 ff.; and formal-nonformal distinction, 177, 186 f.; history of, 24 n.; in Kant, 8 ff., 23 ff., 55; in Lewis, 25 ff.; in nat-

ural language, 231; in pragmatic reconstruction, 248; and reductionism, 12 ff.
Antecedent framework, 59 n., 225 ff., 249; and metaphysics, 255 ff.; and natural language, 231 ff.; of natural language, 233 f.; ultimate, 255 ff.
Application, context of; *see* Context
A priori, 9 ff., 21 f., 23 f., 61 n.
Aristotle, 78
Artificial language, 51 ff., 61 ff., 77, 84 f., 149, 169, 173 f., 189, 195 f., 209, 223, 231, 244; and natural language, 237 ff.
Association, 98; and complication, 106; and psychology, 151 f.
Atomism: and analysis, 94 ff.; logical, 68, 73, 153, 204 ff., 215, 252; and perception, 114 f., 128 f.; and psychology, 151 f.; theoretic, 153
Aufbau, 203, 251
Availability, 72, 77, 83 f., 133, 204, 234 f., 263
Awareness, 92 ff., 101, 131; and memory, 139
Ayer, A. J., 74, 120, 148

Bacon, Francis, 3
Basic proposition, 5, 235
Beck, Lewis White, 81 n.
Benjamin, A. C., 206 n.
Bentley, Arthur F., 128 n., 141 n., 153 n.
Bergmann, Gustav, 4, 62 ff., 67, 70 n., 71, 74 ff., 81 f., 85 n., 86, 104, 191, 203 f., 206, 215, 217, 243, 244 n., 250
Bergson, 3, 121, 132, 144
Berkeley, 104, 174
Black, Max, 206 n.
Blueprint theories, 203 ff., 251 f.
Britten, Benjamin, 123 n.
Broad, C. D., 73 n., 104, 121, 147 n.

269

Bruner, Jerome S., 136 n., 153 n., 163 n.

Can't-get-started argument, 135 f., 161, 162 f.

Cantril, Hadley, 125 n., 154 n., 157 n., 200 n.

Carnap, Rudolf, 3 f., 19 n., 38, 45 ff., 49 ff., 59 n., 60, 62, 69, 86, 120 n., 184, 194 f., 199, 203, 216 n., 218 f., 224, 227 n., 232, 251 n.

Cartesian doubt, 98 f.

Causality, 68 ff., 80, 216, 226 ff.

Certainty, 31, 151

Church, Alonzo, 11, 41, 51 n., 82 n., 239

Circularity, 145 ff., 150 f., 162, 214, 222 ff., 235, 243

Clearness, 88, 205 ff., 234, 252, 258; and distinctness, 206 ff.; and empirical significance, 206, 209

Cobitz, J. L., 12

Cognition, 91, 160 ff., 234; and action, 166 f.; contextual, 160; threshold of, 208

Cognitive-noncognitive distinction, 242, 246 f.

Cohen, Morris R., 168 n.

Collingwood, R. G., 133

Completeness, requirement of, 63 n.

Complication, 105 ff., 117; and synesthesia, 122

Comprehension, 35 n.

Constants: derivative, 53; descriptive, 51, 64, 72, 77, 81, 191, 238; empirical, 77; logical, 33, 40, 51 ff. (see also Logical-nonlogical distinction); nonlogical, 76; primitive, 64, 77, 220 f., 238 (see also Primitive bases)

Construction, 92 ff., 98, 104 n., 113, 159; logical, 98; mental, 98

Containment, 24 ff., 39, 60, 83

Context, 48 f., 78, 84; of application, 218, 234, 250, 258; and conceptual thinking, 160; of discovery, 62, 81, 217 f., 234; and empiricism, 264 f.; and experience, viii f., 155 ff., 175 ff.; and explication, 38; of explication, 63, 81, 217 f., 234; of justification, 62, 81, 217 f., 234; and metaphysics, 255 ff.; and

perception, 153 ff., 160; and precision, 169; and principle of identity, 170 ff.; scientific, 185 ff., 197; and significance, viii, 66 f., 182 ff., 200

Convention, 47 ff., 78, 80, 84, 87, 140, 191 f., 213 f., 227

Copi, Irving M., 11, 99 n.

Copilowish, I. M., 206 n.

Counterfactual conditionals, 68 ff., 203 f., 206, 226 ff.

Dalkey, Norman, 205 n.

Definition, 33 f., 37 ff., 84, 248; in use, 65 f., 182

Degree, 47 ff., 78, 84, 87, 140; of analyticity, 48; of empirical significance, 194 ff., 260; of independent meaning, 46, 194; of synonymy, 37

Déjà vu illusion, 136 n.

Demos, Raphael, 205 n.

Denotation, 35 n. (see also Meaning, extensional)

Depth, perception of, 104 f.

"Derived from," 5, 62, 64

Descartes, 99, 205 n., 209 n.

Determinable-determinate distinction, argument from, 106 ff.; relativity of, 111 n.

Dewey, John, x, 153 n.

Disposition terms, 68 ff., 80, 204, 216, 226 ff.

Distinctions: coextension of, 10 n.; and philosophy, ix

Distinctness, 88, 205 ff. (see also Precision); and clearness, 206 ff.; and epistemological continuum, 207 ff.; scale, 207 ff., 227 f., 233 f.

Duhem, Pierre, 16, 66, 184

Effectiveness, 51 f., 235

Emmet, Dorothy M., 255

Empiricism, vii ff., 3 ff., 11 ff., 72, 86, 144 f., 159 f., 181, 190 ff., 258 ff.; and analyticity, 11 ff., 61; contemporary, 235; and experience, 259 f.; history of, 4 n.; and intersubjectivity, 261 ff.; of knowledge, 7 n.; of meaning, 7 n.; principle of, 5, 10 f., 62, 64, 72, 83, 86, 259 ff.; and rational recon-

struction, 64 ff., 79 f., 85, 192; and reductionism, 12; and science, 260 f., 263 f.; of truth, 7 n.
Epistemological continuum, 159 ff., 174 f., 185 f., 201, 233 f.; and distinctness scale, 207 ff.; and principle of identity, 171
Epistemological inquiry, 92, 100 ff., 112 f., 145 ff.; as conceptual analysis, 148 ff.; criteria of, 94, 98, 100 f.; as noninductive, 145 f.
Epistemological present, 132 ff., 136 ff., 154
Epistemological priority; see Priority
Evidence: epistemological, 101, 113, 145 ff., 241; factual, 101, 113, 119, 145 ff., 241; logical, 56; perceptual, 146 f.
Existence: analytic, 73 f., 93; empirical, 73 f., 93; epistemic, 74 f., 93 f.; epistemological, 73; logical, 73; real, 73; -without-persistence, 75
Experience, vii, 6, 72 ff., 88, 91 ff., 181, 222, 259 ff.; cognitive (see Cognition); and formal-nonformal distinction, 186; noncognitive, 208; perceptual, 96, 99; and time, 132
"Experience," 5 f., 62, 64, 145
Explication, 38, 50 ff., 148 f., 204 f., 217, 230; context of, 63; in Kant, 55
Expressive statement, 5, 235
Extension; see Meaning
Extensional language, 26, 51, 68, 84, 216, 226
External; see Internal and external

Firth, Roderick, 76 n., 92 n., 93 n., 103, 105 n.
Fitzgerald, F. Scott, 126 n., 141
Formal-nonformal distinction, viii, 91 ff., 105, 112, 151, 156 ff., 201, 241; as analytic-synthetic distinction, 177, 186 f.; as formal-empirical distinction, 87 f.; as formal-factual distinction, 87, 143, 212; functional, 158, 187, 245; relativity of, 158
Formalization, 237 ff.
Framework; see Context

Frege, G., 38
Functional absolutes, 157, 187
Functional analysis, 153, 160

Genetic fallacy, 234
Gewirth, Alan, 11, 46 n., 205 n.
Given, the, 73 n., 93, 113, 128 ff., 142, 158, 248 f.; and complication, 106 ff.; and dualism, 127 f.; epistemic, 93; modality of, 125 ff.; as noticed, 131 ff.; and primary recognition, 134; psychological, 93; units of, 115 f.
Gödel, Kurt, 82 n.
Goodman, Nelson, 4, 35 ff., 69 n., 120 n., 235 n.

Hahn, Lewis E., 153 n.
Hartshorne, Charles, 124 n.
Hayek, F. A., 123 n., 124
Hempel, Carl G., 38, 192 f., 197, 202 f., 206 n., 215 n.
Heraclitus, 121
Hobbes, 3
Hofstadter, Albert, 12, 14 ff., 65 n., 183 n., 251 n.
Holism, and perception, 152 f.
Holophrastic meaning; see Meaning
Human nature, uniformity of, 101, 146
Hume, ix, 3 f., 7 f., 10, 65, 79, 99, 174
Husserl, Edmund, 3

"Idea," 5, 7, 62, 65
Ideal language, 63, 65 ff., 75 ff., 191, 203, 215, 217, 238, 244, 254
Identity, principle of: in behavior, 170 ff., 175, 199 ff.; in logic, 169, 175; resistance to, 171 f.; in thought, 170, 175
Idiomatic accuracy; see Accuracy
Inclusion, 25 ff., 39, 83
Independence, requirement of, 53
Indubitability, 72, 76 f., 93, 98 f., 102, 158, 164, 235
Induction, 31, 73 n., 101, 145 f., 159, 218, 235; condensed, 106; justification of, 145 f.; and sensory correlation, 119
Inference: and complication, 105 f.;